Berlitz®

Western
Europe

phrase book & dictionary

Berlitz Publishing
New York   London   Singapore

Contacting the Editors
Every effort has been made to provide accurate information in this publication, but changes are inevitable. The publisher cannot be responsible for any resulting loss, inconvenience or injury. We would appreciate it if readers would call our attention to any errors or outdated information. We also welcome your suggestions; if you come across a relevant expression not in our phrase book, please contact us at: **comments@berlitzpublishing.com**

All Rights Reserved
© 2015 Berlitz Publishing/APA Publications (UK) Ltd.
Berlitz Trademark Reg. U.S. Patent Office and other countries. Marca Registrada. Used under license from Berlitz Investment Corporation.

Second Printing: 2015
Printed in China

Publishing Director: Agnieszka Mizak
Senior Commissioning Editor: Kate Drynan
Translation: updated by Wordbank
Simplified phonetics: updated by Wordbank
Cover & Interior Design: Beverley Speight
Production Manager: Vicky Mullins
Picture Researcher: Beverley Speight
Cover Photo: stained glass Corrie Wingate; honey, Chez Clément sign Kevin Cummins; oven gloves Lydia Evans; vespa Ming-Tang Evans; money and buildings iStockphoto

Interior Photos: p1 Corrie Wingate; p6 Julian Love; p34 Kevin Cummins; p60 Jon Santa Cruz; p88 Glyn Genin; p116 Britta Jaschinski; p142 Lydia Evans; p170 Gregory Wrona; p198 Frank Noon

Contents

How to use this Book

> Sometimes you see two alternatives separated by a slash. Choose the one that's right for your situation.

ESSENTIAL

I'm here on vacation [holiday]/business.	**Ik ben hier met vakantie/voor zaken.** *ihk behn heer meht faa·kahn·see/foar zaa·kuhn*
I'm going to...	**Ik ga naar...** *ihk khaa naar...*
I'm staying at the...Hotel.	**Ik logeer in Hotel...** *ihk loa·zhayr ihn hoa·tehl...*

> Words you may see are shown in YOU MAY SEE boxes.

YOU MAY SEE...

COUVERT	cover charge
DAGSCHOTEL	menu of the day
BEDIENING (NIET) INBEGREPEN	service (not) included

> Any of the words or phrases listed can be plugged into the sentence below.

Tickets

When's...to Amsterdam?	**Wanneer vertrekt...naar Amsterdam?** *vah·nayr fuhr·trehkt...naar ahm·stuhr·dahm*
the (first) bus	**de (eerste) bus** *duh (ayr·stuh) buhs*
the (next) flight	**de (volgende) vlucht** *duh (fohl·khuhn·duh) fluhkht*
the (last) train	**de (laatste) trein** *duh (laat·stuh) trien*

Dutch phrases appear in purple.

Read the simplified pronunciation as if it were English. For more on pronunciation, see page 8.

Romance

Can I join you? **Mag ik bij je komen zitten?**
mahkh ihk bie yuh koa·muhn zih·tuhn

Can I buy you
a drink? **Wil je iets van me drinken?**
vihl yuh eets fahn muh drihng·kuhn

I love you. **Ik vind je leuk.** *ihk fihnd yuh luk.*

For Communications, see page 16.

Related phrases can be found by going to the page number indicated.

In an emergency, dial 112 for police, fire brigade or ambulance.

Information boxes contain relevant country, culture and language tips.

Expressions you may hear are shown in You May Hear boxes.

YOU MAY HEAR...

rechtdoor *rehkht·doar* straight ahead
links *lihnks* left

Color-coded side bars identify each section of the book.

Dutch

Essentials

ESSENTIAL

Hello./Hi!	**Hallo!** *hah·loa*
Goodbye.	**Dag.** *dakh*
Yes/No/Okay.	**Ja/Nee/Oké.** *yaa/nay/okay*
Excuse me! (to get attention)	**Meneer/Mevrouw!** *muh·nayr/muh·frow*
Excuse me. (to get past)	**Pardon.** *pahr·dohn*
I'd like…	**Ik wil graag…** *ihk vihl khraak*
How much?	**Hoeveel kost het?** *hoo·fayl kohst heht*
And/Or.	**En/van.** *ehn/fahn*
Where is/are…?	**Waar is/zijn…?** *vaar ihs/zien*
Please.	**Alstublieft.** *ahls·tew·bleeft*
Thank you.	**Dank u wel.** *dahngk ew vehl*
You're welcome.	**Geen dank.** *khayn dahngk*
I'm going to…	**Ik ga naar…** *ihk khaa naar…*
My name is…	**Mijn naam is…** *mien naam ihs…*
Can you speak more slowly?	**Kunt u iets langzamer spreken?** *kuhnt ew eets lahng·zaa·muhr spray·kuhn*
Can you repeat that?	**Kunt u dat herhalen?** *kuhnt ew daht hehr·haa·luhn*
I don't understand.	**Ik begrijp het niet.** *ihk buh·khrayp heht neet*
Do you speak English?	**Spreekt u Engels?** *spraykt ew ehng·uhls*
I don't speak Dutch.	**Ik spreek geen Nederlands.** *ihk sprayk khayn nay·duhr·lahnds*
Where is the restroom [toilet]?	**Waar is het toilet?** *vaar ihs heht twaa·leht*
Help!	**Help!** *hehlp*

You'll find the pronunciation of the Dutch letters and words written in gray after each sentence to guide you. Simply pronounce these as if they were English, noting that any underlines and bolds indicate an additional emphasis or stress or a lengthening of a vowel sound. As you hear the language being spoken, you will quickly become accustomed to the local pronunciation and dialect.

Numbers

0	**nul**	*nuhl*
1	**één**	*ayn*
2	**twee**	*tvay*
3	**drie**	*dree*
4	**vier**	*feer*
5	**vijf**	*fief*
6	**zes**	*zehs*
7	**zeven**	*zay·fuhn*
8	**acht**	*ahkht*
9	**negen**	*nay·khuhn*
10	**tien**	*teen*
11	**elf**	*ehlf*
12	**twaalf**	*tvaalf*
13	**dertien**	*dehr·teen*
14	**veertien**	*fayr·teen*
15	**vijftien**	*fief·teen*
16	**zestien**	*zehs·teen*
17	**zeventien**	*zay·fuhn·teen*
18	**achttien**	*ahkh·teen*
19	**negentien**	*nay·khuhn·teen*
20	**twintig**	*tvihn·tuhkh*

21	**eenentwintig**	_ayn_•uhn•tvihn•tuhkh
22	**tweeëntwintig**	_tvay_•uhn•tvihn•tuhkh
30	**dertig**	_dehr_•tihkh
31	**eenendertig**	_ayn_•uhn•dehr•tihkh
40	**veertig**	_fayr_•tihkh
50	**vijftig**	_fief_•tihkh
60	**zestig**	zehs•tihkh
70	**zeventig**	zay•fuhn•tihkh
80	**tachtig**	tahkh•tih
90	**negentig**	nay•khuhn•tihkh
100	**honderd**	hohn•duhrt
101	**honderdéén**	hohn•duhrt•ayn
200	**tweehonderd**	tvay•hohn•duhrt
500	**vijfhonderd**	fief•hohn•duhrt
1,000	**duizend**	daw•zuhnt
10,000	**tienduizend**	teen•daw•zuhnt
1,000,000	**één miljoen**	uhn mihl•yoon

Time

What time is it?	**Hoe laat is het?**	hoo laat ihs heht
It's noon [midday].	**Het is twaalf uur 's middags.**	
	heht ihs tvaalf ewr smih•dahkhs	
Twenty after [past] four.	**Tien voor half vijf.** teen foar hahlf fief	
A quarter to nine.	**Kwart voor negen.** kvahrt foar nay•khuhn	
5:30 a.m./p.m.	**Half zes 's morgens/Half zes 's avonds.**	
	hahlf zehs smohr•khuhns/hahlf zehs saa•fohnts	

For Days, see page 10.

Days

Monday	**maandag**	_maan_·dahkh
Tuesday	**dinsdag**	_dihns_·dahkh
Wednesday	**woensdag**	_voons_·dahkh
Thursday	**donderdag**	_dohn_·duhr·dahkh
Friday	**vrijdag**	_frie_·dahkh
Saturday	**zaterdag**	_zaa_·tuhr·dahkh
Sunday	**zondag**	_zohn_·dahkh

Dates

yesterday	**gisteren**	_khihs_·tuh·ruhn
today	**vandaag**	fahn·_daakh_
tomorrow	**morgen**	_mohr_·khuhn
day	**dag**	dahkh
week	**week**	vayk
month	**maand**	maant
year	**jaar**	yaar
Happy New Year!	**Gelukkig Nieuwjaar!**	khe·luw·kig neeew·yaar
Happy Birthday!	**Gelukkig Verjaardag!**	khe·luw·kig fuhr·yaar·dahkh

Months

January	**januari**	_yah_·new·aa·ree
February	**februari**	_fay_·brew·aa·ree
March	**maart**	maart
April	**april**	ah·_prihl_
May	**mei**	mie
June	**juni**	_yew_·nee
July	**juli**	yew·lee
August	**augustus**	ow·_khuhs_·tuhs
September	**september**	sehp·_tehm_·buhr

October	**oktober** ohk•*toa*•buhr
November	**november** noa•*fehm*•buhr
December	**december** day•*sehm*•buhr

Arrival & Departure

I'm here on vacation [holiday]/business.	**Ik ben hier met vakantie/voor zaken.** *ihk behn heer meht faa•kahn•see/foar zaa•kuhn*
I'm going to...	**Ik ga naar...** *ihk khaa naar...*
I'm staying at the...Hotel.	**Ik logeer in Hotel...** *ihk loa•zhayr ihn hoa•tehl...*

Money

Where's...?	**Waar is...?** *vaar ihs...*
the ATM	**de geldautomaat** *duh khehlt•ow•toa•maat*
the bank	**de bank** *duh bahngk*
the currency exchange office	**het geldwisselkantoor** *heht khehlt•vihs•suhl•kahn•toar*
What time does the bank open/close?	**Hoe laat gaat de bank open/dicht?** *hoo laat khaat duh bahngk oa•puhn/dihkht*
I'd like to change some dollars/pounds into euros.	**Ik wil graag wat dollars/ponden in euro's omwisselen.** *ihk vihl khraakh vaht dohl•lahrs/pohn•duhn ihn u•roas ohm•vihs•suh•luhn*
I want to cash some traveler's checks [cheques].	**Ik wil wat reischeques verzilveren.** *ihk vihl vaht ries•shehks fuhr•zihl•fuhr•uhn*

YOU MAY SEE...

Dutch currency is the **euro**, divided into **cents**.
Bills: 5, 10, 20, 50, 100, 500 **euro**
Coins: 1, 2, 5, 10, 20, 50 **cents** and 1 and 2 **euro**

| Can I pay in cash? | **Kan ik contant betalen?** *kahn ihk kohn·tahnt buh·taa·luhn* |
| Can I pay by credit card? | **Kan ik met een creditcard betalen?** *kahn ihk meht uhn khreh·diht·kaart buh·taa·luhn* |

For Numbers, see page 8.

Getting Around

How do I get to town?	**Hoe kom ik in de stad?** *hoo kohm ihk ihn duh staht*
Where's...?	**Waar is...?** *vaar ihs...*
the airport	**het vliegveld** *heht fleekh·fehlt*
the train [railway] station	**het station** *heht staa·shohn*
the bus station	**het busstation** *heht buhs·staa·shohn*
the subway station	**het metrostation** *heht may·troa·staa·shohn*
How far is it?	**Hoe ver is het?** *hoo fehr ihs heht*
Where can I buy tickets?	**Waar kan ik kaartjes kopen?** *vaar kahn ihk kaart·yuhs koa·puhn*
A one-way/return-trip ticket.	**Enkeltje/Retourtje.** *ehng·kuhl·tyuh/ruh·toor·tyuh*
How much?	**Hoeveel kost het?** *hoo·fayl kohst heht*
Which gate/line?	**Welke gate/lijn?** *vehl·kuh gayt/lien*
Which platform?	**Welk spoor?** *vehlk spoar*
Where can I get a taxi?	**Waar kan ik een taxi krijgen?** *vaar kahn ihk uhn tahk·see krie·khuhn*
Could you take me to this address?	**Kunt u me naar dit adres brengen?** *kuhnt ew muh naar diht ah·drehs brehng·uhn*
I'm in a rush.	**Ik heb haast.** *ihk hehp haast*
To...Airport, please.	**Naar...Airport, alstublieft.** *naar...air·pohrt ahls·tew·bleeft*
Can I have a map?	**Heeft u een kaart voor mij?** *hayft ew uhn kaart foar mie*

12

Tickets

When's...to Amsterdam?	**Wanneer vertrekt...naar Amsterdam?** _vah•nayr fuhr•trehkt ...naar ahm•stuhr•dahm_
the (first) bus	**de (eerste) bus** _duh (ayr•stuh) buhs_
the (next) flight	**de (volgende) vlucht** _duh (fohl•khuhn•duh) fluhkht_
the (last) train	**de (laatste) trein** _duh (laat•stuh) trien_
One ticket/Two tickets, please.	**Eén kaartje/Twee kaartjes, alstublieft.** _ayn kaart•yuh/tway kaart•yuhs ahl•stew•bleeft_
For today/tomorrow.	**Voor vandaag/morgen.** _foar fahn•daakh/mohr•khuhn_
A one-way [single]/ round-trip [return] ticket.	**Enkeltje/Retourtje.** _ehng•kuhl•tyuh/ruh•toor•tyuh_
A first-class/ economy-class ticket.	**Kaartje eerste klas/tweede klas.** _kaart•yuh ayr•stuh klahs/tway•duh klahs_
I have an e-ticket.	**Ik heb een e-ticket.** _ihk hehp uhn ee•tih•kuht_
How long is the trip [journey]?	**Hoe lang duurt de reis?** _hoo lahng dewrt duh ries_
Do I have to change trains?	**Moet ik overstappen?** _moot ihk oa•fuhr•stahp•puhn_
Is this the bus to...?	**Is dit de bus naar...?** _is diht duh buhs naar...?_
Can you tell me when to get off?	**Kunt u me waarschuwen wanneer ik moet uitstappen?** _kuhnt ew muh vaar•skhew•vuhn vah•nayr ihk moot awt•stahp•puhn_
I'd like to... my reservation.	**Ik wil graag mijn reservering...** _ihk vihl khraakh mien ray•zehr•vay•rihng..._
cancel	**annuleren** _ah•new•lay•ruhn_
change	**wijzigen** _vie•zih•khuhn_
confirm	**bevestigen** _buh•fehs•tih•khuhn_

For Time, see page 9.

Car Hire

Where can I rent a car?	**Waar kan ik een auto huren?**	
	vaar kahn ihk uhn ow‑toa hew‑ruhn	
I'd like to hire…	**Ik wil graag…huren.** *ihk vihl khraakh…hew‑ruhn*	
a cheap/small car	**een goedkope/kleine auto** *uhn khoot‑koa‑peh‑ow‑toa*	
an automatic/	**een automaat/een handgeschakelde**	
a manual	*uhn ow‑toa‑maat/uhn hahnt‑kheh‑skhah‑kuhl‑duh.*	
a car with air conditioning	**een auto met airco** *uhn ow‑toa meht air‑coa*	
a car seat	**een kinderzitje** *uhn kihn‑duhr‑ziht‑yuh*	
How much…?	**Hoeveel kost het…?** *hoo‑fayl kohst heht…*	
per day/week	**per dag/week** *pehr dahkh/vayk*	

YOU MAY HEAR…

rechtdoor *rehkht‑doar*	straight ahead
links *lihnks*	left
rechts *rehkhts*	right
op/om de hoek *ohp/ohm duh hook*	on/around the corner
tegenover *tay‑khuhn‑oa‑fuhr*	opposite
achter *ahkh‑tuhr*	behind
naast *naast*	next to
na *naa*	after
ten noorden/ten zuiden	north/south
tehn noar‑duhn/tehn zaw‑duhn	
ten oosten/ten westen	east/west
tehn oas‑tuhn/tehn vehs‑tuhn	
bij het stoplicht *bie heht stohp‑lihkht*	at the traffic light
bij de kruising *bie deh kraw‑sihng*	at the intersection

| Are there any discounts for…? | **Zijn er ook kortingen voor…?** |
| | *zien ehr oak <u>kohr</u>·tihng·uhn foar…* |

Places to Stay

Can you recommend a hotel?	**Kunt u een hotel aanbevelen?**
	kuhnt ew uhn hoa·<u>tehl</u> <u>aan</u>·buh·fay·luhn
I have a reservation.	**Ik heb een reservering.**
	ihk hehp uhn <u>ray</u>·zuhr·<u>vay</u>·rihng
My name is…	**Mijn naam is…** *mien naam ihs…*
Do you have a room…?	**Heeft u een kamer…?**
	hayft ew uhn <u>kaa</u>·muhr…
for one	**voor één persoon** *foar ayn puhr·<u>soan</u>*
for two	**voor twee personen** *foar tvay puhr·<u>soa</u>·nuhn*
with a bathroom [toilet]/shower	**met toilet/douche** *meht twaa·<u>leht</u>/doosh*
with air conditioning	**met airco** *meht <u>air</u>·coa*
For tonight.	**Voor vannacht.** *foar fahn·<u>nahkht</u>*
For two nights.	**Voor twee nachten.** *foar tvay <u>nahkh</u>·tuhn*
For one week.	**Voor één week.** *foar ayn vayk*
How much?	**Hoeveel kost het?** *<u>hoo</u>·fayl kohst heht*
Do you have anything cheaper?	**Heeft u iets goedkopers?**
	hayft ew eets khoot·<u>koa</u>·puhrs
When's check-out?	**Hoe laat moeten we uitchecken?**
	hoo laat <u>moo</u>·tuhn vie <u>awt</u>·check·uhn
Can I leave this in the safe?	**Mag ik dit in de kluis bewaren?**
	mahkh ihk diht ihn duh klaws buh·<u>waa</u>·ruhn
Can we leave our bags?	**Mogen we onze bagage hier laten staan?**
	<u>moa</u>·khuhn wie <u>ohn</u>·zuh baa·<u>khaa</u>·zhuh heer <u>laa</u>·tuhn staan
Can I have the bill/ a receipt?	**Mag ik de rekening/bon?**
	mahkh ihk duh <u>ray</u>·kuh·nihng/bonn

| I'll pay in cash/by credit card. | **Ik wil graag contant/met creditcard betalen.** |
| | *ihk vihl khraakh kohn•tahnt/meht kreh•diht•kaart buh•taa•luhn* |

Communications

Where's an internet cafe?	**Waar vind ik een internetcafé?**
	vaar fihnt ihk uhn ihn•tuhr•neht•kaa•fay
Can I access the internet?	**Kan ik hier internetten?**
	kahn ihk heer ihn•tuhr•neh•tuhn
Can I check my email?	**Kan ik mijn e-mail checken?** *kahn ik mien ee•mayl tsheh•kuhn*
How much per hour/ half hour?	**Hoeveel kost het per uur/half uur?**
	hoo•fayl kohst heht pehr ewr/hahlf ewr
How do I connect/ log on?	**Hoe kan ik verbinding maken/inloggen?**
	hoo kahn ihk fuhr•bihn•dihng maa•kuhn/ihn•loh•khun
I'd like a phone card, please.	**Ik wil een telefoonkaart, alstublieft.**
	ihk vihl uhn tay•luh•foan•kaart ahls•tew•bleeft
Can I have your phone number?	**Mag ik uw telefoonnummer?**
	mahkh ihk ew tay•luh•foan•nuh•muhr
Here's my number/ email address.	**Hier is mijn telefoonnummer/e-mailadres.**
	heer ihs mien tay•luh•foan•nuh•muhr/ee•mayl•aa•drehs
Call me.	**Bel me.** *behl muh*
Please text me.	**Ik verzoek u me te sms'en.**
	ihk fuhr•zook ew muh tuh ehs•ehm•ehs•uhn
I'll text you.	**Ik zal u sms'en.** *ihk zahl ew ehs•ehm•ehs•uhn*
E-mail me.	**Stuur me een e-mail.** *stewr muh uhn ee•mayl*
Hello. This is…	**Hallo. U spreekt met…** *hallo ew spraykt meht…*
I'd like to speak to…	**Ik wil graag met…spreken.**
	ihk vihl khraakh meht…spray•kuhn
Can you repeat that?	**Kunt u dat herhalen?** *kuhnt ew daht hehr•haa•luhn*

I'll call back later.	**Ik bel straks wel even terug.**
	ihk behl strahks vehl ay-fuhn truhkh
Bye.	**Dag.** *dahkh*
Where's the post office?	**Waar is het postkantoor?** *vaar ihs heht pohst-kahn-toar*
I'd like to send	**Ik wil dit naar... versturen.**
this to...	*ihk vihl diht naar... fuhr-stew-ruhn*
Can I...?	**Kan ik...?** *kahn ihk...*
access the internet	**hier internetten** *heer ihn-tuhr-neh-tuhn*
check e-mail	**mijn e-mail checken** *mien ee-mayl tsheh-kuhn*
print	**printen** *prihn-tuhn*
plug in/charge my	**mijn laptop/iPhone/iPad/BlackBerry**
laptop/iPhone/	**aansluiten/opladen?** *mien laptop/iPhone/*
iPad/BlackBerry?	*iPad/BlackBerry aan-slaw-tehn/ohp-laa-dehn*
access Skype?	**Skypen?** *skypen*
What is the WiFi	**Wat is het wifi-wachtwoord?**
password?	*vaht is heht wee-fee vahkht-voart*
Is the WiFi free?	**Is wifi gratis?** *is wee-fee khrah-tis*
Do you have bluetooth?	**Heeft u bluetooth?** *hayft ew bluetooth*
Do you have a scanner?	**Heeft u een scanner?** *hayft ew uhn scanner*

Social Media

Are you on Facebook/	**Bent u op Facebook/Twitter?**
Twitter?	*Behnt ew ohp Facebook/Twitter*
What's your user	**Wat is uw gebruikersnaam?**
name?	*waht is ew kheh-braw-kehrs-naam*
I'll add you as a friend.	**Ik zal u toevoegen als vriend.**
	ik sahl ew too-foo-khehn ahls freent
I'll follow you on	**Ik zal u volgen op Twitter.**
Twitter.	*ik sahl ew fohl-khehn op twitter*
Are you following...?	**Volgt u...?** *fohlkht ew...*

| I'll put the pictures on Facebook/Twitter. | **Ik zal de foto's op Facebook/Twitter zetten.** *ihk sahl duh foa·toas op facebook/twitter seh·tehn* |
| I'll tag you in the pictures. | **Ik zal u op de foto's taggen.** *ihk sahl ew ohp duh foa·toas taggen.* |

Conversation

Hello./Hi!	**Hallo./Hoi!** *hah·loa/hoy*
How are you?	**Hoe gaat het met u?** *hoo khaat heht meht ew*
Fine, thanks.	**Prima, dank u.** *pree·maa dangk ew*
Excuse me! (to a man/woman)	**Meneer/Mevrouw!** *muh·nayr/muh·frow*
Do you speak English?	**Spreekt u Engels?** *spraykt ew ehng·uhls*
What's your name?	**Hoe heet u?** *hoo hayt ew*
My name is...	**Mijn naam is...** *mien naam ihs...*
Nice to meet you.	**Aangenaam.** *aan·khuh·naam*
Where are you from?	**Waar komt u vandaan?** *vaar kohmt ew fahn·daan*
I'm from the U.S./U.K.	**Ik kom uit de Verenigde Staten/Groot-Brittannië.** *ihk kohm awt duh fuhr·ay·nihkh·duh staa·tuhn/ khroat·brih·tah·nee·yuh*
What do you do?	**Wat doet u voor werk?** *vaht doot ew foar vehrk*
I work for...	**Ik werk bij...** *ihk vehrk bie...*
I'm a student.	**Ik ben student.** *ihk behn stew·dehnt*
I'm retired.	**Ik ben met pensioen.** *ihk behn meht pehn·shoon*

Romance

| Would you like to go out for a drink/meal? | **Heb je zin om iets te gaan drinken/uit eten te gaan?** *hehp yuh zihn ohm eets tuh gaan drihn·kuhn/ awt ay·tuhn tuh gaan* |
| What are your plans for tonight/tomorrow? | **Wat zijn je plannen voor vanavond/morgen?** *vaht zien yuh plah·nuhn foar fah·naa·fohnt/mohr·khuhn* |

Can I have your phone number?	**Mag ik je telefoonnummer?**
	mahkh ihk yuh tay·luh·foan·nuh·muhr
Can I join you?	**Mag ik bij je komen zitten?**
	mahkh ihk bie yuh koa·muhn zih·tuhn
Can I buy you a drink?	**Wil je iets van me drinken?**
	vihl yuh eets fahn muh drihng·kuhn
I love you.	**Ik vind je leuk.** *ihk fihnd yuh luk.*

Accepting & Rejecting

Thank you. I'd love to.	**Dank je. Dat zou erg leuk zijn.**
	dangk yuh daht zow ehrkh luk zien
Where should we meet?	**Waar zullen we elkaar ontmoeten?**
	vaar zuh·luhn vuh ehl·kaar ohnt·moo·tuhn
I'll meet you at the bar/your hotel.	**Laten we in de bar/jouw hotel afspreken.**
	laa·tuhn vuh ihn duh bahr/yow hoa·tehl ahf·spray·kuhn
I'll come by at. . .	**Ik haal je om. . .uur op.** *ihk haal yuh ohm. . .uwr ohp*
Thank you, but I'm busy.	**Dank je, maar ik heb het te druk.**
	dangk yuh maar ihk hehp heht tuh druhk
I'm not interested.	**Ik heb geen interesse.** *ihk hehp khayn*
	ihn·tuh·reh·suh ihk hehp khayn ihn·tuh·reh·suh
Leave me alone, please.	**Laat me alstublieft met rust.**
	laat muh ahls·tew·bleeft meht ruhst
Stop bothering me.	**Blijf me niet steeds lastig vallen.**
	blief muh neet stayts lahs·tihkh fah·luhn

Close friends may kiss cheeks (left, right, left) and say **Hoe gaat het?** (How are you?) or **Alles goed?** (Is everything alright?). You'll find surnames are used more frequently than first names, even when answering the phone.

Food & Drink

Eating Out

Can you recommend a good restaurant/bar?	**Kunt u een goed restaurant/goede bar aanbevelen?** *kuhnt ew uhn khoot rehs•toa•rahnt/khoo•duh bahr aan•buh•fay•luhn*
Is there a traditional Dutch/an inexpensive restaurant near here?	**Is er een traditioneel Nederlands/goedkoop restaurant in de buurt?** *ihs ehr uhn traa•dee•shoa•nayl nay•duhr•lahnds/khoot•koap rehs•toa•rahnt ihn duh bewrt*
A table for..., please.	**Een tafel voor..., alstublieft.** *uhn taa•fuhl foar...ahls•tew•bleeft*
Can we sit...?	**Kunnen we...zitten?** *kuh•nuhn vuh...zih•tuhn*
here/there	**hier/daar** *heer/daar*
outside	**buiten** *baw•tuhn*
in a non-smoking area	**in het gedeelte voor niet-rokers** *ihn heht khuh•dayl•tuh foar neet•roa•kuhrs*
I'm waiting for someone.	**Ik wacht op iemand.** *ihk vahkht ohp ee•mahnt*
Where are the restrooms/toilets?	**Waar is het toilet?** *vaar ihs heht tvaa•leht*
A menu, please?	**Mag ik een menukaart, alstublieft?** *mahkh ihk uhn muh•new•kaart ahls•tew•bleeft*
What do you recommend?	**Wat kunt u aanbevelen?** *vaht kuhnt ew aan•buh•fay•luhn*
I'd like...	**Ik wil graag...** *ihk vihl khraakh...*
Some more..., please.	**Nog wat..., alstublieft.** *nohkh vaht...ahls•tew•bleeft*
Enjoy your meal.	**Eet smakelijk.** *ayt smaa•kuh•luhk*
Can I have the check [bill]?	**Mag ik de rekening?** *mahkh ihk duh ray•kuh•nihng*

YOU MAY SEE...

COUVERT	cover charge
DAGSCHOTEL	menu of the day
BEDIENING (NIET) INBEGREPEN	service (not) included
SPECIALITEITEN	specials

Is service included?	**Is de bediening inbegrepen?**
	ihs duh buh·dee·nihng ihn·buh·khray·puhn
Can I pay by credit card?	**Kan ik met creditcard betalen?**
	kahn ihk meht khreh·diht·kaart buh·taa·luhn
Can I have a receipt, please?	**Mag ik de bon alstublieft?**
	mahkh ihk duh bon ahls·tew·bleeft

Breakfast

boter *boa·tuhr*	butter
brood *broat*	bread
ei *ie*	egg
roerei *roor·ie*	scrambled egg
honing *hoa·nihng*	honey
jam *zhehm*	jam
toast *toast*	toast
kaas *kaas*	cheese
spek *spehk*	bacon
spiegelei *spee·khuhl·ie*	fried egg
wafel *vaa·fuhl*	waffle
worst *vohrst*	sausage
yoghurt *yoh·khuhrt*	yogurt

YOU MAY HEAR...

kort gebakken *kohrt kuh·bah·kuhn*   rare
medium *may·dee·yuhm*   medium
goed doorbakken *khoot doar·bah·kuhn*   well-done

Appetizers

erwtensoep *ehr·tuhn·soop*   famous thick Dutch pea soup
with pig's knuckle, smoked
sausage and bacon

vissoep *fihs·soop*   fish soup
kippensoep *kih·puhn·soop*   chicken soup
tomatensoep *toa·maa·tuhn·soop*   tomato soup
groentesoep (met balletjes)   vegetable soup
khroon·tuh·soop (meht bah·luh·tyuhs)   (with meatballs)
paté *paa·tay*   paté
salade *saa·laa·duh*   salad

Meat

biefstuk *beef·stuhk*   steak
kalfsvlees *kahlfs·flays*   veal
kip *kihp*   chicken
lamsvlees *lahms·flays*   lamb
rundvlees *ruhnt·flays*   beef
varkensvlees *fahr·kuhns·flays*   pork

Fish & Seafood

garnaal *khahr·naal*   shrimp [prawn]
haring *haa·rihng*   herring [whitebait]
kabeljauw *kaa·buhl·yow*   cod

kreeft *krayft*	lobster
mossel <u>*moh*</u>*·suhl*	mussel
zalm *zahlm*	salmon

Vegetables

aardappel <u>*aar*</u>*·dah·puhl*	potato
champignon *shahm·*<u>*pee*</u>*·yohn*	mushroom
erwt *ehrt*	pea
kool *koal*	cabbage
bonen <u>*boa*</u>*·nuhn*	beans
tomaat *toa·*<u>*maat*</u>	tomato
ui *aw*	onion
wortel <u>*vohr*</u>*·tuhl*	carrot

Sauces & Condiments

zout *zowt*	salt
peper <u>*pay*</u>*·puhr*	pepper
mosterd <u>*moh*</u>*·stehrt*	mustard
ketchup <u>*keht*</u>*·suhp*	ketchup

Fruit & Dessert

aardbei <u>*aart*</u>*·bie*	strawberry
appel <u>*ah*</u>*·puhl*	apple
banaan *baa·*<u>*naan*</u>	banana
sinaasappel <u>*see*</u>*·naas·ah·puhl*	orange
peer *payr*	pear
citroen *see·*<u>*troon*</u>	lemon
room *roam*	cream
roomijs <u>*roam*</u>*·ies*	ice cream
chocolade *shoa·koa·*<u>*laa*</u>*·duh*	chocolate
vanille *vaa·*<u>*nee*</u>*·yuh*	vanilla
gebak *khuh·bahk*	pastry or cake

Drinks

May I see the wine list/drink menu?	**Mag ik de wijnkaart/drankkaart zien?** *mahkh ihk duh <u>vien</u>•kaart/<u>drahnk</u>•kaart zeen*
What do you recommend?	**Wat kunt u aanbevelen?** *vaht kuhnt ew <u>aan</u>•buh•fay•luhn*
I'd like a bottle/glass of red/white wine.	**Ik wil graag een fles/glas rode/witte wijn.** *ihk vihl khraakh uhn flehs/khlahs <u>roa</u>•duh/<u>vih</u>•tuh vien*
The house wine, please.	**Mag ik de huiswijn?** *mahkh ihk duh <u>haws</u>•vien*
Another bottle/ glass, please.	**Nog een fles/glas, alstublieft.** *nohkh uhn flehs/khlahs ahls•tew•<u>bleeft</u>*
I'd like a local beer.	**Ik wil graag een lokaal biertje.** *ihk vihl khraakh uhn loa•<u>kaal beer</u>•tyuh*
Can I buy you a drink?	**Wilt u iets van me drinken?** *vihlt ew eets fahn muh <u>drihng</u>•kuhn*
Cheers!	**Proost!** *proast*
A coffee/tea, please.	**Een koffie/thee, alstublieft.** *uhn <u>koh</u>•fee/tay ahls•tew•<u>bleeft</u>*
With/Without milk.	**Met/Zonder melk.** *meht/<u>zohn</u>•duhr mehlk*
With sugar.	**Met suiker.** *meht <u>zaw</u>•kuhr*
With artificial sweetener.	**Met zoetjes.** *meht <u>zoo</u>•tyuhs*
..., please.	**..., alstublieft.** *... ahls•tew•<u>bleeft</u>*
Juice	**Een vruchtensap** *uhn <u>fruhkh</u>•tuhn•sahp*
Soda [soft drink]	**Een frisdrank** *uhn <u>frihs</u>•drahngk*
(Sparkling/Still) Water	**(Koolzuurhoudend/Koolzuurvrij) Water** *(<u>koal</u>•zewr•<u>how</u>•duhnt/<u>koal</u>•zewr•<u>frie</u>) <u>vaa</u>•tuhr*

Leisure Time

Sightseeing

Where's the tourist information office?	**Waar is het VVV-kantoor?** *vaar ihs heht vay•vay•vay•kahn•toar*
What are the main points of interest?	**Wat zijn de bezienswaardigheden?** *vaht zien duh buh•zeens•waar•dihkh•hay•duhn*
Do you have tours in English?	**Verzorgt u excursies in het Engels?** *fuhr•zohrkht ew ehks•kuhr•sees ihn heht ehng•uhls*
Can I have a map/guide please?	**Mag ik een kaart/gids, alstublieft?** *mahkh ihk uhn kaart/khihts ahls•tew•bleeft*

> **YOU MAY SEE...**
> **OPEN/GESLOTEN**   open/closed
> **INDGANG/UITGANG**   entrance/exit

Shopping

Where is the market/mall [shopping centre]?	**Waar is de markt/het winkelcentrum?** *vaar ihs duh mahrkt/heht vihn•kuhl•sehn•truhm*
I'm just looking.	**Ik kijk alleen.** *ihk kiek ah•layn*
Can you help me?	**Kunt u me helpen?** *kuhnt ew muh hehl•puhn*
I'm being helped.	**Ik word al geholpen.** *ihk vohrt ahl khuh•hohl•puhn*
I'd like...	**Ik wil graag...** *ihk vihl khraak*
How much?	**Hoeveel kost het?** *hoo•fayl kohst heht*
That one.	**Die daar.** *dee daar*
That's all, thanks.	**Das was het, dank u.** *das vas heht dangk ew*
Where do I pay?	**Waar moet ik betalen?** *vaar moot ihk buh•taa•luhn*

I'll pay in cash/ by credit card.	**Ik wil graag contant/met creditcard betalen.** *ihk vihl khraakh kohn·tahnt/meht kreh·diht·kaart buh·taa·luhn*
A receipt, please.	**Mag ik de bon.** *mag ihk duh bon*

Sport & Leisure

When's the game?	**Wanneer is de wedstrijd?** *vah·nayr ihs duh veht·striet*
Where's...?	**Waar is...?** *vaar ihs...*
the beach	**het strand** *heht strahnt*
the park	**het park** *heht pahrk*
the pool	**het zwembad** *heht zvehm·baht*
Is it safe to swim/ dive here?	**Is het veilig om hier te zwemmen/duiken?** *ihs heht fie·lihkh ohm heer tuh zveh·muhn/daw·kuhn*
Can I rent [hire] golf clubs?	**Kan ik golfclubs huren?** *kahn ihk gohlf·kluhps hew·ruhn*
How much per hour?	**Hoeveel kost het per uur?** *hoo·fayl kohst heht pehr ewr*

After dark, the Netherlands has a lot to offer depending on what you're in the mood for. In Amsterdam, the action is centered in three main areas. If you're looking for dance and night clubs, head to **Leidseplein**. For clubs, cabarets and strip shows, go to **Rembrandtplein**. The Red Light District is world-famous for offering a range of alternative activities.

For a low key evening, check out a 'brown' cafe (traditional Dutch bar), pub or bar. Amsterdam is home to about a thousand, so you can easily find one that fits your style.

How far is it to…?	**Hoe ver is het naar…?** *hoo fehr ihs heht naar…*
Can you show me on the map?	**Kunt u me dat op de kaart laten zien?** *kuhnt ew muh daht ohp duh kaart laa•tuhn zeen*

Going Out

What is there to do in the evenings?	**Wat is er 's avonds te doen?** *vaht ihs ehr saa•vohnts tuh doon*
Do you have a program of events?	**Heeft u een evenementenprogramma?** *hayft ew uhn ay•fuh•nuh•mehn•tuhn•proa•krah•maa*
What's playing at the movies [cinema] tonight?	**Welke films draaien er vanavond?** *vehl•kuh fihlms draa•yuhn ehr fah•naa•fohnt*
Where's…?	**Waar is…?** *vaar ihs…*
the downtown area	**het stadscentrum** *heht staht•sehn•truhm*
the bar	**de bar** *duh bahr*
the dance club	**de discotheek** *duh dihs•koa•tayk*
Is this area safe at night?	**Is dit gebied 's nachts veilig?** *ihs diht kheh•beet snahkhs fay•lihkh*

Baby Essentials

Do you have…?	**Heeft u…?** *hayft ew…*
a baby bottle	**een babyfles** *uhn bay•bee•flehs*
baby wipes	**babydoekjes** *bay•bee•dook•yuhs*
a car seat	**een kinderzitje** *uhn kihn•duhr•ziht•yuh*
a children's menu/portion	**een kindermenu/kinderportie** *uhn kihn•duhr•muh•new/kihn•duhr•pohr•see*
a highchair	**een kinderstoel** *uhn kihn•duhr•stool*
a crib/cot	**een wieg/kinderbedje** *uhn veekh/kihn•duhr•beht•yuh*
diapers [nappies]	**luiers** *law•yuhrs*
formula	**flesvoeding** *flehs•foo•dihng*
a pacifier [dummy]	**een fopspeen** *uhn fohp•spayn*

a playpen	**een babybox** uhn bay·bee·bohks
a stroller	**een kinderwagen**
[pushchair]	uhn kihn·duhr·vaa·khun
Can I breastfeed	**Mag ik mijn baby hier de borst geven?**
the baby here?	mahkh ihk mien bay·bee heer duh bohrst khay·fuhn
Where can I	**Waar kan ik de baby verschonen?**
change the baby?	vaar kahn ihk duh bay·bee fuhr·skhoa·nuhn

For Eating Out, see page 20.

Disabled Travelers

Is there access for	**Is het toegankelijk voor gehandicapten?**
the disabled?	is heht too·khahng·kuh·luhk foar
	khuh·hehn·dee·kehp·tuhn
Is there a wheelchair	**Is er een rolstoeloprit?**
ramp?	uhn rohl·stool·ohp·riht
Is there a	**Is er een toilet dat toegankelijk is voor**
handicapped-	**gehandicapten?**
[disabled-]accessible	uhn tvaa·leht daht too·khahng·kuh·luhk ihs foar
toilet?	khuh·hehn·dee·kehp·tuhn
I need...	**Ik heb...nodig.** ihk hehp...noa·dihkh
assistance	**hulp** huhlp
an elevator [lift]	**een lift** uhn lihft
a ground-floor	**een kamer op de begane grond**
room	uhn kaa·muhr ohp duh buh·khaa·nuh khrohnt
Please speak louder.	**Kunt u iets luider spreken, alstublieft?**
	kuhnt ew eets law·dehr spray·kehn, ahls·tuh·bleeft

28

YOU MAY HEAR...

Vul dit formulier in.
fuhl diht fohr•muh•leer ihn

Fill out this form.

Mag ik uw legitimatiebewijs zien?
mahkh ihk ew lay•khee•tee•maat•see zeen

Can I see your identification?

Wanneer/Waar is het gebeurd?
vah•nayr/vaar ihs heht khuh•burt

When/Where did it happen?

Hoe ziet hij *m*/zij *f* eruit?
hoo zeet hie/zie ehr•awt

What does he/she look like?

Emergencies

Help!	**Help!** *hehlp*
Go away!	**Ga weg!** *khaa vehkh*
Stop thief!	**Houd de dief!** *howt duh deef*
Get a doctor!	**Haal een dokter!** *haal uhn dohk•tuhr*
Fire!	**Brand!** *brahnt*
I'm lost.	**Ik ben verdwaald.** *ihk behn fuhr•dvaalt*
Can you help me?	**Kunt u me helpen?** *kuhnt ew muh hehl•puhn*

In an emergency, dial **112** for police, fire brigade or ambulance.

Call the police!	**Bel de politie!** *bel duh poa·leet·see*
Where's the police station?	**Waar is het politiebureau?** *vaar ihs heht poa·leet·see·bew·roa*
My child is missing.	**Ik ben mijn kind kwijt.** *ihk behn mien kihnt kviet*

Health

I'm sick [ill].	**Ik ben ziek.** *ihk behn zeek*
I need an English-speaking doctor.	**Ik zoek een dokter die Engels spreekt.** *ihk zook uhn dohk·tuhr dee ehng·uhls spraykt*
It hurts here.	**Het doet hier pijn.** *heht doot heer pien*
Where's the nearest pharmacy [chemist]?	**Waar is de dichtstbijzijnde apotheek?** *vaar ihs duh dihkhtst·bie·zien·duh ah·poa·tayk*
I'm allergic to antibiotics/penicillin.	**Ik ben allergisch voor antibiotica/penicilline.** *ihk behn ah·lehr·khees foar ahn·tee·bee·oa·tee·kaa/ pay·nee·see·lee·nuh*
I'm on...	**Ik neem...** *ihk naym...*
I'm (...months) pregnant.	**Ik ben (...maanden) zwanger.** *ihk behn (...maandehn) swahng·ehr*

The **apotheek** (pharmacy) fills medical prescriptions and the **drogisterij** (drug store) sells non-prescription items, toiletries and cosmetics. Regular opening hours are Monday to Friday from 8:00 or 9:00 a.m. until 6:00 p.m. On nights and weekends, pharmacies open on a rotating schedule: if the one you are outside is closed, check the sign in the window to find the closest pharmacy that is open.

Dictionary

acetaminophen paracetamol
adapter adapter
address adres
American *n* Amerikaan;
   adj Amerikaans
and en
antiseptic adj antiseptisch
aspirin aspirine
baby baby
backpack rugzak
bad slecht
bag tas
bandage (small) pleister;
   (large) verband
battleground slagmark
beige beige
bikini bikini
blanket sort
bland intetsigende
blue blå
bottle opener flesopener
bowl kom
boy jongen
boyfriend vriend
British *n* Britten; *adj* Brits
bra beha
bra beha
brown brun
camera fototoestel
can opener blikopener
car seat kinderzitje
castle kasteel

cheap goedkoop
cigarette sigaret
cold (chilly) koud;
   (flu) verkoudheid
comb kam
computer computer
condom condoom
contact lens solution
   contactlensvloeistof
corkscrew kurkentrekker
cup kopje
dangerous gevaarlijk
dark donker
date of birth geboortedatum
  deodorant deodorant
diabetic *adj* diabetisch;
   n suikerpatiënt
dirty vies
dog hond
doll pop
driver's license rijbewijs
dry droog
ear oor
ear drops oordruppels
earache oorpijn
early vroeg
earrings oorbellen
east oost
easy makkelijk
eat eten
England Engeland
English Engels

31

female vrouwelijk
ferry veerboot
fever koorts
fine (good) goed; **(well)** prima;
(police) boete
fly *n* vlieg; *v* vliegen
fork vork
fracture breuk
full vol
garbage bag vuilniszak
girl meisje
girlfriend vriendin
glass (drinking) glas
good goed
great prima
green groen
Great Britain Groot-Brittannië
gym fitnessruimte
hairbrush borstel
heating [BE] verwarming
horse paard
hot heet
hurry *n* haast; *v* haasten
hurt *n* pijn; *v* pijn hebben
husband man
ibuprofen ibuprofen
I'd like… Ik wil graag…
Ireland Ierland
inexpensive goedkoop
infect ontsteken
infection infectie
insect repellent insectenspray
insurance verzekering
jeans spijkerbroek

joke grap
kind (pleasant) aardig;
(type) soort
kiss *v* kussen
knife mes
lactose intolerant lactose-
intolerant
large groot
laundry facilities wasmachines
lawyer advocaat
laxative laxerend middel
lighter *adj* lichter; *n* aansteker
long lang
lotion crème
love *n* liefde; (general) *v* dol zijn
op; (romantic) *v* houden van
matches lucifers
medicine geneesmiddel
meet ontmoeten
meeting vergadering
medium medium
mobile phone [BE]
(informal) mobiel;
(formal) mobiele telefoon
moisturizer (cream)
vochtinbrengende crème
mosquito bite muggenbeet
museum museum
nail file nagelvijl
napkin servet
nurse verpleegster
or of
orange orange
park *n* park; *v* parkeren

partner partner
pen pen
pink lyserød
plate bord
purple lilla
pyjamas pyjamas
rain *n* regen; *v* regenen
raincoat regenjas
razor scheerapparaat
red rød
refund *n* terugbetaling;
    v terugbetalen
salty saltet
sandals sandalen
sanitary napkin maandverband
sanitary pad [BE] maandverband
scissors schaar
sea zee
seasick zeeziek
shampoo shampoo
shoe schoen
small klein
sneakers gymschoenen
snow *n* sneeuw; *v* sneeuwen
soap zeep
socks sokken
spicy krydret
spoon lepel
stamp *n* postzegel; *v* stempelen
suitcase koffer
sun zon
sunglasses zonnebril
sunscreen zonnebrandcrème
sweater trui

sweatshirt sweatshirt
swimsuit zwempak
tampon tampon
terrible vreselijk
this dit
those die
tie *n* stropdas
timetable [BE] dienstregeling
tissue tissue
toilet paper toiletpapier
toothbrush tandenborstel
toothpaste tandpasta
tough hårde
toy speelgoed
toy store speelgoedwinkel
T-shirt t-shirt
U.K. Groot-Brittannië
U.S. Verenigde Staten
underwear undertøj
vegan veganist
vegetarian *n* vegetariër;
    adj vegetarisch
Wales Wales
white hvid
wife vrouw
with met
without zonder
yellow gul
your din
zoo dierentuin

French

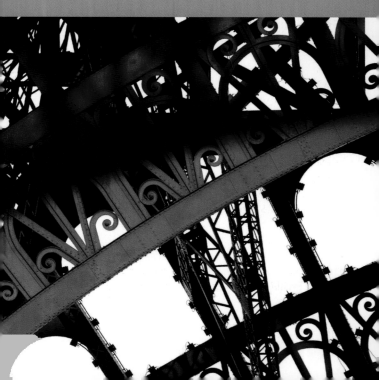

Essentials

Hello.	**Bonjour.** _bohN·zhoor_
Goodbye.	**Au revoir.** _oh ruh·vwahr_
Yes.	**Oui.** _wee_
No.	**Non.** _nohN_
OK.	**D'accord.** _dah·kohr_
Excuse me! (to get attention)	**Excusez-moi!** _ehk·skew·zay·mwah_
Excuse me. (to get past)	**Pardon.** _pahr·dohN_
I'm sorry.	**Je suis désolé** _m_/**désolée** _f_ _zhuh swee day·zoh·lay_
I'd like...	**Je voudrais...** _zhuh voo·dray..._
How much?	**Combien ça coûte?** _kohN·beeyehN sah koot_
And/Or.	**Et/Ou.** _eh/oo_
Where is...?	**Où est...?** _oo ay..._
Please.	**S'il vous plaît.** _seel voo play_
Thank you.	**Merci.** _mehr·see_
You're welcome.	**De rien.** _duh reeyehN_
I'm going to...	**Je vais à/aux...** _zhuh vay ah/oh..._
My name is...	**Mon nom est...** _mohN nohN ay..._
Please speak slowly.	**S'il vous plaît, parlez lentement.** _seel voo play pahr·lay lawN·tuh·mawN_
Can you repeat that?	**Pouvez-vous répéter cela?** _poo·vay·voo ray·pay·tay suh·lah_
I don't understand.	**Je ne comprends pas.** _zhuh nuh kohN·prawN pah_
Do you speak English?	**Parlez-vous anglais?** _pahr·lay·voo awN·glay_
I don't speak French.	**Je ne parle pas français.** _zhuh nuh pahrl pah frawN·say_
Where's the restroom [toilet]?	**Où sont les toilettes?** _oo sohN lay twah·leht_
Help!	**Au secours !** _oh suh·koohr_

French

You'll find the pronunciation of the French letters and words
written in gray after each sentence to guide you. Simply
pronounce these as if they were English, noting where there is a
break in syllables.
As you hear the language being spoken, you will quickly become
accustomed to the local pronunciation and dialect.

Numbers

0	**zéro**	zay·roh
1	**un**	uhN
2	**deux**	duh
3	**trois**	trwah
4	**quatre**	kah·truh
5	**cinq**	sehNk
6	**six**	sees
7	**sept**	seht
8	**huit**	weet
9	**neuf**	nuhf
10	**dix**	dees
11	**onze**	ohNz
12	**douze**	dooz
13	**treize**	trehz
14	**quatorze**	kah·tohrz
15	**quinze**	kehNz
16	**seize**	sehz
17	**dix-sept**	dee·seht
18	**dix-huit**	deez·weet
19	**dix-neuf**	deez·nuhf
20	**vingt**	vehN

21	**vingt-et-un** *vehN·tay·uhN*
22	**vingt-deux** *vehN·duh*
30	**trente** *trawNt*
31	**trente-et-un** *trawN·tay·uhN*
40	**quarante** *kah·rawNt*
50	**cinquante** *sehN·kawNt*
60	**soixante** *swah·zawNt*
70	**soixante-dix** *swah·zawNt·dees*
80	**quatre-vingt** *kah·truh·vehN*
90	**quatre-vingt-dix** *kah·truh·vehN·dees*
100	**cent** *sawN*
101	**cent-un** *sawN·uhN*
200	**deux-cent** *duh·sawN*
500	**cinq-cent** *sehNk·sawN*
1,000	**mille** *meel*
10,000	**dix mille** *dee meel*
1,000,000	**un million** *uhN meel·yohN*

Time

What time is it?	**Quelle heure est-il?** *kehl uhr ay·teel*
It's midday.	**Il est midi.** *ee lay mee·dee*
Five past three.	**Trois heures cinq.** *trwah zuhr sehNk*
A quarter to ten.	**Dix heures moins le quart.** *dee zuhr mwehN luh kahr*
5:30 a.m./p.m.	**Cinq heures et demie du matin/de l'après-midi.** *sehN kuhr eh duh·mee dew mah·tehN/ duh lah·preh·mee·dee*

Days

Monday	**lundi** *luhN·dee*
Tuesday	**mardi** *mahr·dee*
Wednesday	**mercredi** *mehr·kruh·dee*
Thursday	**jeudi** *zhuh·dee*

Friday	**vendredi** *vawN·druh·dee*
Saturday	**samedi** *sahm·dee*
Sunday	**dimanche** *dee·mawNsh*

Dates

yesterday	**hier** *eeyehr*
today	**aujourd'hui** *oh·zhoor·dwee*
tomorrow	**demain** *duh·mehN*
day	**le jour** *luh zhoor*
week	**la semaine** *lah suh·mehN*
month	**le mois** *luh mwah*
year	**l'année/l'an** *lah·nay/lawN*
Happy New Year!	**Bonne année !** *bohN ah·nay*
Happy Birthday!	**Joyeux anniversaire !** *zhoy·uhz ah·nee·vehr·sehr*

For Numbers, see page 36.

Months

January	**janvier** *zhawN·veeyay*
February	**février** *fay·vreeyay*
March	**mars** *mahrs*
April	**avril** *ah·vreel*
May	**mai** *may*
June	**juin** *zhwehN*
July	**juillet** *zhwee·yay*
August	**août** *oot*
September	**septembre** *sehp·tawN·bruh*
October	**octobre** *ohk·toh·bruh*
November	**novembre** *noh·vawN·bruh*
December	**décembre** *day·sawN·bruh*

YOU MAY SEE...

The French currency is the **euro**, **€**, which is divided into 100 **cents**.
Coins: 1, 2, 5, 10, 20 and 50 cents; €1, 2
Bills: €5, 10, 20, 50, 100, 200 and 500

Arrival & Departure

I'm on vacation [holiday]/business.	**Je suis en vacances/voyage d'affaires.** *zhuh swee zawN vah·kawNs/vwah·yahzh dah·fehr*
I'm going to...	**Je vais à/aux...** *zhuh vay ah/oh...*
I'm staying at the...Hotel.	**Je reste à l'hôtel...** *zhuh rehst ah loh·tehl...*

Money

Where's...?	**Où est...?** *oo ay...*
the ATM	**le distributeur automatique de billets** *luh dee·stree·bew·tuhr oh·toh·mah·teek duh bee·yay*
the bank	**la banque** *lah bawNk*
the currency exchange office	**le bureau de change** *luh bew·roh duh shawNzh*
When does the bank open/close?	**Quand est-ce que la banque ouvre/ferme?** *kawN tehs kuh lah bawNk oo·vruh/fehrm*
I'd like to change dollars/pounds sterling into euros.	**Je voudrais échanger des dollars/livres sterling en euros.** *zhuh voo·dray ay·shawN·zhay day doh·lahr/lee·vruh stayr·leeng awN nuh·roh*
I'd like to cash traveler's cheques.	**Je voudrais encaisser des chèques de voyages.** *zhuh voo·dray awN·kay·say day shehk duh vwah·yahzh*
Can I pay by cash?	**Je peux payer en espèces?** *zhuh puh pay·yay awN nehs·pehs?*
Can I pay by credit card?	**Puis-je payer par carte?** *pwee·zhuh pay·yay pahr kahrt*

Getting Around

How do I get to town?	**Comment vais-je en ville?** *koh·mawN vay·zhuh awN veel*
Where's…?	**Où est…?** *oo ay…*
the airport	**l'aéroport** *lah·ay·roh·pohr*
the train station	**la gare** *lah gahr*
the bus station	**la gare routière** *lah gahr roo·tee·yehr*
the Metro station	**le métro** *luh may·troh*
Is it far from here?	**C'est loin d'ici?** *say lwehN dee·see*
Where do I buy a ticket?	**Où puis-je acheter un billet?** *oo pwee·zhuh a ah·shtay uhN bee·yay*
A one-way/return-trip ticket to…	**Un billet aller simple/aller-retour…** *uhN bee·yay ah·lay sehN·pluh/ah·lay·ruh·toor…*
How much?	**Combien ça coûte?** *kohN·beeyehN sah koot*
Which gate/line?	**Quelle porte/ligne?** *kehl pohrt/lee·nyuh*
Which platform?	**Quel quai?** *kehl kay*
Where can I get taxi?	**Où puis-je prendre un taxi?** *oo pwee·zhuh a prawN·druh uhN tahk·see*
Take me to this address.	**Conduisez-moi à cette adresse.** *kohN·dwee·zay·mwah ah seh tah·drehs*
To…Airport, please.	**À l'aéroport de…, s'il vous plaît.** *ah lah·ay·roh·pohr duh…seel voo play*
I'm in a rush.	**Je suis pressé m/pressée f.** *zhuh swee preh·say*
Can I have a map?	**Puis-je avoir une carte?** *pwee·zhuh ah·vwahr ewn kahrt*

Tickets

When's…to Paris?	**Quand est…pour Paris?** *kawN tay…poor pah·ree*
the (first) bus	**le (premier) bus** *luh (pruh·meeay) bews*
the (next) flight	**le (prochain) vol** *luh (proh·shehN) vohl*
the (last) train	**le (dernier) train** *luh (dehr·neeay) trehN*

One/Two ticket(s).	**Un/Deux billet(s).** *uhN/duh bee•yay*
For today/tomorrow.	**Pour aujourd'hui/demain.**
	poor oh•zhoor•dwee/duh•mehN
A…ticket.	**Un billet…** *uhN bee•yay…*
one-way	**aller simple** *nah•lay sehN•pluh*
return trip	**aller-retour** *nah•lay•ruh•toor*
first class	**première classe** *pruh•meeyehr klahs*
I have an e-ticket.	**J'ai un billet électronique.**
	zhay uhN bee•yay ay•lehk•troh•neek
How long is the trip?	**Combien de temps dure le voyage?**
	kohN• beeyehN duh tawN dewr luh vwah•yahzh
Is it a direct train?	**Est-ce que c'est un train direct?**
	ehs kuh say tuhN trehN dee•rehkt
Is this the bus to…?	**Est-ce le bus pour…?** *ehs luh bews poor…*
Can you tell me	**Pouvez-vous me dire quand je dois descendre?**
when to get off?	*poo•vay•voo muh deer kawN zhuh dwah deh•sawN•druh*
I'd like to…	**Je voudrais…ma réservation.**
my reservation.	*zhuh voo•dray…mah ray•zehr•vah•seeyohN*
cancel	**annuler** *ah•new•lay*
change	**échanger** *ay•shawN•zhay*
confirm	**confirmer** *kohN•feer•may*

For Time, see page 37.

Car Hire

Where's the car hire?	**Où est l'agence de location de voitures?**
	oo ay lah•zhawNs duh loh•kah•seeyohN duh vwah•tewr
I'd like…	**Je voudrais…** *zhuh voo•dray…*
a cheap/small car	**une voiture bon marché/petite voiture**
	ewn vwah•tewr bohN mahr•shay/puh•teet vwah•tewr
an automatic/	**une automatique/manuelle**
a manual	*ewn oh•toh•mah•teek/mah•new•ehl*

air conditioning	**la climatisation** *lah klee•mah•tee•zah•seeyohN*
a car seat	**un siège bébé** *uhN seeyehzh bay•bay*
How much…?	**Combien ça coûte…?** *kohN•beeyehN sah koot…*
per day/week	**par jour/semaine** *pahr zhoor/suh•mehN*
Are there any	**Y-a-t-il des réductions?**
discounts?	*yah•teel day ray•dewk•seeyohN*

Places to Stay

Can you recommend	**Pouvez-vous me conseiller un hôtel?**
a hotel?	*poo•vay•voo muh kohN•say•yay uhN noh•tehl*
I made a reservation.	**J'ai fait une réservation.**
	zhay fay ewn ray•zehr•vah•seeyohN
My name is…	**Mon nom est…** *mohN nohN ay…*
Do you have	**Avez-vous une chambre…?**
a room…?	*ah•vay•voo ewn shawN•bruh…*

YOU MAY HEAR…

tout droit *too drwah*	straight ahead
à gauche *ah gohsh*	left
à droite *ah drwaht*	right
au coin *oh kwehN*	around the corner
à l'opposé *ah loh•poh•zay*	opposite
derrière *deh•reeyehr*	behind
près de *pray duh*	next to
après *ah•pray*	after
nord/sud *nohr/sewd*	north/south
est/ouest *ehst/oowehst*	east/west
au feu (tricolore) *oh fuh (tree•koh•lohr)*	at the traffic light
au carrefour *oh cahr-foor*	at the intersection

for one/two	**pour un/deux** *poor uhN/duh*	
with a bathroom	**avec salle de bains** *ah·vehk sahl duh behN*	
with air conditioning	**avec climatisation** *ah·vehk klee·mah·tee·zah·seeyohN*	
For…	**Pour…** *poor…*	
tonight	**ce soir** *suh swahr*	
two nights	**deux nuits** *duh nwee*	
one week	**une semaine** *ewn suh·mehn*	
How much?	**Combien ça coûte?** *kohN·beeyehN sah koot*	
Is there anything cheaper?	**N'y-a-t-il rien de moins cher?** *Nee·yah·teel reeyehN duh mwehN shehr*	
When's check-out?	**Quand dois-je quitter la chambre?** *kawN dwah·zhuh kee·tay lah shawN·bruh*	
Can I leave this in the safe?	**Puis-je laisser ceci dans le coffre?** *pwee·zhuh lay·say suh·see dawN luh koh·fruh*	
Can I leave my bags?	**Puis-je laisser mes bagages?** *pwee·zhuh lay·say meh bah·gahzh*	
Can I have my bill/ a receipt?	**Puis-je avoir ma facture/un reçu?** *pwee·zhuh ah·vwahr mah fahk·tewr/uhN ruh·sew*	
I'll pay in cash/by credit card.	**Je paierai en espèces/par carte de crédit.** *zhuh pay·ray awN nehs·pehs/pahr kahrt duh kray·dee*	

Communications

Where's an internet cafe?	**Où y-a-t-il un cyber café?** *oo yah·teel uhN see·behr kah·fay*
Can I access the internet/check my e-mail?	**Puis-je me connecter à Internet/consulter mes mails?** *pwee·zhuh muh koh·nehk·tay ah ehN·tehr·neht/kohN·sewl·tay may mehyl*
How much per half hour/hour?	**Combien coûte la demi-heure/l'heure?** *kohN·beeyehN koot lah duh·mee·uhr/luhr*

How do I connect/log on?	**Comment est-ce que je me connecte/ j'ouvre une session?** *koh·mawN ehs kuh zhuh muh koh·nehkt/zhoo·vruh ewn seh·seeyohN*
A phone card, please.	**Une carte de téléphone, s'il vous plaît.** *ewn kahrt duh tay·lay·fohn seel voo play*
Can I have your phone number?	**Puis-je avoir votre numéro de téléphone?** *pwee·zhuh ah·vwahr voh·truh new·meh·roh duh tay·lay·fohn*
Here's my number/e-mail.	**Voici mon numéro/mail.** *vwah·see mohN new·meh·roh/mehyl*
Please call/text me.	**S'il vous plaît, appelez-moi/envoyez-moi un SMS.** *seel voo play ah·puh·lay·mwah/ awN·vwah·yay·mwah uhN ehs·ehm·ehs*
I'll call/text you.	**Je vous appellerai/enverrai un SMS.** *zhuh voo zah·peh·luh·ray/zawN·veh·ray uhN nehs·ehm·ehs*
E-mail me.	**Envoie-moi un mail.** *awN·vwah·mwah uhN mehyl*
Hello. This is...	**Bonjour. C'est...** *bohN·zhoor say...*
Can I speak to...?	**Puis-je parler à...?** *pwee·zhuh pahr·lay ah...*
Can you repeat that?	**Pouvez-vous répéter cela?** *poo·vay·voo ray·pay·tay suh·lah*
I'll call back later.	**Je rappellerai plus tard.** *zhuh rah·peh·luh·ray plew tahr*
Bye.	**Au revoir.** *oh ruh·vwahr*
Where's the post office?	**Où est la poste?** *oo ay lah pohst*
I'd like to send this to...	**Je voudrais envoyer ceci à...** *zhuh voo·dray zawN·vwah·yay suh·see ah...*
Can I...?	**Puis-je...?** *pwee·zhuh...*
access the internet	**accéder à Internet** *ahk·seh·day ah ehN·tehrneht*
check my email	**consulter mes mails** *kohN·sewl·tay may mehyl*
print	**imprimer** *ehN·pree·may*

plug in/charge my laptop/iPhone/ iPad/BlackBerry?	**brancher/charger mon ordinateur portable/ iPhone/iPad/Blackberry?** *brawN·shay/ shahr·zhay mohN nohr·dee·nah·tuhr pohr·tah·bluh/ ee·fohn/ee·pahd/black·ber·ee*
access Skype?	**accéder à Skype?** *ah·ksay·day ah skiep*
What is the WiFi password?	**Quel est le mot de passe du WiFi?** *keh lay luh moh duh pahs dew wee·fee*
Is the WiFi free?	**Est-ce que le WiFi est gratuit?** *ehs kuh luh wee·fee ay grah·twee*
Do you have bluetooth?	**Avez-vous Bluetooth?** *ah·vay·voo bloo·toohs*
Do you have a scanner?	**Avez-vous un scanneur?** *ah·vay·voo uhN skah·nuhr*

Social Media

Are you on Facebook/Twitter?	**Etes-vous sur Facebook/Twitter?** *(polite form)* *eht·voo sewr fayhs·book/twee·teuhr*
	Es-tu sur Facebook/Twitter? *(informal form)* *eh·tew sewr fayhs·book/twee·teuhr*
What's your user name?	**Quel est votre nom d'utilisateur?** *(polite form)* *keh lay voh·truh nohN dew·tee·lee·zah·tuhr*
	Quel est ton nom d'utilisateur? *(informal form)* *keh lay tohN nohN dew·tee·lee·zah·tuhr*
I'll add you as a friend.	**Je vous ajouterai comme ami.** *(polite form)* *zhuh voo zah·zhoo·tray kohm ah·mee*
	Je t'ajouterai comme ami. *(informal form)* *zhuh tah·zhoo·tray kohm ah·mee*
I'll follow you on Twitter.	**Je vous suivrai sur Twitter.** *(polite form)* *zhuh voo swee·vray sewr twitter*
	Je te suivrai sur Twitter. *(informal form)* *zhuh tuh swee·vray sewr twitter*

Are you following...?	**Suivez-vous...?** *(polite form)* swee•vay voo
	Suis-tu...? *(informal form)* swee tew
I'll put the pictures on Facebook/Twitter.	**Je mettrai les photos sur Facebook/Twitter.** *zhuh may•tray lay foh•toh sewr fayhs•book/twee•teuhr*
I'll tag you in the pictures.	**Je vous marquerai sur les photos.** *(polite form)* *zhuh voo mahr•kuh•ray sewr lay foh•toh*
	Je te marquerai sur les photos. *(informal form)* *zhuh tuh mahr•kuh•ray sewr lay foh•toh*

Conversation

Hello!/Hi!	**Bonjour!/Salut !** bohN•zhoor/sah•lew
How are you?	**Comment allez-vous?** koh•mawN tah•lay•voo
Fine, thanks.	**Bien, merci.** beeyehN mehr•see
Excuse me!	**Excusez-moi !** ehk•skew•zay•mwah
Do you speak English?	**Parlez-vous anglais?** pahr•lay•voo zawN•glay
What's your name?	**Comment vous appelez-vous?** *koh•mawN voo zah•puh•lay•voo*
My name is...	**Je m'appelle...** zhuh mah•pehl...
Nice to meet you.	**Enchanté** *m*/**Enchantée** *f.* awN•shawN•tay
Where are you from?	**D'où êtes-vous?** doo eht•voo
I'm from the U.K./U.S.	**Je viens du Royaume-Uni/des États-Unis.** *zhuh veeyehN dew rwah•yohm•ew•nee/ day zay•tah•zew•nee*
What do you do for a living?	**Que faites-vous dans la vie?** *kuh feht•voo dawN lah vee*
I work for...	**Je travaille pour...** zhuh trah•vie poor...
I'm a student.	**Je suis étudiant** *m*/**étudiante** *f.* *zhuh swee zay•tew•deeyawN/zay•tew•deeyawnt*
I'm retired.	**Je suis à la retraite.** zhuh swee zah lah ruh•trayt

Romance

Would you like to go out for a drink/dinner?	**Voudriez-vous aller prendre un verre/ sortir dîner?** *voo·dreeyay·voo ah·lay prawN·druh uhN vehr/sohr·teer dee·nay*
What are your plans for tonight/ tomorrow?	**Quels sont vos projets pour ce soir/ demain?** *kehl sohN voh proh·zhay poor suh swahr/duh·mehN*
Can I have your (phone) number?	**Puis-je avoir votre numéro (de téléphone)?** *pwee·zhuh ah·vwahr voh·truh new·may·roh (duh tay·lay·fohn)*
Can I join you?	**Puis-je me joindre à vous?** *pwee·zhuh muh zhwehN·druh ah voo*
Can I buy you a drink?	**Puis-je vous offrir un verre?** *pwee·zhuh voo zoh·freer uhN vehr*
I love you.	**Je t'aime.** *zhuh tehm*

Accepting & Rejecting

I'd love to.	**Avec plaisir.** *ah·vehk play·zeer*
Where should we meet?	**Où devons-nous nous retrouver?** *oo duh·vohN·noo noo ruh·troo·vay*
I'll meet you at the bar/your hotel.	**Je vous retrouverai au bar/à votre hôtel.** *zhuh voo ruh·troo·vuh·ray oh bahr/ah voh·truh oh·tehl*
I'll come by at...	**Je viendrai à...** *zhuh veeyehN·dray ah...*
I'm busy.	**Je suis occupé *m*/occupée *f*.** *zhuh swee zoh·kew·pay*
I'm not interested.	**Je ne suis pas intéressé *m*/intéressée *f*.** *zhuh nuh swee pah ehN·tay·reh·say*
Leave me alone.	**Laissez-moi tranquille.** *leh·say mwah trawN·keel*
Stop bothering me!	**Fichez-moi la paix !** *fee·shay·mwah lah pay*

Food & Drink

Eating Out

Can you recommend a good restaurant/bar?	**Pouvez-vous me conseiller un bon restaurant/bar?** *poo·vay·voo muh kohN·say·yay uhN bohN reh·stoh·rawN/bahr*
Is there a traditional French/an inexpensive restaurant nearby?	**Y-a-t-il un restaurant traditionnel français/ bon marché près d'ici?** *yah·teel uhN reh·stoh·rawN trah·dee·seeyohN·nehl frawN·say/ bohN mahr·shay pray dee·see*
A table for..., please.	**Une table pour..., s'il vous plaît.** *ewn tah·bluh poor...seel voo play*
Can we sit...?	**Pouvons-nous nous asseoir...?** *poo·vohN·noo noo zah·swahr...*
here/there	**ici/là** *ee·see/lah*
outside	**dehors** *duh·ohr*
in a non-smoking area	**en zone non-fumeur** *awN zohn nohN·few·muhr*
I'm waiting for someone.	**J'attends quelqu'un.** *zhah·tawN kehl·kuhN*
Where are the toilets?	**Où sont les toilettes?** *oo sohN lay twah·leht*
A menu, please.	**La carte, s'il vous plaît.** *lah kahrt seel voo play*
What do you recommend?	**Que recommandez-vous?** *kuh reh·koh·mawN·day·voo*
I'd like...	**Je voudrais...** *zhuh voo·dray...*
Some more..., please.	**Un peu plus de..., s'il vous plaît.** *uhN puh plew duh...seel voo play*
Enjoy your meal!	**Bon appétit !** *bohN nah·peh·tee*
The check [bill], please.	**L'addition, s'il vous plaît.** *lah·dee·seeyohN seel voo play*

Is service included?	**Est-ce que le service est compris?**
	ehs kuh luh sehr·vees ay kohN·pree
Can I pay by credit card/have a receipt?	**Puis-je payer par carte de crédit/avoir un reçu?**
	pwee·zhuh pay·yay pahr kahrt duh kray·dee/ ah·vwahr uhN ruh·sew

Breakfast

le bacon *luh beh·kohn*	bacon
le pain *luh pehN*	bread
le beurre *luh buhr*	butter
la charcuterie *lah shahr·kew·tuh·ree*	cold cuts
le fromage *luh froh·mahzh*	cheese
l'œuf... *luhf...*	...egg
dur/à la coque *dewr/ah lah kohk*	hard-/soft-boiled
sur le plat *sewr luh plah*	fried
brouillé *broo·yay*	scrambled
la confiture *lah kohN·fee·tewr*	jam/jelly
l'omelette *lohm·leht*	omelet
le pain grillé *luh pehN gree·yay*	toast
la saucisse *lah soh·sees*	sausage
le yaourt *luh yah·oort*	yogurt

YOU MAY SEE...

COUVERT	cover charge
PRIX FIXE	fixed-price
MENU (DU JOUR)	menu (of the day)
SERVICE (NON) COMPRIS	service (not) included
MENU À LA CARTE	specials

Appetizers

le pâté *luh pah·tay*	liver paté
le potage bilibi *luh poh·tahzh bee·lee·bee*	fish and oyster soup
la soupe aux légumes/a soupe de tomates *lah soop oh lay·gewm/lah soop duh toh·maht*	vegetable/tomato soup
la soupe de volaille *lah soop duh voh·lie*	chicken soup
salade *sah·lahd*	salad

Meat

le bœuf *luh buhf*	beef
le poulet *luh poo·lay*	chicken
l'agneau *lah·nyoh*	lamb
le porc *luh pohr*	pork
le bifteck *luh beef·tehk*	steak
le veau *luh voh*	veal

Fish & Seafood

la morue *lah moh·rew*	cod
le hareng *luh ah·rawN*	herring
le homard *luh oh·mahr*	lobster
le saumon *luh soh·mohN*	salmon
la crevette *lah kruh·veht*	shrimp

YOU MAY HEAR...

saignant *say·nyawN*	rare
à point *ah pwehN*	medium
bien cuit *beeyehN kwee*	well-done

Vegetables

les haricots *lay ah‧ree‧koh*	beans
le chou *luh shoo*	cabbage
la carotte *lah kah‧roht*	carrot
le champignon *luh shawN‧pee‧nyohN*	mushroom
l'oignon *loh‧nyohN*	onion
les petits pois *lay puh‧tee pwah*	peas
la pomme de terre *lah pohm duh tehr*	potato
la tomate *lah toh‧maht*	tomato

Sauces & Condiments

sel *sehl*	salt
poivre *pwah‧vruh*	pepper
moutarde *moo‧tahrd*	mustard
ketchup *Ket‧shuhp*	ketchup

Fruit & Dessert

la pomme *lah pohm*	apple
la banane *lah bah‧nahn*	banana
le citron *luh see‧trohN*	lemon
l'orange *loh‧rawNzh*	orange
la poire *lah pwahr*	pear
la fraise *lah frehz*	strawberry
la glace *lah glahs*	ice cream
le chocolat *luh shoh‧koh‧lah*	chocolate
la vanille *lah vah‧neeyuh*	vanilla
la génoise *lah zhay‧nwahz*	sponge cake
la tarte aux fruits *lah tahrt oh frwee*	fruit pie or tart
la mousse *lah moos*	chocolate mousse
la crème anglaise *lah krehm awN‧glehz*	custard
la crème *lah krehm*	cream

Drinks

Can I see the wine list/ drinks menu, please?	**La carte des vins/boissons, s'il vous plaît.** *lah kahrt day vehN/bwah•sohN seel voo play*
What do you recommend?	**Que me conseillez-vous?** *kuh muh kohN•say•yay•voo*
I'd like a bottle/glass of red/white wine.	**Je voudrais une bouteille/un verre de vin rouge/blanc.** *zhuh voo•dray ewn boo•tehy/uhN vehr duh vehN roozh/blawN*
The house wine, please.	**Le vin de la maison, s'il vous plaît.** *luh vehN duh lah may•zohN seel voo play*
Another bottle/glass, please.	**Une autre bouteille/Un autre verre, s'il vous plaît.** *ewn oh•truh boo•tehy/uhN noh•truh vehr seel voo play*
I'd like a local beer.	**Je voudrais une bière locale.** *zhuh voo•dray ewn beeyehr loh•kahl*
Can I buy you a drink?	**Puis-je vous offrir un verre?** *pwee•zhuh voo zoh•freer uhN vehr*
Cheers!	**Santé !** *sawN•tay*
A coffee/tea, please.	**Un café/thé, s'il vous plaît.** *uhN kah•fay/tay seel voo play*
Black.	**Noir.** *nwahr*
With…	**Avec…** *ah•vehk…*
milk	**du lait** *dew lay*
sugar	**du sucre** *dew sew•kruh*
artificial sweetener	**de l'édulcorant** *duh lay•dewl•koh•rawN*
A…, please.	**Un…, s'il vous plaît.** *uhN… seel voo play*
juice	**jus de fruit** *zhew duh frwee*
soda	**soda** *soh•dah*
sparkling/still water	**de l'eau gazeuse/plate** *duh loh gah•zuhz/plaht*

Leisure Time

Sightseeing

Where's the tourist information office?	**Où est l'office de tourisme?** *oo ay loh·fees duh too·ree·smuh*
What are the main sights?	**Quelles sont les choses importantes à voir?** *kehl sohN lay shoh zehN·pohr·tawN tah vwahr*
Do you offer tours in English?	**Proposez-vous des visites en anglais?** *Proh·poh·zay·voo day vee·zeet awN nawN·glay*
Can I have a map/guide?	**Puis-je avoir une carte/un guide?** *pwee·zhuh ah·vwahr ewn kahrt/uhN geed*

Shopping

Where's the market/mall?	**Où est le marché/centre commercial?** *oo ay luh mahr·shay/sawN·truh koh·mehr·seeyahl*
I'm just looking.	**Je regarde seulement.** *zhuh ruh·gahrd suhl·mawN*
Can you help me?	**Pouvez-vous m'aider?** *poo·vay·voo meh·day*
I'm being helped.	**On s'occupe de moi.** *ohN soh·kewp duh mwah*
How much?	**Combien ça coûte?** *kohN·beeyehN sah koot*
That one, please.	**Celui-ci** *m*/**Celle-ci** *f*, **s'il vous plaît.** *suh·lwee·see/sehl see seel voo play*
I'd like...	**Je voudrais...** *zhuh voo·dray...*
That's all.	**C'est tout.** *say too*
Where can I pay?	**Où puis-je payer?** *oo pwee·zhuh pay·yay*
I'll pay in cash/by credit card.	**Je paierai en espèces/par carte de crédit.** *zhuh pay·ray awN neh·spehs/pahr kahrt duh kray·dee*
A receipt, please.	**Un reçu, s'il vous plaît.** *uhN ruh·sew seel voo play*

YOU MAY SEE...

OUVERT/FERMÉ	open/closed
ENTRÉE/SORTIE	entrance/exit

Sport & Leisure

When's the game?	**Quand a lieu le match?** *kawN tah leeyuh luh mahtch*
Where's…?	**Où est…?** *oo ay…*
the beach	**la plage** *lah plazh*
the park	**le parc** *luh pahrk*
the pool	**la piscine** *lah pee-seen*
Is it safe to swim here?	**Est-ce que c'est sans danger de nager ici?** *ehs kuh say sawN dawN-zhay duh nah-zhay ee-see*
Can I hire clubs?	**Puis-je louer des clubs?** *pwee-zhuh looway day kluhb*
How much per hour?	**Combien ça coûte par heure?** *kohN-beeyehN sah koot pahr uhr*
How far is it to…?	**À quelle distance se trouve…?** *ah kehl dees-tawNs suh troov…*
Show me on the map, please.	**Montrez-moi sur la carte, s'il vous plaît.** *mohN-tray-mwah sewr lah kahrt seel voo play*

Going Out

What's there to do at night?	**Que peut-on faire le soir?** *kuh puh-tohN fehr luh swahr*
Do you have a program of events?	**Avez-vous un programme des festivités?** *ah-vay-voo uhN proh-grahm day fehs-tee-vee-tay*
What's playing tonight?	**Qui joue ce soir?** *kee zhoo suh swahr*
Where's…?	**Où est…?** *oo ay…*
the downtown area	**le centre ville** *luh sawN-truh veel*
the bar	**le bar** *luh bahr*
the dance club	**la discothèque** *lah dees-koh-tehk*
Is this area safe at night?	**Est-ce que cet endroit est sûr la nuit?** *ehs kuh seht awN-drwah ay sewr lah nwee*

Baby Essentials

Do you have...?	**Avez-vous...?** *ah·vay·voo...*
a baby bottle	**un biberon** *uhN bee·buh·rohN*
baby food	**des petits pots** *day puh·tee poh*
baby wipes	**des lingettes pour bébé** *day lehN·zhet poor bay·bay*
a car seat	**un siège bébé** *uhN seeyehzh bay·bay*
a children's menu/portion	**un menu/des portions pour enfants** *uhN muh·new/day pohr·seeyohN poo rawN·fawN*
a child's seat/highchair	**un siège bébé/une chaise haute** *uhN seeyehzh bay·bay/ewn shehz oht*
a crib/cot	**un berceau/lit pliant** *uhN behr·soh/lee pleeyawN*
diapers [nappies]	**des couches** *day koosh*
formula	**du lait pour bébé** *dew lay poor bay·bay*
a pacifier [dummy]	**une tétine** *ewn tay·teen*
a playpen	**un parc pour enfant** *uhN pahrk poo rawN·fawN*
a stroller [pushchair]	**une poussette** *ewn poo·seht*
Can I breastfeed the baby here?	**Puis-je allaiter le bébé ici?** *pwee·zhuh ah·leh·tay luh bay·bay ee·see*
Where can I breastfeed/change the baby?	**Où puis-je allaiter/changer le bébé?** *oo pwee·zhuh ah·leh·tay/shawN·zhay luh bay·bay*

For Eating Out, see page 48.

Disabled Travelers

Is there...?	**Y-a-t-il...?** *yah·teel...*
access for the disabled	**un accès pour handicapés** *uhN nahk·seh poor awN·dee·kah·pay*
a wheelchair ramp	**un accès pour chaises roulantes** *uhN nahk·say poor shehz roo·lawNt*
a disabled-accessible toilet	**des toilettes accessibles aux handicapés** *day twah·leht ahk·seh·see·bluh oh zawN·dee·kah·pay*

I need...	**J'ai besoin...** *zhay buh·zwehN...*
assistance	**d'aide** *dehd*
an elevator [a lift]	**d'un ascenseur** *duhN nah·sawN·suhr*
a ground-floor room	**d'une chambre au rez-de-chaussée** *dewn shawN·bruh oh ray·duh·shoh·say*
Please speak louder.	**S'il vous plaît, parlez plus fort.** *seel voo play pahr·lay plew fohr*

Health & Emergencies

Emergencies

Help!	**Au secours!** *oh suh·koor*
Go away!	**Allez-vous en!** *ah·lay·voo zawN*
Stop, thief!	**Arrêtez, au voleur!** *ah·reh·tay oh voh·luhr*
Get a doctor!	**Allez chercher un docteur!** *ah·lay shehr·shay uhN dohk·tuhr*
Fire!	**Au feu!** *oh fuh*
I'm lost.	**Je suis perdu *m*/perdue *f*.** *zhuh swee pehr·dew*
Can you help me?	**Pouvez-vous m'aider?** *poo·vay·voo may·day*
Call the police!	**Appelez la police!** *ah·puh·lay lah poh·lees*
Where's the police station?	**Où est le commissariat de police?** *oo ay luh koh·mee·sah·reeyah duh poh·lees*
My child is missing.	**Mon enfant a disparu.** *mohN nawN·fawN ah dees·pah·rew*

In an emergency, dial: **17** for the police
18 for the fire brigade
15 for the ambulance

YOU MAY HEAR...

Remplissez ce formulaire.
rawN•plee•say suh fohr•mew•lehr
Fill out this form.

Vos papiers d'identité, s'il vous plaît.
voh pah•peeyay dee•dawN•tee•tay seel voo play
Your ID, please.

Quand/Où cela s'est-il produit?
kawN/oo suh•lah say•teel proh•dwee
When/Where did it happen?

À quoi ressemble-t-il *m*/ressemble-t-elle *f*?
ah kwah ruh•sawN•bluh•teel/ruh•sawN•bluh•tehl
What does he/she look like?

Health

I'm sick.	**Je suis malade.** *zhuh swee mah•lahd*
I need an English-speaking doctor.	**J'ai besoin d'un docteur qui parle anglais.** *zhay buh•zwehN duhN dohk•tuhr kee pahrl awN•glay*
It hurts here.	**Ça fait mal ici.** *sah fay mahl ee•see*
Where's the pharmacy?	**Où est la pharmacie?** *oo ay lah fahr•mah•see*
I'm (...months) pregnant.	**Je suis enceinte (de...mois).** *zhuh swee zawN•sehNt (duh...mwah)*
I'm on...	**Je prends...** *zhuh prawN...*
I'm allergic to antibiotics/penicillin.	**Je suis allergique aux antibiotiques/ à la pénicilline.** *zhuh swee zah•lehr•zheek oh zawN•tee•beeyoh•teek/ah lah pay•nee•see•leen*

Dictionary

a un *m*/une *f*
acetaminophen le paracétamol
adapter l'adaptateur
and et
antiseptic cream la crème antiseptique
aspirin l'aspirine
baby le bébé
backpack le sac à dos
bad mauvais(e)
bag le sac
bandage le pansement
battleground le champ de bataille
beige beige
bikini le bikini
bird l'oiseau
black noir
bland sans goût
blue bleu
bottle opener l'ouvre-bouteille
bowl le saladier
boy le garçon
boyfriend le petit-ami
bra le soutien-gorge
brown marron
camera l'appareil photo;
can opener le l'ouvre-boîte
castle le château
charger charger
cigarette la cigarette
cold (sickness) le rhume;
 ~ **(temperature)** froid

comb le peigne
computer l'ordinateur
condom le préservatif
contact lens solution la solution pour lentilles de contact
corkscrew le tire-bouchon
cup la tasse
dangerous dangereux
deodorant le déodorant
diabetic diabétique
doll la poupée
fly la mouche
fork la fourchette
girl la fille
girlfriend la petite-amie
glass le verre;
good adj bon
gray gris
green vert
hairbrush la brosse
hairspray la laque
hot (spicy) épicé;
 ~ **(temperature)** chaud;
husband le mari
ice la glace
icy glacé
injection la piqûre
I'd like… Je voudrais…
insect repellent la lotion anti-insectes
jeans le jean
knife le couteau

lactose intolerant allergique au lactose
large grand
lighter le briquet
lotion la crème
love v **(someone)** aimer; ~ n amour
matches d'allumettes
medium (size) moyen
museum le musée
nail file la lime á ongle
napkin la serviette
nurse l'infirmier
orange (color) orange
park v se garer; ~ n le parc
pen le stylo
plate l'assiette
purple pourpre
pajamas un pyjama
rain la pluie
raincoat l'imperméable
razor blade la lame de rasoir
razor, disposable un rasoir (jetable)
red rouge
salty salé
sandals les sandales
sauna le sauna
sanitary napkin la serviette hygiénique
scissors les ciseaux
shampoo/conditioner du shampooing/de l'après shampooing
shoes les chaussures
small petit(e)
snake le serpent

sneakers les tennis
snowy neigeux
soap le savon
sock la chaussette
spicy épicé
spider l'araignée (f)
spoon la cuillère
stamp n **(postage)** le timbre
suitcase la valise
sun le soleil
sunblock l'écran solaire
sunglasses les lunettes de soleil
sweater le pull
sweatshirt le sweat-shirt
swimsuit le maillot de bain
tampon le tampon
terrible terrible
tie (clothing) la cravate
tissues les Kleenex
toilet paper le papier toilette
toothbrush la brosse
toothpaste le dentifrice
tough (food) dur
toy le jouet
underwear les sous-vêtements
vegan végétalien m/végétalienne f
vegetarian végétarien
white blanc
wife l'épouse
with avec
without sans
yellow jaune
your votre
zoo le zoo

German

Essentials

Hello.	**Hallo.** *hah-loh*
Goodbye.	**Auf Wiedersehen.** *owf vee-dehr-zehn*
Yes/No/OK	**Ja/Nein/Okay.** *yah/nien/oh-keh*
Excuse me! (to get attention, to get past)	**Entschuldigung!** *ehnt-shool-dee-goong*
I'm sorry.	**Tut mir leid.** *toot meer lied*
I'd like...	**Ich möchte ...** *eekh merkh-tuh ...*
How much?	**Wie viel?** *vee feel*
And/or	**Und/oder** *oont/oh-duhr*
Please.	**Bitte.** *biht-tuh*
Thank you.	**Danke.** *dahn-kuh*
You're welcome.	**Gern geschehen.** *gehrn guh-sheh-uhn*
Where is...?	**Wo ist ...?** *voh ihst ...*
I'm going to	**Ich reise nach ...** *eekh riez-uh nahkh ...*
My name is	**Mein Name ist ...** *mien nahm-uh ihst ...*
Please speak slowly.	**Bitte sprechen Sie langsam.** *biht-tuh shpreh-khehn zee lahng-zahm*
Can you repeat that?	**Können Sie das wiederholen?** *kehr-nuhn zee dahs vee-dehr-hoh-luhn*
I don't understand.	**Ich verstehe nicht.** *eekh fehr-shteh-uh neekht*
Do you speak English?	**Sprechen Sie Englisch?** *shpreh-khen zee ehn-gleesh*
I don't speak German	**Ich spreche kein Deutsch.** *eekh shpreh-khuh kien doych*
Where's the restroom [toilet]?	**Wo ist die Toilette?** *voh ihst dee toy-leh-tuh*
Help!	**Hilfe!** *hihl-fuh*

You'll find the pronunciation of the German letters and words written in gray after each sentence to guide you. Simply pronounce these as if they were English, noting that any underlines and bolds indicate an additional emphasis or stress or a lengthening of a vowel sound. As you hear the language being spoken, you will quickly become accustomed to the local pronunciation and dialect.

Numbers

0	**null** *nool*
1	**eins** *iens*
2	**zwei** *tsvie*
3	**drei** *drie*
4	**vier** *feer*
5	**fünf** *fewnf*
6	**sechs** *zehks*
7	**sieben** *zeeb·uhn*
8	**acht** *ahkht*
9	**neun** *noyn*
10	**zehn** *tsehn*
11	**elf** *ehlf*
12	**zwölf** *tsverlf*
13	**dreizehn** *drie·sehn*
14	**vierzehn** *feert·sehn*
15	**fünfzehn** *fewnf·tsehn*
16	**sechszehn** *zehk·tsehn*
17	**siebzehn** *zeep·tsehn*
18	**achtzehn** *ahkht·tsehn*
19	**neunzehn** *noyn·tsehn*
20	**zwanzig** *tsvahnt·seek*

21	**einundzwanzig** _ien_·oond·tsvahn·tseek
30	**dreißig** _drie_·seekh
40	**vierzig** _feert_·seek
50	**fünfzig** _fewnf_·tseeg
60	**sechzig** _zehkht_·seeg
70	**siebzig** _zeeb_·tseeg
80	**achtzig** _ahkht_·tseeg
90	**neunzig** _noynt_·seek
100	**einhundert** _ien_·hoon·dehrt
101	**einhunderteins** _ien_·hoon·dehr·tiens
200	**zweihundert** _tsvie_·hoon·dehrt
500	**fünfhundert** _fewnf_·hoon·dehrt
1,000	**eintausend** _ien_·tow·zuhnt
10,000	**zehntausend** _tsehn_·tow·zuhnt
1,000,000	**eine Million** _ien_·uh mihl·_yohn_

Time

What time is it?	**Wie spät ist es?** _vee shpayt ihst ehs_
It's midday.	**Es ist zwölf.** _ehs ihst tsverlf_
Five past three.	**Fünf nach drei.** _fewnf nahkh drie_
A quarter to four.	**Viertel vor vier.** _feert_·uhl fohr feer
5:30 a.m./5:30 p.m.	**Fünf Uhr dreißig/Siebzehn Uhr dreißig.**
	_fewnf oohr _drie_·seeg/_zeeb_·tsuhn oohr _drie_·seeg_

Days

Monday	**Montag** _mohn_·tahk
Tuesday	**Dienstag** _deens_·tahk
Wednesday	**Mittwoch** _miht_·vohkh
Thursday	**Donnerstag** _dohn_·ehrs·tahk
Friday	**Freitag** _frie_·tahk
Saturday	**Samstag** _zahms_·tahk
Sunday	**Sonntag** _zohn_·tahk

Dates

yesterday	**gestern** _gehs_·tehrn	
today	**heute** _hoy_·tuh	
tomorrow	**morgen** _mohr_·guhn	
day	**Tag** tahk	
week	**Woche** _vohkh_·uh	
month	**Monat** _moh_·naht	
year	**Jahr** yahr	
Happy New Year!	**Frohes neues Jahr!** fro·uhs noy·uhs yahr	
Happy Birthday!	**Alles gute zum geburtstag!**	
	ahl·uhs _goo_·tuh tsoom _geh_·boors·tahk	

Months

January	**Januar** _yahn_·wahr
February	**Februar** _fehb_·rooahr
March	**März** mehrts
April	**April** ah·_prihl_
May	**Mai** mie
June	**Juni** _yoo_·nee
July	**Juli** _yoo_·lee
August	**August** _ow_·goost
September	**September** zehp·_tehm_·behr
October	**Oktober** ohk·_toh_·behr
November	**November** noh·_vehm_·behr
December	**Dezember** deh·_tsehm_·behr

Arrival & Departure

I'm on vacation [holiday].	**Ich mache Urlaub.** eekh _mahkh_·uh _oor_·lowb
I'm on business.	**Ich bin auf Geschäftsreise.** eekh bihn owf guh·_shehfts_·rie·zuh
I'm going to...	**Ich reise nach ...** eekh _rie_·zuh nahkh ...

| I'm staying at the...Hotel. | **Ich übernachte im Hotel ...** *eekh ew•buhr•nahkh•tuh ihm hoh•tehl ...* |

Money

Where's...?	**Wo ist ...?** *voh ihst ...*
the ATM	**der Bankautomat** *dehr bahnk•ow•toh•maht*
the bank	**die Bank** *dee bahnk*
the currency exchange office	**die Wechselstube** *dee vehkh•zuhl•shtoo•buh*
When does the bank open/close?	**Wann öffnet/schließt die Bank?** *vahn erf•nuht/ shleest dee bahnk*
I'd like to change dollars/pounds into euros.	**Ich möchte Dollar/Pfund in Euro wechseln.** *eekh mehrkh•tuh doh•lahr/pfoont ihn oy•roh vehkh•zuhln*
I'd like to cash traveler's checks [cheques].	**Ich möchte Reiseschecks einlösen.** *eekh mehrkh•tuh rie•zuh•shehks ien•ler•zuhn*
Can I pay in cash?	**Kann ich bar bezahlen?** *kahn eekh bahr beht•sahl•uhn*
Can I pay by credit card?	**Kann ich mit Kreditkarte bezahlen?** *kahn eekh miht kreh•deet•kahr•tuh beht•sahl•uhn*

For Numbers, see page 62.

YOU MAY SEE...

German currency is the **Euro €**, divided into 100 **Cent**.
Coins: 1, 2, 5, 10, 20, 50 **Cent**; €1, 2
Notes: €5, 10, 20, 50, 100, 200, 500

Getting Around

How do I get to town?	**Wie komme ich in die Stadt?**
	vee <u>koh</u>•muh eekh ihn dee shtaht
Where's. . .?	**Wo ist . . .?** *voh ihst . . .*
the airport	**der Flughafen** *dehr <u>flook</u>•hah•fuhn*
the train station	**der Bahnhof** *dehr <u>bahn</u>•hohf*
the bus station	**die Bushaltestelle** *dee boos•hahl•tuh•shteh•luh*
the subway [underground] station	**die U-Bahn-Haltestelle** *dee <u>oo</u>•bahn•<u>hahl</u>•tuh•shteh•luh*
Is it far from here?	**Wie weit ist es?** *vee viet ihst ehs*
Where do I buy a ticket?	**Wo kann ich eine Fahrkarte kaufen?** *voh kahn eekh <u>ie</u>•nuh <u>fahr</u>•kahr•tuh <u>kow</u>•fuhn*
A one-way/ return ticket to. . .	**Ein Einzelticket/Eine Fahrkarte für Hin und Rückfahrt nach . . .** *ien <u>ien</u>•tsehl•tee•kuht/ <u>ie</u>•nuh <u>fahr</u>•kahr•tuh fewr hihn oond <u>rewk</u>•fahrt nahkh. . .*
How much?	**Wie viel kostet es?** *vee feel <u>kohs</u>•tuht ehs*
Which gate/line?	**Welches Gate/Linie?** *<u>vehl</u>•khehs <u>geht</u>/<u>leen</u>•yah*
Which platform?	**Welcher Bahnsteig?** *<u>vehl</u>•khehr <u>bahn</u>•shtieg*
Where can I get a taxi?	**Wo finde ich ein Taxi?** *voh <u>fihn</u>•duh eekh ien <u>tahk</u>•see*
Take me to this address, please.	**Bitte fahren Sie mich zu dieser Adresse.** *<u>biht</u>•tuh <u>fah</u>•ruhn zee meekh tsoo <u>dee</u>•zehr ah•<u>dreh</u>•suh*
To. . .Airport, please.	**Zum Flughafen . . ., bitte.** *tsoom <u>flook</u>•hah•fuhn . . . <u>biht</u>•tuh*
I'm in a rush.	**Ich habe es eilig.** *eekh <u>hah</u>•buh ehs <u>ie</u>•leek*
Can I have a map, please?	**Können Sie mir bitte einen Stadtplan geben?** *<u>ker</u>•nuhn zee mihr <u>biht</u>•tuh <u>ien</u>•uhn <u>shtaht</u>•plahn <u>geh</u>•behn*

Tickets

When's...to Berlin?	**Wann geht ... nach Berlin?**
	vahn geht ... nahkh behr-leen
the (first) bus	**der (erste) Bus** *dehr (ehr-stuh) boos*
the (next) flight	**der (nächste) Flug** *dehr (nehks-tuh) floog*
the (last) train	**der (letzte) Zug** *dehr (lehts-tuh) tsoog*
One/two ticket(s), please.	**Ein/Zwei Ticket(s), bitte.** *ien/tsvie tee-kuht(s) biht-tuh*
For today/tomorrow.	**Für heute/morgen.** *fewr hoy-tuh/mohr-guhn*
A...ticket.	**Ein ... Ticket.** *ien ... tee-kuht*
one-way	**einfaches** *ien-fah-khuhs*
return trip	**Hin- und Rückflug-** *hihn oont rewk-floog*
first class	**Erste-Klasse-** *ehr-stuh-klah-suh*
I have an e-ticket.	**Ich habe ein E-Ticket/Online-Ticket.**
	eekh hah-buh ien ay-tee-keht/ohn-lien-tee-keht
How long is the trip?	**Wie lange dauert die Fahrt?** *vee lahng-uh dow-ehrt dee fahrt*
Is it a direct train?	**Ist das eine direkte Zugverbindung?**
	ihst dahs ien-uh dee-rehkt tsoog-ver-bind-ungh
Is this the bus to...?	**Ist das der Bus nach ...?** *ihst dahs dehr boos nahkh...*
Can you tell me when to get off?	**Können Sie mir sagen, wann ich aussteigen muss?** *kehrn-uhn zee meer zahg-uhn vahn eekh ows-shtieg-uhn moos*
I'd like to... my reservation.	**Ich möchte meine Reservierung ...** *eekh merkh-tuh mie-nuh reh-zehr-vee-roong ...*
cancel	**stornieren** *shtohr-nee-ruhn*
change	**ändern** *ehn-dehrn*
confirm	**bestätigen** *beh-shtay-tee-guhn*

For Time, see page 63.

Car Hire

Where's the car hire?	**Wo ist die Autovermietung?** *voh ihst dee ow·toh·fehr·miet·oong*
I'd like…	**Ich möchte …** *eekh merkh·tuh …*
a cheap/small car	**ein billiges/kleines Auto** *ien bihl·lee·guhs/klien·uhs ow·toh*
an automatic/ a manual car	**ein Auto mit Automatikschaltung/ Gangschaltung** *ien ow·toh miht ow·toh·mah·teek·shahl·toong/gahng·shahl·toong*
air conditioning	**ein Auto mit Klimaanlage** *ien ow·toh miht klee·mah·ahn·lah·guh*
a car seat	**einen Kindersitz** *ien·uhn kihnd·ehr·zihts*

YOU MAY HEAR…

geradeaus *geh·rahd·uh·ows*	straight ahead
links *leenks*	left
rechts *rehkhts*	right
an der/um die Ecke *ahn dehr/oom dee eh·kuh*	on/around the corner
gegenüber *geh·guhn·ew·behr*	opposite
hinter *hihnt·ehr*	behind
neben *nehb·uhn*	next to
nach *nahkh*	after
nördlich/südlich *nerd·leekh/zewd·leekh*	north/south
östlich/westlich *erst·leekh/vehst·leekh*	east/west
an der Ampel *ahn dehr ahmp·ehl*	at the traffic light
an der Kreuzung *ahn dehr kroytz·oong*	at the intersection

How much...?	**Wie viel kostet es ...?** *vee feel <u>kohs</u>•tuht ehs ...*
per day/week	**pro Tag/Woche** *proh tahk/<u>vohkh</u>•uh*
Are there any discounts?	**Gibt es irgendwelche Ermäßigungen?**
	gihpt ehs <u>eer</u>•guhnd•vehlkh•uh ehr•<u>meh</u>•see•goong•uhn

Places to Stay

Can you recommend a hotel?	**Können Sie ein Hotel empfehlen?**
	ker•nuhn zee ien hoh•<u>tehl</u> ehm•<u>pfeh</u>•luhn
I have a reservation.	**Ich habe eine Reservierung.** *eekh <u>hahb</u>•uh*
	<u>ien</u>•uh rehz•ehr•<u>veer</u>•oong
My name is...	**Mein Name ist ...** *mien <u>nahm</u>•uh ihst ...*
Do you have a room...?	**Haben Sie ein Zimmer ...?** *<u>hah</u>•buhn zee ien*
	<u>tsihm</u>•mehr ...
for one person/ two people	**für eine Person/zwei Personen**
	fewr <u>ien</u>•uh pehr•<u>sohn</u>/tsvie pehr•<u>sohn</u>•uhn
with a bathroom	**mit Bad** *miht bahd*
with air conditioning	**mit Klimaanlage** *miht <u>kleem</u>•uh•ahn•lahg•uh*
For...	**Für ...** *fewr ...*
tonight	**heute Nacht** *<u>hoy</u>•tuh nahkht*
two nights	**zwei Nächte** *tsvie <u>nehkht</u>•uh*
one week	**eine Woche** *<u>ien</u>•uh <u>vohkh</u>•uh*
How much?	**Wie viel kostet es?** *vee feel <u>kohs</u>•tuht ehs*
Is there anything cheaper?	**Gibt es etwas Billigeres?** *gihpt ehs*
	<u>eht</u>•vahs <u>bihl</u>•lee•geh•ruhs
When's check-out?	**Wann ist der Check-out?** *vahn ihst dehr <u>tshehk</u>•owt*
Can I leave this in the safe?	**Kann ich das im Safe lassen?** *kahn eekh*
	dahs ihm sehf <u>lahs</u>•suhn
Can I leave my bags?	**Kann ich meine Taschen hierlassen?**
	kahn eekh <u>mien</u>•uh <u>tahsh</u>•uhn <u>heer</u>•lahs•suhn

Can I have my bill/a receipt?	**Kann ich meine Rechnung/eine Quittung haben?** *kahn eekh mien-uh rehkh-noong/ ien-uh kveet-oong hah-buhn*
I'll pay in cash/by credit card.	**Ich bezahle bar/mit Kreditkarte.** *eekh beht-sahl-uh bahr/miht kreh-deet-kahr-tuh*

Communications

Where's an internet cafe?	**Wo gibt es ein Internetcafé?** *voh gihpt ehs ien ihnt-ehr-neht-kah-feh*
Can I access the internet/check e-mail?	**Kann ich das Internet benutzen/meine E-Mails lesen?** *kahn eekh dahs ihnt-ehr-neht beh-noot-suhn/mien-uh ee-miels lehz-uhn*
How much per (half) hour?	**Wie viel kostet eine (halbe) Stunde?** *vee feel kohst-uht ien-uh (hahlb-uh) shtoond-uh*
A phone card, please.	**Eine Telefonkarte, bitte.** *ien-uh tehl-uh-fohn-kahrt-uh biht-tuh*
Can I have your phone number?	**Kann ich Ihre Telefonnummer haben?** *kahn eekh eehr-uh tehl-uh-fohn-noom-ehr hah-buhn*
Here's my number/e-mail.	**Hier ist meine Telefonnummer/E-Mail.** *heer ihst mien-uh tehl-uh-fohn-noom-ehr/ee-miel*
Call me/text me.	**Rufen Sie mich an/Schicken Sie mir eine SMS.** *roo-fuhn zee meekh ahn/shihk-uhn zee meer ien-uh ehs-ehm-ehs*
I'll text you.	**Ich werde Ihnen eine SMS schicken.** *eekh vehrd-uh eehn-uhn ien-uh ehs-ehm-ehs shihk-uhn*
E-mail me.	**Mailen Sie mir.** *miel-uhn zee meer*
Hello. This is…	**Hallo. Hier ist …** *hah-loh heer ihst …*
Can I speak to…?	**Kann ich mit … sprechen?** *kahn eekh miht … shprehkh-uhn*
Can you repeat that, please?	**Könnten Sie das bitte wiederholen?** *kern-tuhn zee dahs biht-tuh veed-ehr-hohl-uhn*

I'll call back later.	**Ich rufe später zurück.**
	eekh roof·uh shpeht·ehr tsoo·rewkh
Bye.	**Auf Wiederhören.** *owf veed·ehr·her·ruhn*
Where's the post office?	**Wo ist die Post?** *voh ihst dee pohst*
I'd like to send this to...	**Ich möchte das nach ... schicken.**
	eekh merkh·tuh dahs nahkh ... shihk·uhn
Can I...?	**Kann ich ...?** *kahn eekh ...*
access the internet	**das Internet benutzen** *dahs ihnt·ehr·neht beh·noot·suhn*
check e-mail	**E-Mails lesen** *ee·miels lehz·uhn*
print	**drucken** *drook·uhn*
plug in/charge my laptop/iPhone/iPad/BlackBerry?	**meinen Laptop/mein iPhone/iPad/BlackBerry aufladen?** *kahn eekh mien·uhn lap·top/mien iphone/ipad/blackberry owf·lahd·uhn*
access Skype?	**Skype verwenden?** *skype fuhr· vehn· dehn*
What is the WiFi password?	**Wie lautet das WLAN-Passwort?** *vee low·teht dahs veh·lahn·pahs·vohrt*
Is the WiFi free?	**Ist der WLAN-Zugang gratis?** *ihst dehr veh·lahn·tsoo·gahng grah·tihs*
Do you have bluetooth?	**Haben Sie Bluetooth?** *hah·buhn zee bloo·tooth*
Do you have a scanner?	**Haben Sie einen Scanner?** *hah·buhn zee ien·uhn scan·nuhr*

71

Social Media

Are you on Facebook/Twitter?	**Sind Sie bei Facebook/Twitter?** *(polite form)*
	zihnt zee by face·book/twit·ter
	Bist du bei Facebook/Twitter? *(informal form)*
	bihst doo by face·book/twit·ter
What's your user name?	**Was ist Ihr Benutzername?** *(polite form)*
	vahs ihst eehr beh·noots·uhr·nah·muh

Was ist dein Benutzername? *(informal form)*
vahs ihst dien beh·noots·uhr·nah·muh

I'll follow you
on Twitter.
Ich werde Ihre Twitter-Einträge verfolgen.
(polite form) eekh vehr·duh eer·he
twit·ter·ien·treh·ghe fehr·folg·hun

Ich werde deine Twitter-Einträge verfolgen.
(informal form) eekh vehr·duh die·nuh
twit·ter·ien·treh·ghe fehr·folg·hun

Are you following...? **Verfolgen Sie ...?** *(polite form) fehr·folg·hun zee ...*
Verfolgst du ...? *(informal form) fehr·folgst doo ...*

I'll add you
as a friend.
Ich werde Sie als Freund/Freundin hinzufügen.
(polite form) eekh vehrd·uh zee ahls froynd/
froyn·dihn hihn·tsoo·few·guhn

Ich werde dich als Freund/Freundin hinzufügen.
(informal form) eekh vehrd·uh deekh ahls froynd/
froyn·dihn hihn·tsoo·few·guhn

I'll put the pictures
on Facebook/Twitter.
**Ich werde die Fotos auf Facebook/Twitter
hochladen.** *eekh vehr·duh dee foh·tohs owf face·book/*
twit·ter hokh·lah·duhn

I'll tag you in
the pictures.
Ich werde Sie auf den Fotos markieren.
(polite form) eekh vehr·duh zee owf dehn foh·tohs
mahr·kih·ruhn

Ich werde dich auf den Fotos markieren.
(informal form) eekh vehr·duh deekh owf dehn
foh·tohs mahr·kih·ruhn

Conversation

Hello!	**Hallo!** *hah·loh*	
How are you?	**Wie geht es Ihnen?** *vee geht ehs eehn·uhn*	
Fine, thanks.	**Gut, danke.** *goot dahn·kuh*	
Excuse me!	**Entschuldigung!** *ehnt·shool·dee·goong*	

Do you speak English?	**Sprechen Sie Englisch?** _shpreh•khuhn zee ehn•gleesh_
What's your name?	**Wie heißen Sie?** _vee hie•suhn zee_
My name is...	**Mein Name ist ...** _mien nahm•uh ihst ..._
Nice to meet you.	**Schön, Sie kennenzulernen.** _shern zee keh•nehn•tsoo•lehr•nehn_
Where are you from?	**Woher kommen Sie?** _voh•hehr koh•muhn zee_
I'm from the U.S./U.K.	**Ich komme aus den USA/Großbritannien.** _eekh koh•muh ows dehn oo•ehs•ah/ grohs•bree•tah•nee•ehn_
What do you do for a living?	**Was machen Sie beruflich?** _vahs mah•khuhn zee beh•roof•likh_
I work for...	**Ich arbeite für ...** _eekh ahr•bie•tuh fewr ..._
I'm a student.	**Ich bin Student.** _eekh bihn shtoo•dehnt_
I'm retired.	**Ich bin Rentner.** _eekh been rehnt•nehr_

Romance

Would you like to go out for a drink/dinner?	**Möchten Sie mit mir auf einen Drink/zum Essen gehen?** _merkh•tuhn zee miht meer owf ien•uhn treenk/tsoom eh•suhn geh•uhn_
What are your plans for tonight/tomorrow?	**Was haben Sie heute Abend/morgen vor?** _vahs hah•buhn zee hoy•tuh ah•buhnt/mohr•guhn fohr_
Can I have your number?	**Kann ich Ihre Telefonnummer haben?** _kahn eekh ee•ruh teh•leh•fohn•noo•mehr hah•buhn_
Can I join you?	**Kann ich mitkommen?** _kahn eekh miht•koh•muhn_
Can I get you a drink?	**Darf ich Ihnen einen Drink ausgeben?** _dahrf eekh eehn•uhn ien•uhn treenk ows•geh•buhn_
I like/love you.	**Ich mag/liebe dich.** _eekh mahk/lee•buh deekh_

Accepting & Rejecting

I'd love to.	**Gerne.** _gehr•nuh_
Where should we meet?	**Wo wollen wir uns treffen?** _voh voh•luhn veer oons treh•fuhn_
I'll meet you at the bar/your hotel.	**Ich treffe Sie an der Bar/Ihrem Hotel.** _eekh treh•fuh zee ahn dehr bahr/ee•ruhm hoh•tehl_
I'll come by at…	**Ich komme um … vorbei.** _eekh koh•muh oom … fohr•bie_
I'm busy.	**Ich bin beschäftigt.** _eekh been beh•shehf•teekt_
I'm not interested.	**Ich habe kein Interesse.** _eekh hah•buh kien ihn•teh•reh•suh_
Leave me alone.	**Lassen Sie mich in Ruhe.** _lah•sehn zee meekh ihn roo•uh_
Stop bothering me!	**Hören Sie auf, mich zu belästigen!** _her•ruhn zee owf meekh tsoo buh•lay•steeg•uhn_

Food & Drink

Eating Out

Can you recommend a good restaurant/ bar?	**Können Sie ein gutes Restaurant/eine gute Bar empfehlen?** _ker•nuhn zee ien goo•tuhs reh•stow•rahnt/ien•uh goo•tuh bahr ehm•pfeh•luhn_
Is there a traditional German/an inexpensive restaurant nearby?	**Gibt es in der Nähe ein typisch deutsches/ preisgünstiges Restaurant?** _gihpt ehs ihn dehr neh•uh ien tew•peesh doy•chuhs/ pries•gewn•stee•guhs reh•stow•rahnt_
A table for…, please.	**Bitte einen Tisch für …** _biht•tuh ien•uhn tihsh fewr …_
Can we sit…?	**Können wir … sitzen?** _ker•nuhn veer … ziht•tsuhn_
here/there	**hier/dort** _heer/dohrt_

outside	**draußen** _drow_•suhn
in a non-smoking area	**in einem Nichtraucherbereich** ihn _ien_•uhm neekht•_row_•khehr•beh•riehk
I'm waiting for someone.	**Ich warte auf jemanden.** eekh _vahr_•tuh owf _yeh_•mahnd•uhn
Where are the toilets?	**Wo ist die Toilette?** voh ihst dee toy•_leh_•tuh
A menu, please.	**Die Speisekarte, bitte.** dee _shpie_•zuh•kahr•tuh _biht_•tuh
What do you recommend?	**Was empfehlen Sie?** vahs ehm•_pfeh_•luhn zee
I'd like...	**Ich möchte ...** eekh _merkh_•tuh ...
Some more..., please.	**Etwas mehr ..., bitte.** _eht_•vahs mehr ... _biht_•tuh
Enjoy your meal!	**Guten Appetit!** _goo_•tuhn ah•puh•_teet_
The check [bill], please.	**Die Rechnung, bitte.** dee _rehkh_•noonk _biht_•tuh
Is service included?	**Ist die Bedienung im Preis enthalten?** ihsht dee buh•_dee_•nung ihm pries _ehnt_•hahl•tuhn
Can I pay by credit card/have a receipt?	**Kann ich mit Kreditkarte bezahlen/eine Quittung haben?** kahn eekh miht kreh•_deet_•kahr•tuh beht•_sahl_•uhn/ien•uh _kvee_•toonk _hah_•buhn

YOU MAY SEE...

SPEISEKARTE	menu
TAGESMENÜ	menu of the day
SPEZIALITÄTEN	specials
EINTRITTSGEBÜHR	cover charge
FESTPREIS	fixed price
SERVICE (NICHT IM PREIS) ENTHALTEN	service (not) included

Breakfast

der Schinkenspeck *dehr <u>shihn</u>•kuhn•shpehk*	bacon
das Brot *dahs broht*	bread
die Butter *dee <u>boo</u>•tehr*	butter
der Aufschnitt *dehr <u>owf</u>•shniht*	cold cuts [charcuterie]
der Käse *dehr <u>kay</u>•zuh*	cheese
das ... Ei *dahs ... ie*	...egg
hart/weich gekochte	hard-/soft-boiled
hahrt/viekh guh•<u>kohkh</u>•tuh	
das Rührei *dahs <u>rew</u>•rie*	scrambled egg
die Marmelade *dee mahr•muh•<u>lah</u>•duh*	jam/jelly
das Omelett *dahs <u>ohm</u>•luht*	omelet
der Toast *dehr tohst*	toast
die Wurst *dee voorst*	sausage
der Joghurt *dehr <u>yoh</u>•goort*	yogurt

Appetizers

die Pastete *dee pah•steh•tuh*	pâté
die Fishsuppe *fihsh• zuh•zoo•puh*	fish soup
die Gemüsesuppe *dee guh•<u>mew</u>•zuh•zoo•puh*	vegetable soup
die Tomatensuppe *dee toh•<u>mah</u>•tuhn•zoo•puh*	tomato soup
die Hühnersuppe *dee <u>hewn</u>•ehr•zoo•puh*	chicken soup
der Salat *dehr sah•<u>laht</u>*	salad

Meat

das Rindfleisch *dahs <u>rihnt</u>•fliesh*	beef
das Hühnchen *dahs <u>hewn</u>•khuhn*	chicken
das Lamm *dahs lahm*	lamb
das Schweinefleisch *dahs <u>shvien</u>•uh•fliesh*	pork
das Steak *dahs shtayhk*	steak
das Kalbfleisch *dahs <u>kahlb</u>•fliesh*	veal

Fish & Seafood

der Dorsch *dehr dohrsh*	cod
der Hering *dehr heh·rihng*	herring
der Hummer *dehr hoo·mehr*	lobster
der Lachs *dehr lahks*	salmon
die Garnele *dee gahr·neh·luh*	shrimp

Vegetables

die Bohnen *dee boh·nuhn*	beans
der Kohl *dehr kohl*	cabbage
die Möhre *dee mer·ruh*	carrot
der Pilz *dehr pihlts*	mushroom
die Zwiebel *dee tsvee·buhl*	onion
die Erbse *dee ehrb·zuh*	pea
die Kartoffeln *dee kahr·toh·fehl·ehn*	potatoes
die Tomate *dee toh·mah·teh*	tomato

Sauces & Condiments

salt	**salz** *sahlts*
pepper	**pfeffer** *pfehf·fehr*
mustard	**senf** *sehnf*
ketchup	**ketchup** *ket·shahp*

Fruit & Dessert

der Apfel *dehr ahp·fuhl*	apple
die Apfelsine *dee ah·pfehl·zee·nuh*	orange
die Banane *dee bah·nah·nuh*	banana
die Birne *dee beer·nuh*	pear
die Erdbeere *dee ehrd·beh·ruh*	strawberry
die Zitrone *dee tsee·troh·nuh*	lemon
das Eis *dahs ies*	ice cream
die Schokolade *dee shoh·koh·lah·duh*	chocolate
die Vanille *dee vah·nee·luh*	vanilla
der Kuchen *dehr kookh·uhn*	cake/tart
die Rote Grütze *dee roh·tuh grewt·zuh*	berry pudding
die Schwarzwälder Kirschtorte *dee schvahrts·vahl·dehr keersh·tohr·tuh*	Black Forest chocolate cake with cherries

Drinks

The wine list/drink menu, please.	**Die Weinkarte/Getränkekarte, bitte.** *dee vien·kahr·tuh/geh·trehnk·uh·kahr·tuh biht·tuh*
What do you recommend?	**Was empfehlen Sie?** *vahs ehm·pfeh·luhn zee*
I'd like a bottle/ glass of red/ white wine.	**Ich möchte gern eine Flasche/ein Glas Rotwein/Weißwein.** *eekh merkh·tuh gehrn ien·uh flah·shuh/ien glahs roht·vien/vies·vien*
The house wine, please.	**Den Hauswein, bitte.** *dehn hows·vien biht·tuh*
Another bottle/glass, please.	**Noch eine Flasche/ein Glas, bitte.** *nohkh ien·uh flah·shuh/ien glahs biht·tuh*
I'd like a local beer.	**Ich möchte gern ein Bier aus der Region.** *eekh merkh·tuh gehrn ien beer ows dehr rehg·yohn*
Can I buy you a drink?	**Darf ich Ihnen einen ausgeben?** *dahrf eekh eehn·uhn ows·geh·buhn*

Cheers!	**Prost!** *prohst*
A coffee/tea, please.	**Einen Kaffee/Tee, bitte.**
	ien-uhn kah-feh/tee biht-tuh
Black.	**Schwarz.** *shvahrts*
With...	**Mit ...** *miht ...*
milk	**Milch** *mihlkh*
sugar	**Zucker** *tsoo-kehr*
artificial sweetener	**Süßstoff** *zews-shtohf*
..., please.	**..., bitte.** *... biht-tuh*
A juice	**Einen Saft** *ien-uhn zahft*
A soda	**Eine Cola** *ien-uh koh-lah*
A still/sparkling water	**Ein stilles Wasser/Wasser mit Kohlensäure**
	ien shtihl-uhs vah-sehr/ vah-sehr miht kohl-ehn-zoy-ruh

Leisure Time

Sightseeing

Where's the tourist information office?	**Wo ist das Touristeninformationsbüro?** *voh ihst dahs too-ree-stuhn-een-fohr-mah-syohns-bew-roh*
What are the main sights?	**Was sind die wichtigsten Sehenswürdigkeiten?** *vahs zihnt dee veekh-teeg-stuhn zeh-uhns-vewr-deekh-kie-tuhn*
Do you offer tours in English?	**Haben Sie Führungen in Englisch?** *hah-buhn zee few-roong-uhn een ehn-gleesh*
Can I have a map/ guide?	**Kann ich einen Stadtplan/Reiseführer haben?** *kahn eekh ien-uhn shtaht-plahn/ rie-seh-fewhr-ehr hah-buhn*

YOU MAY SEE...

GEÖFFNET/GESCHLOSSEN	open/closed
EINGANG/AUSGANG	entrance/exit

Shopping

Where's the market/mall [shopping centre]?	**Wo ist der Markt/das Einkaufszentrum?** *voh ihst dehr mahrkt/dahs* *ien•kowfs•tsehn•troom*
I'm just looking.	**Ich schaue mich nur um.** *eekh show•uh meekh noor oom*
Can you help me?	**Können Sie mir helfen?** *kern•uhn zee meer hehlf•uhn*
I'm being helped.	**Ich werde schon bedient.** *eekh vehrd•uh shohn beh•deent*
How much?	**Wie viel kostet das?** *vee feel kohs•tuht dahs*
I'd like...	**Ich möchte ...** *eekh merkht•uh ...*
That's all.	**Das ist alles.** *dahs ihst ahl•uhs*
Where can I pay?	**Wo kann ich bezahlen?** *voh kahn eekh beh•tsahl•uhn*
I'll pay in cash/by credit card.	**Ich zahle bar/mit Kreditkarte.** *eekh tsahl•uh bahr/miht kreh•deet•kahr•tuh*
A receipt, please.	**Eine Quittung, bitte.** *ien•uh kvih•toong biht•tuh*

Sport & Leisure

When's the game?	**Wann findet das Spiel statt?** *vahn fihnd•uht dahs shpeel shtaht*
Where's ...?	**Wo ist ...?** *voh ihst ...*
the beach	**der Strand** *dehr shtrahnd*
the park	**der Park** *dehr pahrk*
the pool	**der Pool** *dehr pool*

Is it safe to swim here?	**Kann man hier schwimmen?** *kahn mahn heer shvihm•uhn*	
Can I hire golf clubs?	**Kann ich Golfschläger ausleihen?** *kahn eekh gohlf•shlelig•ehr ows•lie•uhn*	
How much per hour?	**Wie viel kostet es pro Stunde?** *vee feel kohs•tuht ehs proh shtoond•uh*	
How far is it to...?	**Wie weit ist es bis zum *m*/zur *f* ...?** *vee viet ihst ehs bihs tsoom/tsoor ...*	
Show me on the map, please.	**Zeigen Sie es mir bitte auf dem Stadtplan.** *tsieg•uhn zee ehs meer biht•tuh owf dehm shtaht•plahn*	

Going Out

What's there to do at night?	**Was kann man dort abends unternehmen?** *vahs kahn mahn dohrt ahb•uhnds oon•tehr•nehm•uhn*
Do you have a program of events?	**Haben Sie ein Veranstaltungsprogramm?** *hah•buhn zee ien fehr•ahn•shtahlt•oongs•prohg•rahm*
What's playing tonight?	**Was wird heute Abend aufgeführt?** *vahs vihrd hoyt•uh ahb•uhnd owf•guh•fewrt*
Where's...?	**Wo ist ...?** *voh ihst ...*
the downtown area	**das Stadtzentrum** *dahs shtadt•tsehn•troom*
the bar	**die Bar** *dee bahr*
the dance club	**der Tanzclub** *dee tahnts•kloop*
Is this area safe at night?	**Ist dieses Gebiet bei Nacht sicher?** *ihst dee•zuhs geh•beet bie nahkht zeek•hehr*

Baby Essentials

Do you have...?	**Haben Sie ...?** *hah•buhn zee ...*
a baby bottle	**eine Babyflasche** *ien•uh beh•bee•flahsh•uh*
baby food	**Babynahrung** *beh•bee•nahr•oong*
baby wipes	**feuchte Babytücher** *foykh•tuh beh•bee•tewkh•ehr*
a car seat	**einen Kindersitz** *ien•uhn kihnd•ehr•zihts*

a children's menu/	**ein Kindermenü/eine Kinderportion**
portion	_ien•uhn kihnd•ehr•meh•new/ien•uh_
	kihnd•ehr•pohrtz•yohn•uhn
a child's seat/	**einen Kindersitz/Kinderstuhl**
highchair	_ien•uhn kihnd•ehr•zihts/kihnd•ehr•shtoohl_
a crib/cot	**ein Gitterbett/Kinderbett**
	ien giht•tehr•beht/kihnd•ehr•beht
diapers [nappies]	**Windeln** _vihnd•uhln_
formula [baby food]	**Babynahrung** _beh•bee•nah•roong_
a pacifier [dummy]	**einen Schnuller** _ien•uhn shnool•ehr_
a playpen	**einen Laufstall** _ien•uhn lowf•shtahl_
a stroller	**einen Kinderwagen** _ien•uhn_
[pushchair]	_kihnd•ehr•vahg•uhn_
Can I breastfeed	**Kann ich das Baby hier stillen?** _kahn eekh_
the baby here?	_dahs beh•bee heer shtihl•uhn_
Where can I	**Wo kann ich das Baby stillen/wickeln?**
breastfeed/change	_voh kahn eekh dahs beh•bee shtihl•uhn/vihk•uhln_
the baby?	

For Eating Out, see page 74.

Disabled Travelers

Is there...?	**Gibt es ...?** _gihpt ehs ..._
access for the	**einen Zugang für Behinderte** _ien•uhn_
disabled	_tsoo•gahng fewr beh•hihnd•ehrt•uh_
a wheelchair ramp	**eine Rollstuhlrampe**
	ien•uh rohl•shtool•rahm•puh
a disabled-	**eine Behindertentoilette**
accessible toilet	_ien•uh beh•hihn•dehrt•uhn•toy•leh•tuh_
I need...	**Ich brauche ...** _eekh browkh•uh ..._
assistance	**Hilfe** _hihlf•uh_
an elevator [a lift]	**einen Fahrstuhl** _ien•uhn fahr•shtoohl_

a ground-floor room	**ein Zimmer im Erdgeschoss** *ien tsihm·ehr ihm ehrd·guh·shohs*
Please speak louder.	**Bitte sprechen Sie lauter.** *biht·tuh shprehkh·uhn zee lowt·ehr*

Health & Emergencies

Emergencies

Help!	**Hilfe!** *hihlf·uh*
Go away!	**Gehen Sie weg!** *geh·uhn zee vehk*
Stop, thief!	**Haltet den Dieb!** *hahlt·uht dehn deeb*
Get a doctor!	**Holen Sie einen Arzt!** *hohl·uhn zee ien·uhn ahrtst*
Fire!	**Feuer!** *foy·ehr*
I'm lost.	**Ich habe mich verlaufen.** *eekh hahb·uh meekh fehr·lowf·uhn*
Can you help me?	**Können Sie mir helfen?** *kern·uhn zee meer hehlf·uhn*
Call the police!	**Rufen Sie die Polizei!** *roof·uhn zee dee poh·leet·sie*
Where's the police station?	**Wo ist das Polizeirevier?** *voh ihst dahs poh·leet·sie·ruh·veer*
My child is missing.	**Mein Kind ist weg.** *mien kihnt ihst vehk*

In an emergency, dial: **110** for the police
112 for the fire brigade
115 for the ambulance

83

YOU MAY HEAR...

Füllen Sie dieses Formular aus.
fewl•uhn zee deez•uhs fohr•moo•lahr ows

Fill out this form.

Ihren Ausweis, bitte.
eehr•uhn ows•vies biht•tuh

Your ID, please.

Wann/Wo ist es passiert?
vahn/voh ihst ehs pah•seert

When/Where did it happen?

Wie sah er m/sie f aus?
vee zah ehr/zee ows

What does he/she look like?

Health

I'm sick.	**Ich bin krank.** *eekh bihn krahnk*
I need an English-speaking doctor.	**Ich brauche einen englischsprechenden Arzt.** *eekh browkh•uh ien•uhn ehng•glihsh•shprehkh•ehnd•uhn ahrtst*
It hurts here.	**Es tut hier weh.** *ehs toot heer veh*
Where's the pharmacy?	**Wo ist die Apotheke?** *voh ihst dee ah•poh•tehk•uh*
I'm (one/two/three/four/five/six/seven/eight/nine months) pregnant.	**Ich bin (im ersten/zweiten/dritten/vierten/fünften/sechsten/siebten/achten/neunten Monat) schwanger.** *eekh bihn (ihm ehrs•thun/tsvai•thun/dree•thun/feer•thun/ewnf•thun/sehks•thun/seeb•thun/ahkh•thun/noyn•thun moh•naht) shvahn•guhr*
I'm on...	**Ich nehme ...** *eekh nehm•uh ...*
I'm allergic to antibiotics/penicillin.	**Ich bin allergisch auf Antibiotika/Penicillin.** *eekh bihn ah•lehrg•eesh owf ahn•tee•bee•oh•tee•kah/peh•nih•sihl•ihn*

Dictionary

adapter der Adapter
American *adj* amerikanisch
and und
antiseptic cream die antiseptische Creme
aspirin das Aspirin
baby das Baby;
  a backpack der Rucksack
bad schlecht
bag die Tasche
Band-Aid das Pflaster
bandage die Bandagen
battleground das Schlachtfeld
bee die Biene
bikini der Bikini
bird der Vogel
black *adj* schwarz
bladder die Blase
bland fad
blue *adj* blau
bottle *n* die Flasche;
  ~ opener der Flaschenöffner
bowl *n* die Schüssel
boy der Junge;
  ~friend der Freund
bra der BH
brown *adj* braun
camera die Kamera
can opener der Dosenöffner
cat die Katze
castle das Schloss
charger das Ladegerät

cheap billig; **~er** billiger
cigarettes die Zigaretten
clean *v* reinigen; **~** *adj*
  (clothes) sauber; **~ing**
  product das Reinigungsmittel
cold *n* **(sickness)** die Erkältung;
  ~ *adj* **(temperature)** kalt
comb *n* der Kamm
come *v* kommen
computer der Computer
condom das Kondom
contact lens die Kontaktlinse;
  ~ solution Kontaktlinsenlösung
corkscrew *n* der Korkenzieher
cup *n* die Tasse
dangerous gefährlich
deodorant das Deodorant
diabetic *adj* diabetisch; *n* der
  Diabetiker
difficult schwierig
dog der Hund
doll die Puppe
early früh
expensive teuer
fee *n* die Gebühr
fever *n* das Fieber
fly *v* fliegen
fork *n* die Gabel
form *n* **(document)** das Formular
girl das Mädchen; **~friend**
  die Freundin
glass das Glas

good *adj* gut; ~ *n* die Ware;
~ **afternoon** guten Tag
~ **day** guten Tag; ~ **evening**
guten
Abend; ~ **morning** guten Morgen;
~**bye** auf Wiedersehen
gray *adj* grau
great *adj* super
green *adj* grün
hairbrush die Haarbürste
hairspray das Haarspray
horse das Pferd
hot (spicy) scharf;
~ **(temperature)** heiß;
how wie; ~ **much** wie viel
hug *v* umarmen
hungry hungrig
hurt *v* wehtun
husband der Ehemann
ibuprofen das Ibuprofen
ice *n* das Eis; ~ **hockey** das
Eishockey
icy eisig
injection die Einspritzung
I'd like Ich würde gerne
insect repellent der
Insektenschutz
interesting interessant
Ireland das Irland
Irish *adj* irisch
jeans die Jeans
knife das (Steak)Messer
kosher *adj* koscher

lactose intolerant
laktoseintolerant
large groß
last *adj* letzte
late (time) spät
lighter *n* das Feuerzeug
lion der Löwe
lotion die Lotion
love *v* **(someone)** lieben;
~ *n* die Liebe
matches die Spiele
medium (steak) medium
monkey der Affe
moped das Moped
more mehr
morning *n* der Morgen
museum das Museum
my meine
nail file die Nagelfeile
napkin die Serviette
nauseous übel
near nahe; ~**-sighted** kurzsichtig
nearby in der Nähe von
nurse *n* die Krankenschwester
or oder
orange die Orange
park der Park
partner der Partner
pen *n* der Stift
penicillin das Penicillin
pink *adj* rosa
plate *n* der Teller
purple *adj* violett
pyjamas der Schlafanzug

rain *n* der Regen; **~coat** die Regenjacke
razor blade die Rasierklinge
red *adj* rot
rental car das Mietauto
repair *v* reparieren
repeat *v* wiederholen
reservation die Reservierung; **~ desk** der Reservierungsschalter
reserve *v* (**hotel**) reservieren
restaurant das Restaurant
safari die safari
salty salzig
sandals die Sandalen
sauna die Sauna
scissors die Schere
sea das Meer
seat *n* der Sitzplatz
security die Sicherheit
see *v* sehen
self-service *n* die Selbstbedienung
sell *v* verkaufen
shampoo *n* das Shampoo
shoe der Schuh
small klein
snake die Schlange
sneakers die Turnschuhe
snow der Schnee
soap *n* die Seife
sock die Socke
south *n* der Süden
spicy scharf; ~ (**not bland**) würzig
spider die Spinne
spoon *n* der Löffel

sweater der Pullover
stamps die Briefmarken
suitcase der Koffer
sun die Sonne
sunglasses die Sonnenbrille
sweatshirt das Sweatshirt
swimsuit der Badeanzug
tampon *n* der Tampon
terrible schrecklich
tie die Krawatte
tissue das Gewebe
toilet paper das Toilettenpapier
toothbrush die Zahnbürste
toothpaste die Zahnpaste
tough *adj* (**food**) zäh
town die Stadt; ~ **hall** das Rathaus; ~ **map** der Stadtplan;
toy das Spielzeug;
underwear die Unterwäsche
United Kingdom (U.K.) das Großbritannien
United States (U.S.) die Vereinigten Staaten
vegan *n* der Veganer; ~ *adj* vegan
vegetarian *n* der Vegetarier; ~ *adj* vegetarisch
white *adj* weiß
wife die Ehefrau
without ohne
yellow *adj* gelb
your dein/Ihr
zoo der Zoo

Greek

Essentials

Hello.	**Χαίρετε.** _kheh_•reh•teh
Goodbye.	**Γεια σας.** yah sahs
Yes/No/OK	**Ναι/Όχι/Εντάξει** neh/_oh_•khee/ehn•_dah_•ksee
Excuse me! (to get attention)	**Παρακαλώ!** pah•rah•kah•_loh_
Excuse me. (to get past)	**Συγνώμη.** see•_ghnoh_•mee
I'd like...	**Θα ήθελα...** thah ee•theh•lah...
How much?	**Πόσο;** _poh_•soh
And/or	**και/ή** kah/_ee_
Where is...?	**Πού είναι...;** poo ee•neh...
I'm going to...	**Θα...** thah...
Please.	**Παρακαλώ.** pah•rah•kah•_loh_
Thank you.	**Ευχαριστώ.** ehf•khahr•ee•_stoh_
You're welcome.	**Παρακαλώ.** pah•rah•kah•_loh_
Could you speak more slowly?	**Μπορείτε να μιλάτε πιο αργά;** boh•_ree_•teh nah mee•_lah_•teh pioh ahr•_ghah_
Could you repeat that?	**Μπορείτε να το επαναλάβετε;** boh•_ree_•teh nah toh eh•pah•nah•_lah_•veh•teh
I don't understand.	**Δεν καταλαβαίνω.** THehn kah•tah•lah•lah•_veh_•noh
Do you speak English?	**Μιλάτε Αγγλικά;** mee•_lah_•teh ahn•glee•_kah_
I don't speak. Greek	**Δεν μιλώ Ελληνικά.** THehn mee•_loh_ eh•lee•nee•_kah_
Where is the restroom [toilet]?	**Πού είναι η τουαλέτα;** poo ee•neh ee too•ah•_leh_•tah
Help!	**Βοήθεια!** voh•_ee_•thee•ah

You'll find the pronunciation of the Greek letters and words written in gray after each sentence to guide you. Simply pronounce these as if they were English, noting that any underlines and bolds indicate an additional emphasis or stress or a lengthening of a vowel sound. As you hear the language being spoken, you will quickly become accustomed to the local pronunciation and dialect.

Numbers

0	**μηδέν**	mee·THehn
1	**ένας**	eh·nahs
2	**δύο**	THee·oh
3	**τρεις**	trees
4	**τέσσερις**	teh·seh·rees
5	**πέντε**	pehn·deh
6	**έξι**	eh·ksee
7	**επτά**	eh·ptah
8	**οκτώ**	oh·ktoh
9	**εννέα**	eh·neh·ah
10	**δέκα**	THeh·kah
11	**έντεκα**	ehn·deh·kah
12	**δώδεκα**	THoh·THeh·kah
13	**δεκατρία**	THeh·kah·tree·ah
14	**δεκατέσσερα**	THeh·kah·teh·seh·rah
15	**δεκαπέντε**	THeh·kah·pehn·deh
16	**δεκαέξι**	THeh·kah·eh·ksee
17	**δεκαεπτά**	THeh·kah·eh·ptah
18	**δεκαοκτώ**	THeh·kah·oh·ktoh
19	**δεκαεννέα**	THeh·kah·eh·neh·ah

20	**είκοσι** _ee_·koh·see
21	**είκοσι ένα** _ee_·koh·see _eh_·nah
30	**τριάντα** tree·_ahn_·dah
40	**σαράντα** sah·_rahn_·dah
50	**πενήντα** peh·_neen_·dah
60	**εξήντα** eh·_kseen_·dah
70	**εβδομήντα** ehv·THoh·_meen_·dah
80	**ογδόντα** ohgh·_THohn_·dah
90	**ενενήντα** eh·neh·_neen_·dah
100	**εκατό** eh·kah·_toh_
101	**εκατόν ένα** eh·kah·_tohn_ _eh_·nah
200	**διακόσια** THee·ah·_koh_·siah
500	**πεντακόσια** pehn·dah·_koh_·siah
1,000	**χίλια** _khee_·liah
10,000	**δέκα χιλιάδες** _THeh_·kah khee·_liah_·THehs
1,000,000	**ένα εκατομμύριο** _eh_·nah eh·kah·toh·_mee_·ree·oh

Time

What time is it?	**Τι ώρα είναι;** tee _oh_·rah _ee_·neh
It's noon [midday].	**Είναι μεσημέρι.** _ee_·neh meh·see·_meh_·ree
Twenty after [past] four.	**Τέσσερις και είκοσι.** _teh_·seh·rees keh _ee_·koh·see
A quarter to nine.	**Εννέα παρά τέταρτο.** eh·_neh_·ah pah·_rah_ _teh_·tahr·toh
5:30 a.m./p.m.	**Πεντέμιση π.μ./μ.μ.** pehn·_deh_·mee·see proh meh·seem·_vree_·ahs/meh·_tah_ meh·seem·_vree_·ahs

Days

Monday	**Δευτέρα** THehf·_teh_·rah
Tuesday	**Τρίτη** _tree_·tee
Wednesday	**Τετάρτη** teh·_tahr_·tee

Thursday	**Πέμπτη** _pehm_·tee
Friday	**Παρασκευή** pah·rahs·keh·_vee_
Saturday	**Σάββατο** _sah_·vah·toh
Sunday	**Κυριακή** keer·yah·_kee_

Dates

yesterday	**χτες** khtehs
today	**σήμερα** _see_·meh·rah
tomorrow	**αύριο** _ahv_·ree·oh
day	**ημέρα** ee·_meh_·rah
week	**εβδομάδα** ehv·THoh·_mah_·THah
month	**μήνας** _mee_·nahs
year	**χρόνος** _khroh_·nohs
Happy New Year!	**Καλή χρονιά! !** kah·_lee_ hron·nah
Happy Birthday!	**Χρόνια πολλά!** _khroh_·nah poo·theh·ah

Months

January	**Ιανουάριος** ee·ah·noo·_ah_·ree·ohs
February	**Φεβρουάριος** fehv·roo·_ah_·ree·ohs
March	**Μάρτιος** _mahr_·tee·ohs
April	**Απρίλιος** ahp·_ree_·lee·ohs
May	**Μάιος** _mah_·ee·ohs
June	**Ιούνιος** ee·_oo_·nee·ohs
July	**Ιούλιος** ee·_oo_·lee·ohs
August	**Αύγουστος** _ahv_·ghoo·stohs
September	**Σεπτέμβριος** sehp·_tehm_·vree·ohs
October	**Οκτώβριος** ohk·_toh_·vree·ohs
November	**Νοέμβριος** noh·_ehm_·vree·ohs
December	**Δεκέμβριος** THeh·_kehm_·vree·ohs

Arrival & Departure

I'm here on vacation [holiday]/business.	**Είμαι εδώ για διακοπές/δουλειά.** _ee_·meh eh·_THoh_ yah THiah·koh·_pehs_/THoo·_liah_
I'm going to...	**Θα...** thah...
I'm staying at the...Hotel.	**Μένω στο...ξενοδοχείο.** _meh_·noh stoh... kseh·noh·THoh·_khee_·oh

Money

Where is...?	**Πού είναι...;** poo _ee_·neh...
the ATM	**το αυτόματο μηχάνημα ανάληψης** toh ahf·_toh_·mee·_khah_·nee·mah ah·_nah_·lee·psees
the bank	**η τράπεζα** ee _trah_·peh·zah
the currency exchange office	**γραφείο ανταλλαγής συναλλάγματος** ghrah·_fee_·oh ahn·dah·lah·_ghees_ see·nah·_lahgh_·mah·tohs
What time does the bank open/close?	**Τι ώρα ανοίγει/κλείνει η τράπεζα;** tee _oh_·rah ah·_nee_·ghee/_klee_·nee ee _trah_·peh·zah
I'd like to change dollars/pounds into euros.	**Θα ήθελα να αλλάξω μερικά δολάρια/λίρες σε ευρώ.** thah _ee_·theh·lah nah ah·_lah_·ksoh meh·ree·_kah_ THoh·_lah_·ree·ah/meh·ree·_kehs_ _lee_·rehs seh ehv·roh
I want to cash some traveler's checks [cheques].	**Θα ήθελα να εξαργυρώσω μερικές ταξιδιωτικές επιταγές.** thah _ee_·theh·lah nah eh·ksahr·yee·_roh_·soh meh·ree·_kehs_ tah·ksee THee·oh·tee·_kehs_ eh·pee·tah·_yehs_

93

YOU MAY SEE...

In 2002, the Greek drachma was replaced with the European Union currency, euro, € (**ευρώ** ehv·_roh_), which is divided into 100 cents (**λεπτό** lehp·_toh_).
Coins: 1, 2, 5, 10, 20, 50 **cents**; €1, 2
Notes: €5, 10, 20, 50, 100, 200, 500

| Can I pay in cash? | **Μπορώ να πληρώσω μετρητά;** boh·_roh_ nah plee·_roh_·soh meht·ree·_tah_ |
| Can I pay by credit card? | **Μπορώ να πληρώσω με αυτήν την πιστωτική κάρτα;** boh·_roh_ nah plee·_roh_·soh meh ahf·_teen_ teen pees·toh·tee·_kee_ kahr·tah |

For Numbers, see page 90.

Getting Around

How do I get to town?	**Πώς μπορώ να πάω στην πόλη;** pohs boh·_roh_ nah _pah_·oh steen _poh_·lee
Where's...?	**Πού είναι...;** poo ee·neh...
the airport	**το αεροδρόμιο** toh ah·eh·roh·_THroh_·mee·oh
the train station	**ο σταθμός των τρένων** oh stahth·_mohs_ ton _treh_·nohn
the bus station	**ο σταθμός των λεωφορείων** oh stahth·_mohs_ tohn leh·oh·foh·_ree_·ohn
the metro station	**ο σταθμός του μετρό** oh stahth·_mohs_ too meh·_troh_
How far is it?	**Πόσο απέχει;** _poh_·soh ah·_peh_·khee
Where can I buy tickets?	**Από πού μπορώ να αγοράσω εισιτήρια;** ah·_poh_ poo boh·_roh_ nah ah·ghoh·_rah_·soh ee·see·_tee_·ree·ah
A one-way/ return-trip ticket.	**Ένα απλό εισιτήριο/εισιτήριο με επιστροφή** _eh_·nah ahp·_loh_ ee·see·_tee_·ree·oh/ee·see·_tee_·ree·oh meh eh·pees·troh·_fee_
How much?	**Πόσο;** _poh_·soh
Which...?	**Ποια...;** piah...
gate	**είσοδος** _ee_·soh·_THohs_
line	**γραμμή** ghrah·_mee_
platform	**πλατφόρμα** plaht·_fohr_·mah
Where can I get a taxi?	**Πού μπορώ να βρω ταξί;** poo boh·_roh_ nah vroh tah·_ksee_

Please take me to this address.	**Παρακαλώ πηγαίνετέ με σε αυτή τη διεύθυνση.**
	pah·rah·kah·loh pee·yeh·neh·the meh seh ahf·tee tee THee·ehf·theen·see
To...Airport, please.	**Στο...αεροδρόμιο, παρακαλώ.**
	stoh...ah·eh·roh·THroh·mee·oh pah·rah·kah·loh
I'm in a rush.	**Βιάζομαι.** *vee·ah·zoh·meh*
Can I have a map?	**Μπορώ να έχω ένα χάρτη;**
	boh·roh nah eh·khoh eh·nah khahr·tee

Tickets

When's...to Athens?	**Πότε αναχωρεί...για Αθήνα;**
	poh·the ah·nah·khoh·ree...yah ah·thee·nah
the (first) bus	**το (πρώτο) λεωφορείο** *toh (proh·toh)*
	leh·oh·foh·ree·oh
the (next) flight	**η (επόμενη) πτήση** *ee (eh·poh·meh·nee) ptee·see*
the (last) train	**το (τελευταίο) τρένο** *toh (teh·lehf·teh·oh) treh·noh*
One ticket./Two tickets.	**Ένα εισιτήριο./Δύο εισιτήρια.**
	eh·nah ee·see·tee·ree·oh/THee·oh ee·see·tee·ree·ah
For today/tomorrow.	**Για σήμερα/αύριο.** *yah see·meh·rah/ahv·ree·oh*
A...ticket.	**Ένα εισιτήριο....** *eh·nah ee·see·tee·ree·oh*
one-way	**χωρίς επιστροφή** *khoh·rees eh·pee·stroh·fee*
return trip	**με επιστροφή** *meh eh·pee·stroh·fee*
business class	**για θέση business** *yah theh·see business*
I have an e-ticket.	**Έχω e-ticket.** *eh·khoh ee tee·keht*
How long is the trip?	**Πόση ώρα διαρκεί το ταξίδι;** *poh·see oh·rah*
	THee·ahr·kee toh tah·ksee·THee
Is it a direct train?	**Είναι απευθείας τρένο;** *ee·neh ah·pehf·thee·ahs*
	treh·noh
Is this the bus to...?	**Είναι αυτό το λεωφορείο για...;** *ee·neh ahf·toh*
	toh leh·oh·foh·ree·oh yah...

Could you tell me when to get off? | **Μπορείτε να μου πείτε πού να κατέβω;**
boh•ree•teh nah moo pee•teh poo nah kah•teh•voh

I'd like to…my reservation. | **Θα ήθελα να…την κράτησή μου.** *Thah ee•theh•lah nah…teen krah•tee•see moo*

   cancel | **ακυρώσω** *ah•kee•roh•soh*

   change | **αλλάξω** *ah•lah•ksoh*

   confirm | **επιβεβαιώσω** *eh•pee•veh•veh•oh•soh*

For Time, see page 91.

Car Hire

Where can I hire a car? | **Πού μπορώ να νοικιάσω ένα αυτοκίνητο;**
poo boh•roh nah nee•kiah•soh eh•nah ahf•toh•kee•nee•toh

YOU MAY HEAR...

ευθεία/ίσια *ehf•thee•ah/ee•see•ah*	straight ahead
στα αριστερά *stah ah•rees•teh•rah*	on the left
στα δεξιά *stah THeh•ksee•ah*	on the right
στη/μετά τη γωνία *stee/meh•tah tee ghoh•nee•ah*	on/around the corner
απέναντι *ah•peh•nahn•dee*	opposite
πίσω *pee•soh*	behind
δίπλα *THee•plah*	next to
μετά *meh•tah*	after
βόρεια/νότεια *voh•ree•ah/noh•tee•ah*	north/south
ανατολικά/δυτικά *ah•nah•toh•lee•kah/THee•tee•kah*	east/west
στο φανάρι *stoh fah•nah•ree*	at the traffic light
στη διασταύρωση *stee THee•ah•stahv•roh•see*	at the intersection

I'd like to hire...	**Θα ήθελα να νοικιάσω ένα...** *thah ee·theh·lah nah nee·kiah·soh eh·nah...*
a cheap/small car	**ένα φτηνό/μικρό αυτοκίνητο** *eh·nah ftee·noh/ mee·kroh ahf·toh·kee·nee·toh*
an automatic/ manual car	**αυτόματο αυτοκίνητο/αυτοκίνητο με συμπλέκτη** *ahf·toh·mah·toh ahf·toh·kee·nee·toh/ahf·toh·kee· nee·toh meh see·bleh·ktee*
a car with air-conditioning	**αυτοκίνητο με κλιματισμό** *ahf·toh·kee·nee·toh meh klee·mah·tee·smoh*
a car seat	**παιδικό κάθισμα αυτοκινήτου** *peh·THee·koh kah·thee·smah ahf·toh·kee·nee·too*
How much...?	**Πόσο κάνει...;** *poh·soh kah·nee...*
per day/week	**την ημέρα/ενδομάδα** *teen ee·meh·rah/ehv·THoh· mah·THah*
Are there any	**Υπάρχει έκπτωση;** *ee·pahr·khee ehk·ptoh·see*

Places to Stay

Can you recommend a hotel?	**Μπορείτε να μου συστήσετε ένα ξενοδοχείο;** *boh·ree·teh nah moo sees·tee·seh·teh eh·nah kseh·noh·THoh·khee·oh*
I have a reservation.	**Έχω κλείσει δωμάτιο.** *eh·khoh klee·see THoh·mah·tee·oh*
My name is...	**Λέγομαι...** *leh·ghoh·meh...*
Do you have a room...?	**Έχετε ελεύθερο δωμάτιο...;** *eh·kheh·the eh·lehf·theh·roh THoh·mah·tee·oh...*
for one/two	**μονόκλινο/δίκλινο** *moh·noh·klee·noh/THee·klee·noh*
with a bathroom	**με μπάνιο** *meh bah·nioh*
with air-conditioning	**με κλιματισμό** *meh klee·mah·teez·moh*
For tonight.	**Γι' απόψε.** *yah·poh·pseh*
For two nights.	**Για δύο βράδια.** *yah THee·oh vrah·THee·ah*
For one week.	**Για μια εβδομάδα.** *yah mee·ah ev·THoh·mah·THah*

Greek

Essentials

How much?	**Πόσο;** *poh•soh*
Do you have anything cheaper?	**Έχετε τίποτα φθηνότερο;** *eh•kheh•the tee•poh•tah fthee•noh•teh•roh*
When's check-out?	**Τι ώρα πρέπει να αδειάσουμε το δωμάτιο;** *tee oh•rah preh•pee nah ah•THee•ah•soo•meh toh THoh•mah•tee•oh*
Can I leave this in the safe?	**Μπορώ να αφήσω αυτό στη θυρίδα;** *boh•roh nah ah•fee•soh ahf•toh stee thee•ree•THah*
Could we leave our baggage here until…?	**Μπορούμε να αφήσουμε τα πράγματά μας εδώ ως τις…;** *boh•roo•meh nah ah•fee•soo•meh tah prahgh•mah•tah mahs eh•THoh ohs tees…*
Could I have the bill/a receipt?	**Μπορώ να έχω τον λογαριασμό/μιααπόδειξη;** *boh•roh nah eh•hoh tohn loh•ghahr•yahs•moh/miah ah•poh•THeek•see*
I'll pay in cash/by credit card.	**Θα πληρώσω τοις μετρητοίς/με πιστωτική κάρτα.** *thah plee•roh•soh tees meht•ree•tees/meh pees•toh•tee•kee kahr•tah*

Communications

98

Where's an internet cafe?	**Πού υπάρχει internet cafe;** *poo ee•pahr•khee een•tehr•neht kah•feh*
Can I access the internet/check e-mail here?	**Μπορώ να μπω στο internet/να ελέγξω τα e-mail μου εδώ;** *boh•roh nah boh stoh een•tehr•neht/nah eh•lehng•ksoh tah ee•meh•eel moo eh•THoh*
How much per hour/half hour?	**Πόσο χρεώνεται η ώρα/μισή ώρα;** *poh•soh hreh•oh•neh•teh ee oh•rah/mee•see oh•rah*
How do I connect/log on?	**Πώς μπορώ να συνδεθώ/μπω;** *pohs boh•roh nah seehn•THeh•thoh/boh*
I'd like a phone card.	**Θα ήθελα μια τηλεκάρτα.** *thah ee•theh•lah miah tee•leh•kahr•tah*

Can I have your phone number?	**Μπορώ να έχω τον αριθμό τηλεφώνου σας;** *boh·roh nah eh·hoh tohn ah·reeth·moh tee·leh·foh·noo sahs*
Here's my number /e-mail address.	**Ορίστε το τηλέφωνό μου/e-mail μου.** *oh·rees·teh toh tee·leh·foh·noh moo/ee·meh·eel moo*
Call me/Text me.	**Πάρτε με τηλέφωνο/στείλτε μου μήνυμα.** *pahr·teh meh tee·leh·foh·noh/pah·rah·kah·loh steel·teh moo mee·nee·mah*
I'll text you.	**Θα σου γράψω.** *thah soo grap·soh*
E-mail me.	**Στείλτε μου e-mail.** *steel·teh moo ee·meh·eel*
Hello. This is…	**Εμπρός. Είμαι…** *ehm·brohs ee·meh…*
I'd like to speak to…	**Θα ήθελα να μιλήσω με…** *thah ee·theh·lah nah mee·lee·soh meh…*
Repeat that, please.	**Επαναλάβετέ το, παρακαλώ.** *eh·pah·nah·lah·veh·teh toh pah·rah·kah·loh*
I'll be in touch.	**Θα επικοινωνήσω μαζί σας.** *thah eh·pee·kee·noh·nee·soh mah·zee sahs*
Bye.	**Αντίο.** *ah·dee·oh*
Where is the nearest/ main post office?	**Πού είναι το κοντινότερο/κεντρικό ταχυδρομείο;** *poo ee·neh toh koh·ndee·noh·teh·roh/kehn·dree·koh tah·khee·THroh·mee·oh*
I'd like to send this to…	**Θα ήθελα να στείλω αυτό σε…** *thah ee·theh·lah nah stee·loh ahf·toh seh…*
What is the WiFi password?	**Ποιος είναι ο κωδικός πρόσβασης για το WiFi;** *piohs ee·neh oh koh·THee·kohs proh·svah·sees yah toh WiFi*
Is the WiFi free?	**Το WiFi είναι δωρεάν;** *toh WiFi ee·neh THo·reh·ahn*
Do you have bluetooth?	**Έχετε bluetooth;** *eh·kheh·teh bluetooth*
Can I…?	**Μπορώ…;** *boh·roh…*
access the internet here	**να έχω πρόσβαση στο internet από εδώ** *nah eh·hoh prohs·vah·see stoh een·tehr·neht ah·poh eh·THoh*

check e-mail	**να ελέγξω τα e-mail μου** nah eh-<u>leng</u>-ksoh tah ee-<u>meh</u>-eel moo
print	**εκτυπώσω** ehk-tee-<u>poh</u>-soh
plug in/charge my laptop/iPhone/iPad /BlackBerry?	**να συνδέσω/φορτίσω το laptop/iPhone/iPad/ BlackBerry;** nah seen-<u>THeh</u>-soh toh laptop/iPhone/ iPad/BlackBerry
access Skype?	**να μπω στο Skype;** nah <u>boh</u> stoh Skype
Do you have a scanner?	**Έχεις σαρωτή;** <u>ee</u>-cheis sa-<u>ro</u>-ti

Social Media

Are you on Facebook /Twitter?	**Είστε στο Facebook/Twitter;** <u>ee</u>-steh stoh Facebook/Twitter
What's your user name?	**Ποιο είναι το όνομα χρήστη;** pioh <u>ee</u>-neh toh <u>oh</u>-noh-mah <u>khree</u>-stee
I'll add you as a friend.	**Θα σε προσθέσω ως φίλο.** thah seh proh-<u>stheh</u>-soh ohs <u>fee</u>-loh
I'll follow you on Twitter.	**Θα σε ακολουθώ στο Twitter.** thah seh ah-koh-loo-<u>thoh</u> stoh Twitter
Are you following...?	**Ακολουθείς...;** ah-koh-loo-<u>thees</u>
I'll put the pictures on Facebook/Twitter.	**Θα βάλω τις φωτογραφίες στο Facebook/Twitter.** thah <u>vah</u>-loh tees foh-toh-ghrah-<u>fee</u>-ehs sto Facebook/ Twitter
I'll tag you in the pictures.	**Θα σε σημειώσω στις φωτογραφίες.** thah seh see-mee-<u>oh</u>-soh stees foh-toh-ghrah-<u>fee</u>-ehs

Conversation

Hello.	**Χαίρετε.** <u>kheh</u>-reh-teh
How are you?	**Πώς είστε;** pohs <u>ee</u>-steh
Fine, thanks. And you?	**Καλά, ευχαριστώ. Εσείς;** kah-<u>lah</u> ehf-khah-ree-<u>stoh</u> eh-<u>sees</u>
Excuse me!	**Συγγνώμη!** seegh-<u>noh</u>-mee

Do you speak English?	**Μιλάτε Αγγλικά;** *mee-lah-the ahng-lee-kah*
What's your name?	**Πώς λέγεστε;** *pohs leh-yeh-steh*
My name is…	**Λέγομαι…** *leh-ghoh-meh…*
Nice to meet you.	**Χαίρω πολύ.** *kheh-roh poh-lee*
Where are you from?	**Από πού είστε;** *ah-poh poo ee-steh*
I'm from the U.S./U.K.	**Είμαι από τις Ηνωμένες Πολιτείες/το Ηνωμένο Βασίλειο.** *ee-meh ah-poh tees ee-noh-meh-nehs poh-lee-tee-ehs/toh ee-noh-meh-noh vah-see-lee-oh*
What do you do?	**Τι δουλειά κάνετε;** *tee THoo-liah kah-neh-teh*
I work for…	**Δουλεύω για…** *THoo-leh-voh yah…*
I'm a student.	**Είμαι φοιτητής m/φοιτήτρια f.** *ee-meh fee-tee-tees/fee-tee-tree-ah*
I'm retired.	**Είμαι συνταξιούχος.** *ee-meh seen-dah-ksee-oo-khohs*

Romance

Would you like to go out for a drink/dinner?	**Θέλετε να βγούμε για ποτό/φαγητό;** *theh-leh-teh nah vghoo-meh yah poh-toh/fah-yee-toh*
What are your plans for tonight/tomorrow?	**Ποια είναι τα σχέδιά σας για απόψε/αύριο;** *piah ee-neh tah skheh-THee-ah sahs yah ah-poh-pseh/ahv-ree-oh*
Can I have your number?	**Μπορώ να έχω τον αριθμό τηλεφώνου σας;** *boh-roh nah eh-khoh tohn ah-reeth-moh tee-leh-foh-noo sahs*
May we join you?	**Να έρθουμε μαζί σας;** *nah ehr-thoo-meh mah-zee sahs*
Let me buy you a drink.	**Να σε κεράσω ένα ποτό.** *nah seh keh-rah-soh eh-nah poh-toh*
I love you.	**Σ' αγαπώ.** *sah-ghah-poh*

Accepting & Rejecting

I'd love to.	**Θα το ήθελα πολύ.** *ehf•khah•rees•toh thah toh ee•theh•lah poh•lee*
Where should we meet?	**Πού θα συναντηθούμε;** *poo thah see•nahn•dee•thoo•meh*
I'll meet you at the bar/your hotel.	**Θα σε συναντήσω στο μπαρ/στο ξενοδοχείο σου.** *thah seh see•nahn•dee•soh stoh bahr/stoh kseh•noh•THoh•khee•oh soo*
I'll come by at...	**Θα περάσω στις...** *thah peh•rah•soh stees...*
Thank you, but I'm busy.	**Σας ευχαριστώ, αλλά είμαι πολύ απασχολημένος m/απασχολημένη f.** *sahs ehf•khah•rees•toh ah•lah ee•meh poh•lee ah•pahs•khoh•lee•meh•nohs/ah•pahs•khoh•lee•meh•nee*
I'm not interested.	**Δεν ενδιαφέρομαι.** *THehn ehn•THee•ah•feh•roh•meh*
Leave me alone, please!	**Σας παρακαλώ, αφήστε με ήσυχο m/ήσυχη f!** *sahs pah•rah•kah•loh ah•fees•the meh ee•see•khoh/ee•see•khee*
Stop bothering me!	**Σταματείστε να με ενοχλείτε!** *stah•mah•tee•steh nah meh eh•noh•khlee•the*

Food & Drink

Eating Out

| Can you recommend a good restaurant/bar? | **Μπορείτε να συστήσετε ένα καλό εστιατόριο/ μπαρ;** *boh•ree•teh nah sees•tee•seh•teh eh•nah kah•loh ehs•tee•ah•toh•ree•oh/bahr* |
| Is there a traditional Greek/ an inexpensive restaurant near here? | **Υπάρχει κανένα ελληνικό/φθηνό εστιατόριο εδώ κοντά;** *ee•pahr•khee kah•neh•nah eh•lee•nee•koh/ fthee•noh ehs•tee•ah•toh•ree•oh eh•THoh kohn•dah* |

YOU MAY SEE...

ΚΟΥΒΕΡ	cover charge
ΣΤΑΘΕΡΗ ΤΙΜΗ	fixed-price
ΚΑΤΑΛΟΓΟΣ	menu
ΜΕΝΟΥ ΤΗΣ ΗΜΕΡΑΣ	menu of the day
Η ΕΞΥΠΗΡΕΤΗΣΗ (ΔΕΝ)	service (not)
ΠΕΡΙΛΑΜΒΑΝΕΤΑΙ	included
ΠΙΑΤΑ ΤΗΣ ΗΜΕΡΑΣ	specials

A table for..., please.	**Ένα τραπέζι για..., παρακαλώ.** _eh•nah trah•peh•zee yah...pah•rah•kah•loh_
Could we sit...?	**Μπορούμε να καθήσουμε...;** _boh•roo•meh nah kah•thee•soo•meh..._
here/there	**εδώ/εκεί** _eh•THoh/eh•kee_
outside	**έξω** _eh•ksoh_
in a non-smoking area	**σε έναν χώρο για μη καπνίζοντες** _seh eh•nahnk hoh•roh yah mee kahp•nee•zohn•dehs_
I'm waiting for someone.	**Περιμένω κάποιον.** _peh•ree•meh•noh kah•piohn_
Where are the toilets	**Πού είναι η τουαλέτα;** _poo ee•neh ee too•ah•leh•tah_
A menu, please.	**Έναν κατάλογο, παρακαλώ.** _eh•nahn kah•tah•loh•ghoh pah•rah•kah•loh_
What do you recommend?	**Τι προτείνετε;** _tee proh•tee•neh•the_
I'd like...	**Θα ήθελα...** _thah ee•theh•lah..._
Some more..., please.	**Λίγο ακόμη..., παρακαλώ.** _lee•ghoh ah•koh•mee... pah•rah•kah•loh_
Enjoy your meal!	**Καλή όρεξη!** _kah•lee oh•reh•ksee_

YOU MAY HEAR...

με το αίμα του, σενιάν	rare
meh toh eh-mah too seh-nian	
μέτρια ψημένο *meht-ree-ah psee-meh-noh*	medium
καλοψημένο *kah-loh-psee-meh-noh*	well-done

The check [bill], please.	**Τον λογαριασμό, παρακαλώ.**
	tohn loh-ghah-riahs-moh pah-rah-kah-loh
Is service included?	**Συμπεριλαμβάνεται και το φιλοδώρημα;**
	seem-beh-ree-lahm-vah-neh-teh keh toh
	fee-loh-THoh-ree-mah
Can I pay by credit card?	**Μπορώ να πληρώσω με πιστωτική κάρτα;**
	boh-roh nah plee-roh-soh meh pee-stoh-tee-kee kahr-tah
Can I have a receipt?	**Μπορώ να έχω απόδειξη;** *boh-roh nah*
	eh-khoh ah-poh-THee-ksee

Breakfast

bacon	**μπέικον** *beh-ee-kohn*	
bread	**ψωμί** *psoh-mee*	
butter	**βούτυρο** *voo-tee-roh*	
cold cuts [charcuterie]	**αλλαντικά** *ah-lah-ndee-kah*	
cheese	**τυρί** *tee-ree*	
...eggs	**αυγά...** *ahv-ghah...*	
soft-boiled	**μελάτα** *meh-lah-tah*	
hard-boiled	**σφικτά** *sfeekh-tah*	
fried	**τηγανητά μάτια** *tee-ghah-nee-tah mah-tiah*	
scrambled eggs	**ομελέτα** *oh-meh-leh-tah*	

| omelet | **ομελέτα** oh·meh·<u>leh</u>·tah |
| toast | **ψωμί φρυγανιά** psoh·<u>mee</u> free·ghah·<u>niah</u> |

Appetizers

pâté	**πατέ** pah·<u>teh</u>
fish soup thickened	**ψαρόσουπα αυγολέμονο** psah·<u>roh</u>·soo·pah
with egg and lemon	ahv·ghoh·<u>leh</u>·moh·noh
tomato soup	**τοματόσουπα** toh·mah·<u>toh</u>·soo·pah
vegetable soup	**χορτόσουπα** khohr·<u>toh</u>·soo·pah
chicken soup	**κοτόσουπα** koh·<u>toh</u>·soo·pah
salad	**σαλάτα** sah·<u>lah</u>·tah
stuffed grape leaves	**ντολμαδάκι** dohl·mah·<u>THah</u>·kee
tzatziki	**τζατζίκι** jah·<u>jee</u>·kee

Meat

beef	**βοδινό** voh·<u>THee</u>·<u>noh</u>
chicken	**κοτόπουλο** koh·<u>toh</u>·poo·loh
lamb	**αρνί** ahr·<u>nee</u>
pork	**χοιρινό** khee·ree·<u>noh</u>
rabbit	**κουνέλι** koo·<u>neh</u>·lee
veal	**μοσχάρι** mohs·<u>khah</u>·ree
veal/pork steak	**μπριζόλα μοσχαρίσια/χοιρινή**
	bree·<u>zoh</u>·lah mohs·khah·<u>ree</u>·siah/khee·ree·<u>nee</u>

Fish & Seafood

fresh cod	**μπακαλιάρος** bah·kah·<u>liah</u>·rohs
herring (smoked)	**ρέγγα (καπνιστή)** <u>rehn</u>·gah (kahp·nees·<u>tee</u>)
lobster	**αστακός** ahs·tah·<u>kohs</u>
shrimp [prawn]	**γαρίδα** <u>ghah</u>·ree·THah
swordfish	**ξιφίας** ksee·<u>fee</u>·ahs

Vegetables

broad beans	**κουκί**	koo-_kee_
cabbage	**λάχανο**	_lah_-khah-noh
carrot	**καρότο**	kah-_roh_-toh
mushroom	**μανιτάρι**	mah-nee-_tah_-ree
onion	**κρεμμύδι**	kreh-_mee_-THee
peas	**αρακάς**	ah-rah-_kahs_
potato	**πατάτα**	pah-_tah_-tah
tomato	**ντομάτα**	ndoh-_mah_-tah

Sauces & Condiments

salt	**Αλάτι**	ah-_lah_-tee
pepper	**Πιπέρι**	pee-_peh_-ree
mustard	**Μουστάρδα**	moo-_stahr_-THah
ketchup	**Κέτσαπ**	_keh_-tsahp

Fruit & Dessert

apple	**μήλο**	_mee_-loh
banana	**μπανάνα**	bah-_nah_-nah
lemon	**λεμόνι**	leh-_moh_-nee
orange	**πορτοκάλι**	pohr-toh-_kah_-lee
pear	**αχλάδι**	akh-_lah_-THee
watermelon	**καρπούζι**	kahr-_poo_-zee
ice cream	**παγωτό**	pah-ghoh-_toh_
a chocolate bar	**σοκολάτα**	soh-koh-_lah_-tah
fruit salad	**φρουτοσαλάτα**	froo-toh-sah-_lah_-tah
rice pudding	**ρυζόγαλο**	ree-_zoh_-ghah-loh
caramel custard	**κρέμα καραμελέ**	_kreh_-mah kah-rah-meh-_leh_
baklava pastry with nut filling	**μπακλαβάς**	bah-klah-_vahs_

Drinks

May I see the wine list/drinks menu?	**Μπορώ να δω τον κατάλογο με τα κρασιά/ποτά;** *boh-roh nah THoh tohn kah-tah-loh-ghoh meh tah krah-siah/poh-tah*
What do you recommend?	**Τι συστήνετε;** *tee see-stee-neh-the*
I'd like a bottle/ glass of red/white wine.	**Θα ήθελα ένα μπουκάλι/ποτήρι κόκκινο/ λευκό κρασί.** *thah ee-theh-lah eh-nah boo-kah-lee/ poh-tee-ree koh-kee-noh/lehf-koh krah-see*
The house wine, please.	**Το κρασί του καταστήματος, παρακαλώ.** *toh krah-see too kah-tah-stee-mah-tohs pah-rah-kah-loh*
Another bottle/ glass, please.	**Άλλο ένα μπουκάλι/ποτήρι, παρακαλώ.** *ah-loh eh-nah boo-kah-lee/poh-tee-ree pah-rah-kah-loh*
I'd like a local beer.	**Θα ήθελα μια τοπική μπύρα.** *thah ee-theh-lah miah toh-pee-kee bee-rah*
Let me buy you a drink.	**Να σασκεράσω ένα ποτό.** *nah sahs keh-rah-soh eh-nah poh-toh*
Cheers!	**Στην υγειά σας!** *steen ee-ghiah sahs*
A coffee/tea, please.	**Έναν καφέ/Ένα τσάι, παρακαλώ.** *eh-nahn kah-feh/ eh-nah tsah-ee pah-rah-kah-loh*
Black.	**Σκέτος.** *skeh-tohs*
With...	**Με...** *meh...*
milk	**γάλα** *ghah-lah*
sugar	**ζάχαρη** *zah-khah-ree*
artificial sweetener	**ζαχαρίνη** *zah-khah-ree-nee*
..., please.	**..., παρακαλώ.** *...pah-rah-kah-loh*
A juice	**Ένα χυμό** *eh-nah khee-moh*
A soda	**Μία σόδα** *mee-ah soh-THah*

| A sparkling water | **Ενα ανθρακούχο νερό** <u>eh</u>·nah ahn·thrah·<u>koo</u>·khoh neh·<u>roh</u> |
| A still water | **Ενα νερό χωρίς ανθρακικό** <u>eh</u>·nah neh·<u>roh</u> khoh·<u>rees</u> ahn·thrah·kee·<u>koh</u> |

Leisure Time

Sightseeing

Where's the tourist information office?	**Πού είναι το γραφείο τουρισμού;** poo <u>ee</u>·neh toh ghrah·<u>fee</u>·oh too·reez·<u>moo</u>
What are the main points of interest?	**Ποια είναι τα κυριότερα αξιοθέατα;** piah <u>ee</u>·neh tah kee·ree·<u>oh</u>·teh·rah ah·ksee·oh·<u>theh</u>·ah·tah
Do you have tours in English?	**Γίνονται ξεναγήσεις στα αγγλικά;** <u>ghee</u>·nohn·deh kseh·nah·<u>ghee</u>·sees stah ahng·lee·<u>kah</u>
Could I have a map/guide?	**Μπορώ να έχω έναν χάρτη/οδηγό;** boh·<u>roh</u> nah <u>eh</u>·khoh <u>eh</u>·nahn <u>khahr</u>·tee/oh·<u>THee</u>·ghoh

Shopping

Where is the market/mall?	**Πού είναι η αγορά/το εμπορικό κέντρο;** poo <u>ee</u>·neh ee ah·ghoh·<u>rah</u>/toh ehm·boh·ree·<u>koh</u> <u>kehn</u>·droh
I'm just looking.	**Απλώς κοιτάω.** ahp·<u>lohs</u> kee·<u>tah</u>·oh
Can you help me?	**Μπορείτε να με βοηθήσετε;** boh·<u>ree</u>·teh nah meh voh·ee·<u>thee</u>·seh·teh
I'm being helped.	**Με εξυπηρετούν.** meh eh·ksee·pee·reh·<u>toon</u>
How much?	**Πόσο;** <u>poh</u>·soh
This/That one, thanks.	**Αυτό/Εκείνο, παρακαλώ.** ahf·<u>toh</u>/eh·<u>kee</u>·noh pah·rah·kah·<u>loh</u>
I'd like…	**Θα ήθελα…** thah <u>ee</u>·theh·lah…
That's all, thanks.	**Τίποτε άλλο, ευχαριστώ.** <u>tee</u>·poh·teh <u>ah</u>·loh ehf·khah·rees·<u>toh</u>

YOU MAY SEE...

ανοιχτό/κλειστό	open/closed
έξοδος	entrance/exit

Where do I pay?	**Πού πληρώνω;** *poo plee·roh·noh*
I'll pay in cash/by credit card.	**Θα πληρώσω τοις μετρητοίς/με πιστωτική κάρτα.** *thah plee·roh·soh tees meht·ree·tees/meh pees·toh· tee·kee kahr·tah*
A receipt, please.	**Μια απόδειξη, παρακαλώ.** *miah ah·poh·THee·ksee pah·rah·kah·loh*

Sport & Leisure

When's the game?	**Πότε είναι ο αγώνας;** *poh·teh ee·neh oh ah·ghoh·nahs*
Where's...?	**Πού είναι...;** *poo ee·neh...*
the beach	**η παραλία** *ee pah·rah·lee·ah*
the park	**το πάρκο** *toh pahr·koh*
the pool	**η πισίνα** *ee pee·see·nah*
Is it safe to swim/ dive here?	**Είναι ασφαλές εδώ για κολύμπι/κατάδυση;** *ee·neh ahs·fah·lehs eh·THoh yah koh·leem·bee/ kah·tah·THee·see*
Can I hire golf clubs?	**Μπορώ να νοικιάσω μπαστούνια του γκόλφ;** *boh·roh nah nee·kiah·soh bahs·too·niah too gohlf*
How much per hour?	**Πόσο χρεώνεται η ώρα;** *poh·soh khreh·oh·neh·teh ee oh·rah*
How far is it to...?	**Πόσο μακριά είναι για...;** *poh·soh mahk·ree·ah ee·neh yah...*
Can you show me on the map?	**Μπορείτε να μου δείξετε στο χάρτη;** *boh·ree·teh nah moo THee·kseh·teh stoh khahr·tee*

Going Out

What's there to do in the evenings?	**Τι μπορώ να κάνω τα βράδια;** *tee boh•roh nah kah•noh tah vrahTH•yah*
Do you have a program of events?	**Έχετε ένα πρόγραμμα εκδηλώσεων;** *eh•kheh•teh eh•nah prohgh•rah•mah ehk•THee•loh•seh•ohn*
What's playing at the movies [cinema] tonight?	**Τι παίζει ο κινηματογράφος απόψε;** *tee peh•zee oh kee•nee•mah•tohgh•rah•fohs ah•poh•pseh*
Where's...?	**Πού είναι...;** *poo ee•neh...*
the downtown area	**το κέντρο της πόλης** *toh kehn•droh tees poh•lees*
the bar	**το μπαρ** *toh bahr*
the dance club	**η ντισκοτέκ** *ee dees•koh•tehk*
Is this area safe at night?	**Η περιοχή είναι ασφαλής τη νύχτα;** *ee peh•ree•oh•khee ee•neh ah•sfah•lees tee nee•khtah*

Baby Essentials

Do you have...?	**Έχετε...;** *eh•kheh•teh...*
a baby bottle	**ένα μπιμπερό** *eh•nah bee•beh•roh*
baby food	**παιδικές τροφές** *peh•THee•kehs troh•fehs*
baby wipes	**υγρά μαντηλάκια** *eegh•rah mahn•dee•lah•kiah*
a car seat	**ένα παιδικό κάθισμα** *eh•nah peh•THee•koh kah•thee•smah*
a children's menu	**έναν παιδικό κατάλογο** *eh•nahn peh•THee•koh kah•tah•loh•ghoh*
a child's portion	**μια παιδική μερίδα** *miah peh•THee•kee meh•ree•THah*
a child's seat/ highchair	**ένα παιδικό κάθισμα/καρεκλάκι** *eh•nah peh•ee•koh kah•theez•mah/kah•rehk•lah•kee moh•roo*
a crib/cot	**μια κούνια/ένα παιδικό κρεβάτι** *miah koo•niah/ eh•nah peh•THee•koh kreh•vah•tee*
diapers [nappies]	**πάνες μωρού** *ee pah•nehs moh•roo*

formula	**βρεφικό γάλα** vreh·fee·koh ghah·lah
a pacifier [dummy]	**μια πιπίλα** miah pee·pee·lah
a playpen	**ένα παιδικό παρκάκι** eh·nah peh·THee·koh pahr·kah·kee
a stroller [pushchair]	**ένα καροτσάκι** eh·nah kah·roh·tsah·kee
Can I breastfeed the baby here?	**Μπορώ να θηλάσω το μωρό εδώ;** boh·roh nah thee·lah·soh toh moh·roh eh·THoh
Where can I change the baby?	**Πού μπορώ να αλλάξω το μωρό;** poo boh·roh nah ah·lah·ksoh toh moh·roh

For Eating Out, see page 102.

Disabled Travelers

Is there...?	**Υπάρχει...;** ee·pahr·khee...
access for the disabled	**πρόσβαση για άτομα με ειδικές ανάγκες;** prohz·vah·see yah ah·toh·mah meh ee·THee·kehs ah·nahn·gehs
a wheelchair ramp	**ράμπα για αναπηρικό καρότσι** rahm·bah yah ah·nah·pee·ree·koh kah·roh·tsee
a disabled-accessible toilet	**προσβάσιμη τουαλέτα για ανάπηρους** prohs·vah·see·mee too·ah·leh·tah yah ah·nah·pee·roos
I need...	**Χρειάζομαι...** khree·ah·zoh·meh...
assistance	**βοήθεια** voh·ee·thiah
an elevator [lift]	**ασανσέρ** ah·sahn·sehr
a ground-floor room	**ισόγειο** ee·soh·yee·oh
Please speak louder.	**Μιλήστε πιο δυνατά.** mee·lee·steh pioh THee·nah·tah

In an emergency, dial: **100** for the police, **199** for the fire brigade and **166** for the ambulance. Or you can also dial the European SOS number: **112**

Health & Emergencies

Emergencies

Help!	**Βοήθεια!**	*voh·ee·thee·ah*
Go away!	**Φύγετε!**	*fee·yeh·teh*
Stop, thief!	**Σταματήστε τον κλέφτη!**	*stah·mah·tees·teh tohn klehf·tee*
Get a doctor!	**Φωνάξτε ένα γιατρό!**	*foh·nahks·teh eh·nah yaht·roh*
Fire!	**Φωτιά!**	*foh·tiah*
I'm lost.	**Έχω χαθεί.**	*eh·khoh khah·thee*
Can you help me?	**Μπορείτε να με βοηθήσετε;**	*boh·ree·teh nah meh voh·ee·thee·seh·the*
Call the police!	**Φωνάξτε την αστυνομία!**	*foh·nahks·teh teen ahs·tee·noh·mee·ah*

YOU MAY HEAR...

Παρακαλώ συμπληρώστε αυτό το έντυπο. *pah·rah·kah·loh sehm·blee·rohs·teh ahf·toh toh ehn·tee·poh*	Please fill out this form.
Την ταυτότητά σας, παρακαλώ. *teen tahf·toh·tee·tah sahs pah·rah·kah·loh*	Your identification, please.
Πότε/Πού έγινε; *poh·teh/poo eh·yee·neh*	When/Where did it happen?
Πώς είναι εμφανισιακά; *pohs ee·neh ehm·fah·nee·see·ah·kah*	What does he/she look like?

| Where's the nearest police station? | **Πού είναι το κοντινότερο αστυνομικό τμήμα;** *poo ee·neh toh kohn·dee·noh·teh·roh ahs·tee·noh·mee·koh tmee·mah* |
| My child is missing. | **Λείπει το παιδί μου.** *lee·pee toh peh·THee moo* |

Health

I'm sick [ill].	**Είμαι άρρωστος.** *ee·meh ah·rohs·tohs*
I need an English-speaking doctor.	**Χρειάζομαι έναν γιατρό που να μιλάει αγγλικά.** *khree·ah·zoh·meh eh·nahn yaht·roh poo nah mee·lah·ee ang·lee·kah*
It hurts here.	**Με πονάει εδώ.** *meh poh·nah·ee eh·THoh*
Where's the nearest pharmacy?	**Πού είναι το κοντινότερο φαρμακείο;** *poo ee·neh toh kohn·dee·noh·teh·roh fahr·mah·kee·oh*
I'm (...months) pregnant.	**Είμαι (...μηνών) έγκυος.** *ee·meh (...mee·nohn) eh·gee·ohs*
I'm on...	**Παίρνω...** *pehr·noh...*
I'm allergic to antibiotics/penicillin.	**Είμαι αλλεργικός στα αντιβιωτικά/στην πενικιλίνη.** *ee·meh ah·lehr·yee·kohs stah ahn·dee·vee·oh·tee·kah/ steen peh·nee·kee·lee·nee*

Dictionary

adaptor προσαρμοστής proh·sahr·moh·stees
antiseptic cream αντισηπτική κρέμα ahn·dee·seep·tee·kee kreh·mah
baby μωρό moh·roh
bad κακός kah·kohs
bandage γάζα ghah·zah
beige μπεζ behz
bikini μπικίνι bee·kee·nee

bird πουλί poo·lee
black μαύρο mahv·roh
blue μπλε bleh
bottle opener τιρμπουσόν teer·boo·sohn
bowls τα μπωλ tah bohl
boy αγόρι ah·ghoh·ree
boyfriend φίλος fee·lohs
bra σουτιέν soo·tiehn
brown καφέ kah·feh

camera φωτογραφική μηχανή foh·tohgh·rah·fee·<u>kee</u> mee·khah·<u>nee</u>

can opener ανοιχτήρι ah·neekh·<u>tee</u>·ree

castle κάστρο <u>kahs</u>·troh

cold adj (temperature) **κρύος** <u>kree</u>·ohs; n (chill) **κρυολόγημα** kree·oh·<u>loh</u>·yee·mah

comb n **χτένα** <u>khteh</u>·nah; v **χτενίζω** khteh·<u>nee</u>·zoh

computer υπολογιστής ee·poh·loh·yee·<u>stees</u>

condom προφυλακτικό proh·fee·lah·ktee·<u>koh</u>

contact lens φακός επαφής fah·<u>kohs</u> eh·pah·<u>fees</u>

corkscrew τιρμπουσόν teer·boo·<u>sohn</u>

dangerous επικίνδυνος eh·pee·<u>keen</u>·THee·nohs

deodorant αποσμητικό ah·pohz·mee·tee·<u>koh</u>

diabetes διαβήτης THee·ah·<u>vee</u>·tees

doll κούκλα <u>kook</u>·lah

earache πόνος στο αυτί <u>poh</u>·nohs stoh ahf·<u>tee</u>

early νωρίς noh·<u>rees</u>

east ανατολικά ah·nah·toh·lee·<u>kah</u>

fly n **μύγα** <u>mee</u>·ghah; v **πετάω** peh·<u>tah</u>·oh

forks τα πηρούνια tah pee·<u>roo</u>·niah

girl κορίτσι koh·<u>ree</u>·tsee

girlfriend φίλη <u>fee</u>·lee

glass (container) ποτήρι poh·<u>tee</u>·ree

good καλός kah·<u>lohs</u>

gray γκρι gree

green πράσινο <u>prah</u>·see·noh

hairbrush βούρτσα <u>voor</u>·tsah

hot (weather) ζεστός zehs·<u>tohs</u>

husband σύζυγος <u>see</u>·zee·ghohs

ice n **πάγος** <u>pah</u>·ghohs

injection ένεση <u>eh</u>·neh·see

I'd like Θα ήθελα… thah <u>ee</u>·theh·lah…

insect repellent εντομοαπωθητικό ehn·doh·moh·ah·poh·thee·tee·<u>koh</u>

jeans μπλου-τζην bloo·<u>jeen</u>

knife μαχαίρι mah·<u>kheh</u>·ree

lactose intolerant έχω ευαισθησία στα γαλακτοκομικά eh·khoh eh·vehs·thee·see·ah stah ghah·lahk·toh·koh·mee·kah

large adj **μεγάλος** meh·<u>ghah</u>·lohs

lighter adj **ανοιχτότερος** ah·neekh·<u>toh</u>·teh·rohs; n **αναπτήρας** ah·nahp·<u>tee</u>·rahs

lotion λοσιόν loh·<u>siohn</u>

love v **αγαπώ** ah·ghah·<u>poh</u>

match (fire starter) σπίρτο <u>speer</u>·toh

medium μέτρια ψημένο <u>meht</u>·ree·ah psee·<u>meh</u>·noh

museum μουσείο moo·<u>see</u>·oh

napkin πετσέτα peh·<u>tseh</u>·tah

nurse *n* **νοσοκόμα** noh·soh·<u>koh</u>·mah
orange πορτοκάλι pohr·toh·kah·lee
park *n* **πάρκο** <u>pahr</u>·koh
pen *n* **στυλό** stee·<u>loh</u>
pink ροζ rohz
rain *n* **βροχή** vroh·<u>khee</u>; *v* **βρέχει** <u>vreh</u>·khee
raincoat αδιάβροχο ah·<u>THee·ahv</u>·roh·khoh
razor ξυραφάκι ksee·rah·<u>fah</u>·kee
razor blade ξυραφάκι ksee·rah·<u>fah</u>·kee
red κόκκινο <u>koh</u>·kee·noh
sandals πέδιλα <u>peh</u>·THee·lah
sanitary napkin σερβιέτα sehr·vee·<u>eh</u>·tah
sauna σάουνα <u>sah</u>·oo·nah
scissors ψαλίδι psah·<u>lee</u>·THee
shampoo *n* **σαμπουάν** sahm·poo·<u>ahn</u>
shoe παπούτσι pah·<u>poo</u>·tsee
small μικρός meek·<u>rohs</u>
sneakers αθλητικά παπούτσια ath·lee·tee·<u>kah</u> pah·<u>poo</u>·tsiah
snow *v* **χιονίζει** khioh·<u>nee</u>·zee
soap *n* **σαπούνι** sah·<u>poo</u>·nee
socks κάλτσες <u>kahl</u>·tsehs
spoon *n* **κουτάλι** koo·<u>tah</u>·lee
stamp *n* **(postage) γραμματόσημο** ghrah·mah·<u>toh</u>·see·moh
sunburn ηλίου ee·<u>lee</u>·oo
sunglasses γυαλιά ηλίου yah·<u>liah</u> ee·<u>lee</u>·oo
sunscreen αντιηλιακό ahn·dee·ee·lee·ah·<u>koh</u>

sweatshirt φούτερ <u>foo</u>·tehr
swimsuit μαγιό mah·<u>yoh</u>
tampon ταμπόν tahm·<u>bohn</u>
terrible φοβερός foh·veh·<u>rohs</u>
thin *adj* **λεπτός** lehp·<u>tohs</u>
think νομίζω noh·<u>mee</u>·zoh
thirsty διψάω THee·<u>psah</u>·oh
those εκείνα eh·<u>kee</u>·nah
tie *n* **γραβάτα** ghrah·<u>vah</u>·tah
tissue χαρτομάντηλο khahr·toh·<u>mahn</u>·dee·loh
toilet paper χαρτί υγείας khahr·<u>tee</u> ee·<u>yee</u>·ahs
toothbrush οδοντόβουρτσα oh·THohn·<u>doh</u>·voor·tsah
toothpaste οδοντόπαστα oh·THohn·<u>doh</u>·pahs·tah
toy κατάστημα kah·<u>tahs</u>·tee·mah
T-shirt μπλουζάκι bloo·<u>zah</u>·kee
underpants [BE] κυλοτάκι kee·loh·<u>tah</u>·kee
vacancy ελεύθερο δωμάτιο eh·<u>lehf</u>·theh·roh THoh·<u>mah</u>·tee·oh
vegetarian χορτοφάγος khohr·toh·<u>fah</u>·ghohs
water *n* **νερό** neh·<u>roh</u>
white άσπρο <u>ahs</u>·proh
wife σύζυγος <u>see</u>·zee·ghohs
with με meh
without χωρίς khoh·<u>rees</u>
yellow κίτρινος <u>keet</u>·ree·nohs
zoo ζωολογικός κήπος zoh·oh·loh·yee·<u>kohs</u> <u>kee</u>·pohs

Italian

Essentials

Hello.	**Salve.** _sahl_•veh
Goodbye.	**Arrivederla.** ahr•ree•veh•_dehr_•lah
Yes/No/OK	**Sì/No/OK.** see/noh/oh•_kay_
Excuse me! (to get attention)	**Scusi!** _skoo_•zee
Excuse me. (to get past)	**Permesso.** pehr•_mehs_•soh
I'm sorry.	**Mi dispiace.** mee dees•_pyah_•cheh
I'd like…	**Vorrei…** vohr•_ray_…
How much?	**Quant'è?** kwahn•_teh_
And/or	**E/o** eh/o
Where is…?	**Dov'è…?** doh•_veh_…
I'm going to…	**Vado…** _vah_•doh…
My name is…	**Mi chiamo…** mee _kyah_•moh…
Please.	**Per favore.** pehr fah•_voh_•reh
Thank you.	**Grazie.** _grah_•tsyeh
You're welcome.	**Prego.** _preh_•goh
Please speak slowly.	**Parli lentamente per favore.** _pahr_•lee lehn•tah•_mehn_•teh pehr fah•_voh_•reh
Can you repeat that?	**Può ripetere?** pwoh ree•_peh_•teh•reh
I don't understand.	**Non capisco.** nohn kah•_pees_•koh
Do you speak English?	**Parla inglese?** _pahr_•lah een•_gleh_•zeh
I don't speak Italian.	**Non parlo italiano.** nohn _pahr_•loh ee•tah•_lyah_•noh
Where's the restroom [toilet]?	**Dov'è la toilette?** doh•_veh_ lah _twah_•leht
Help!	**Aiuto!** ah•_yoo_•toh

You'll find the pronunciation of the Italian letters and words written in gray after each sentence to guide you. Simply pronounce these as if they were English, noting that any underlines and bolds indicate an additional emphasis or stress or a lengthening of a vowel sound. As you hear the language being spoken, you will quickly become accustomed to the local pronunciation and dialect.

Numbers

0	**zero** _dzeh_·roh
1	**uno** _oo_·noh
2	**due** _doo_·eh
3	**tre** treh
4	**quattro** _kwaht_·troh
5	**cinque** _cheen_·kweh
6	**sei** say
7	**sette** _seht_·teh
8	**otto** _oht_·toh
9	**nove** _noh_·veh
10	**dieci** _dyeh_·chee
11	**undici** _oon_·dee·chee
12	**dodici** _doh_·dee·chee
13	**tredici** _treh_·dee·chee
14	**quattordici** kwaht·_tohr_·dee·chee
15	**quindici** _kween_·dee·chee
16	**sedici** _seh_·dee·chee
17	**diciassette** dee·chyahs·_seht_·teh
18	**diciotto** dee·_chyoht_·toh
19	**diciannove** dee·chyahn·_noh_·veh
20	**venti** _vehn_·tee

21	**ventuno** vehn·_too_·noh
30	**trenta** _trehn_·tah
40	**quaranta** kwah·_rahn_·tah
50	**cinquanta** cheen·_kwahn_·tah
60	**sessanta** sehs·_sahn_·tah
70	**settanta** seht·_tahn_·tah
80	**ottanta** oht·_tahn_·tah
90	**novanta** noh·_vahn_·tah
100	**cento** _chehn_·toh
101	**centuno** chehn·_too_·noh
200	**duecento** doo·eh·_chehn_·toh
500	**cinquecento** cheen·kweh·_chehn_·toh
1,000	**mille** _meel_·leh
10,000	**diecimila** dyeh·chee·_mee_·lah
1,000,000	**milione** mee·_lyoh_·neh

Time

What time is it?	**Che ore sono?** keh _oh_·reh _soh_·noh
It's noon [midday].	**È mezzogiorno.** eh meh·dzoh·_jyohr_·noh
Five after [past] three.	**Le tre e cinque.** leh treh eh _cheen_·kweh
A quarter to three.	**Sono le tre meno un quarto.** _soh_·noh leh treh _meh_·noh oon _kwahr_·toh
5:30 a.m./5:30 p.m.	**Le cinque e mezzo/Le diciassette e trenta.** leh _cheen_·kweh eh _meh_·dzoh/ leh _dee_·chyahs·_seht_·teh eh _trehn_·tah

Days

Monday	**lunedì** loon·eh·_dee_
Tuesday	**martedì** mahr·teh·_dee_
Wednesday	**mercoledì** mehr·koh·leh·_dee_
Thursday	**giovedì** jyoh·veh·_dee_
Friday	**venerdì** veh·nehr·_dee_

| Saturday | **sabato** _sah_·bah·toh |
| Sunday | **domenica** doh·_meh_·nee·kah |

Dates

yesterday	**ieri** _yeh_·ree
today	**oggi** _oh_·djee
tomorrow	**domani** doh·_mah_·nee
day	**giorno** _jyohr_·noh
week	**settimana** seht·tee·_mah_·nah
month	**mese** _meh_·zeh
year	**anno** _ahn_·noh
Happy New Year	**Buno Anno Nuovo.** bwohn _ahn_·noh noo·ovo
Happy Birthday	**Buon Compleanno.** bwohn comp·lee·_ahn_·noh

Months

January	**gennaio** jehn·_nah_·yoh
February	**febbraio** fehb·_brah_·yoh
March	**marzo** _mahr_·tsoh
April	**aprile** ah·_pree_·leh
May	**maggio** _mah_·djoh
June	**giugno** _jyoo_·nyoh
July	**luglio** _loo_·llyoh
August	**agosto** ah·_goh_·stoh
September	**settembre** seht·_tehm_·breh
October	**ottobre** oht·_toh_·breh
November	**novembre** noh·_vehm_·breh
December	**dicembre** dee·_chem_·breh

Arrival & Departure

| I'm on vacation [holiday]/business. | **Sono in vacanza/viaggio d'affari.** _soh_·noh een vah·_kahn_·tsah/_vyah_·djoh dahf·_fah_·ree |
| I'm going to... | **Vado a...** _vah_·doh ah... |

YOU MAY SEE...

Italian currency is the **euro €**, divided into 100 **centesimi**.
Coins: 1, 2, 5, 10, 20, 50 **cent.**; **€**1, 2
Notes: €5, 10, 20, 50, 100, 200, 500

I'm staying at the...Hotel.	**Sono all'hotel...** _soh_•noh ahl•loh•_tehl_...

Money

Where's...?	**Dov'è...?** doh•_veh_...
the ATM	**il bancomat** eel _bahn_•koh•maht
the bank	**la banca** lah _bahn_•kah
the currency exchange office	**l'ufficio di cambio** loof•_fee_•chyoh dee _kahm_•byoh
When does the bank open/close?	**A che ora apre/chiude la banca?** ah keh _oh_•rah _ah_•preh/_kyoo_•deh lah _bahn_•kah
I'd like to change dollars/pounds into euros.	**Vorrei cambiare dei dollari/delle sterline in euro.** vohr•_ray_ kahm•_byah_•reh day _dohl_•lah•ree/_dehl_•leh stehr•_lee_•neh een _eh_•oo•roh
I'd like to cash traveler's checks [cheques].	**Vorrei riscuotere dei travellers cheques.** vohr•_ray_ ree•skwoh•_teh_•reh day _trah_•vehl•lehrs chehks
I'll pay in cash/by credit card.	**Pago in contanti/con carta di credito.** _pah_•goh een kohn•_tahn_•tee/kohn _kahr_•tah dee _kreh_•dee•toh

For Numbers, see page 118.

Getting Around

How do I get to town?	**Come si arriva in città?** _koh_•meh see ahr•_ree_•vah een cheet•_tah_
Where's...?	**Dov'è...?** doh•_veh_...
the airport	**l'aeroporto** lah•eh•roh•_pohr_•toh

the train [railway] station	**la stazione ferroviaria** *lah stah·tsyoh·neh fehr·roh·vyah·ryah*
the bus station	**la stazione degli autobus** *lah stah·tsyoh·neh deh·llyee ow·toh·boos*
the metro [underground] station	**la stazione della metropolitana** *lah stah·tsyoh·neh dehl·lah meh·troh·poh·lee·tah·nah*
How far is it?	**Quanto dista?** *kwahn·toh dees·tah*
Where do I buy a ticket?	**Dove si comprano i biglietti?** *doh·veh see kohm·prah·noh ee bee·llyeht·tee*
A one-way/ return-trip ticket to...	**Un biglietto di andata/di andata e ritorno per...** *oon bee·llyeht·toh dee ahn·dah·tah/ dee ahn·dah·tah eh ree·tohr·noh pehr...*
How much?	**Quant'è?** *kwahn·teh*
Which...?	**Quale...?** *kwah·leh...*
gate	**uscita** *oo·shee·tah*
line	**linea** *lee·neh·ah*
platform	**binario** *bee·nah·ryoh*
Where can I get a taxi?	**Dove posso trovare un taxi?** *doh·veh pohs·soh troh·vah·reh oon tah·ksee*
Take me to this address.	**Mi porti a questo indirizzo.** *mee pohr·tee ah kweh·stoh een·dee·ree·tsoh*
To...Airport, please.	**All'aeroporto di..., per favore.** *ahl·lah·eh·roh·pohr·toh dee... pehr fah·voh·reh*
I'm in a rush.	**Ho fretta.** *oh freht·tah*
Can I have a map?	**Può darmi una cartina?** *pwoh dahr·mee oo·nah kahr·tee·nah*

Tickets

| When's the...to Milan? | **A che ora è il/l'...per Milano?** *ah keh oh·rah eh eel/l...pehr mee·lah·noh* |

(first) bus	**(primo) autobus** (_pree_•moh) _ow_•toh•boos
(next) flight	**(prossimo) volo** (_prohs_•see•moh) _voh_•loh
(last) train	**(ultimo) treno** (_ool_•tee•moh) _treh_•noh
Where do I buy a ticket?	**Dove si comprano i biglietti?** _doh_•veh see _kohm_•prah•noh ee bee•_llyeht_•tee
One/Two ticket(s), please.	**Un biglietto/Due biglietti, per favore.** oon bee•_llyeht_•toh/_doo_•eh bee•_llyeht_•tee pehr fah•_voh_•reh
For today/tomorrow.	**Per oggi/domani.** pehr _oh_•djee/doh•_mah_•nee
A…ticket.	**Un biglietto…** oon bee•_llyeht_•toh…
one-way	**di andata** dee ahn•_dah_•tah
return-trip	**di andata e ritorno** dee ahn•_dah_•tah eh ree•_tohr_•noh
first class	**di prima classe** dee _pree_•mah _klahs_•seh
I have an e-ticket.	**Ho un biglietto elettronico.** oh oon bee•_llyeht_•toh eh•leht•_troh_•nee•koh
How long is the trip?	**Quanto dura il viaggio?** _kwahn_•toh _doo_•rah eel _vyah_•djoh
Is it a direct train?	**Il treno è diretto?** eel trehno eh dee•_rayt_•toh
Is this the bus to…?	**È l'autobus per…?** eh _low_•toh•boos pehr…
Can you tell me when to get off?	**Può dirmi quando scendere?** pwoh _deer_•mee _kwahn_•doh _shehn_•deh•reh
I'd like to…my reservation.	**Vorrei…la prenotazione.** vohr•_ray_…lah preh•noh•tah•_tsyoh_•neh
cancel	**annullare** ahn•nool•_lah_•reh
change	**cambiare** kahm•_byah_•reh
confirm	**confermare** kohn•fehr•_mah_•reh

For Time, see page 119.

Car Hire

| Where's the car rental [hire]? | **Dov'è un autonoleggio?** doh•_veh_ oon _ow_•toh•noh•_leh_•djoh |

I'd like…	**Vorrei…** *vohr·ray…*
a cheap/small car	**un'auto economica/piccola** *oo·now·toh eh·koh·noh·mee·kah/peek·koh·lah*
an automatic/ a manual	**un'auto con il cambio automatico/manuale** *oo·now·toh kohn eel kahm·byoh ow·toh·mah·tee·koh/ mah·nwah·leh*
air conditioning	**un'auto con l'aria condizionata** *oo·now·toh kohn lah·ryah kohn·dee·tsyoh·nah·tah*
a car seat	**un sedile** *oon seh·dee·leh*
How much…?	**Qual è la tariffa…?** *kwah·leh lah tah·reef·fah…*
per day/week	**per un giorno/una settimana** *pehr oon jyohr·noh/ oo·nah seht·tee·mah·nah*
Are there discounts?	**Fate sconti?** *fah·teh skohn·tee*

YOU MAY HEAR…

sempre dritto *sehm·preh dreet·toh*	straight ahead
a sinistra *ah see·nee·strah*	left
a destra *ah deh·strah*	right
all'angolo/dietro l'angolo *ahl·lahn·goh·loh/dyeh·troh lahn·goh·loh*	on the corner/around the corner
di fronte a *dee frohn·teh ah*	opposite
dietro a *dyeh·troh ah*	behind
accanto a *ahk·kahn·toh ah*	next to
dopo *doh·poh*	after
a nord/sud *ah nohrd/sood*	north/south
a est/ovest *ah ehst/oh·vehst*	east/west
al semaforo *ahl seh·mah·foh·roh*	at the traffic light
all'incrocio *ahl·leen·kroh·chyoh*	at the intersection

Places to Stay

Can you recommend a hotel?	**Può consigliarmi un hotel?** *pwoh kohn•see•llyahr•mee oon oh•tehl*
I have a reservation.	**Ho una prenotazione.** *oh oo•nah preh•noh•tah•tsyoh•neh*
My name is…	**Mi chiamo…** *mee kyah•moh…*
Do you have a room…?	**Avete una camera…?** *ah•veh•teh oo•nah kah•meh•rah…*
for one/two	**singola/doppia** *seen•goh•lah/dohp•pyah*
with a bathroom	**con bagno** *kohn bah•nyoh*
with air conditioning	**con aria condizionata** *kohn ah•ryah kohn•dee•tsyoh•nah•tah*
For…	**Per…** *pehr…*
tonight	**stanotte** *stah•noht•teh*
two nights	**due notti** *doo•eh noht•tee*
one week	**una settimana** *oo•nah seht•tee•mah•nah*
How much?	**Quanto costa?** *kwahn•toh koh•stah*
Is there anything cheaper?	**C'è qualcosa di più economico?** *cheh kwahl•koh•zah dee pyoo eh•koh•noh•mee•koh*
When's check-out?	**A che ora devo lasciare la camera?** *ah keh oh•rah deh•voh lah•shah•reh lah kah•meh•rah*
Can I leave this in the safe?	**Posso lasciare questo nella cassaforte?** *pohs•soh lah•shah•reh kweh•stoh nehl•lah kahs•sah•fohr•teh*
Can I leave my bags?	**Posso lasciare le valigie?** *pohs•soh lah•shah•reh leh vah•lee•jyeh*
I'd like the bill/receipt.	**Vorrei il conto/la ricevuta.** *vohr•ray eel kohn•toh/lah ree•cheh•voo•tah*
I'll pay in cash/by credit card.	**Pago in contanti/con carta di credito.** *pah•goh een kohn•tahn•tee/kohn kahr•tah dee kreh•dee•toh*

Communications

Where's an internet cafe?	**Dov'è un Internet caffè?** *doh·veh oon een·tehr·neht kahf·feh*
Can I access the internet/check e-mail?	**Posso collegarmi a Internet/controllare le e-mail?** *pohs·soh kohl·leh·gahr·mee ah een·tehr·neht/kohn·trohl·lah·reh leh ee·mayl*
How much per hour/half hour?	**Quanto costa per un'ora/mezz'ora?** *kwahn·toh koh·stah pehr oon·oh·rah/mehdz·oh·rah*
How do I log on?	**Come si fa il login?** *koh·meh see fah eel loh·geen*
A phone card, please.	**Una scheda telefonica, per favore.** *oo·nah skeh·dah teh·leh·foh·nee·kah pehr fah·voh·reh*
Can I have your number, please?	**Mi può dare il suo numero, per favore?** *mee pwoh dah·reh eel soo·oh noo·meh·roh pehr fah·voh·reh*
Here's my number/e-mail.	**Ecco il mio numero/la mia e-mail.** *ehk·koh eel mee·oh noo·meh·roh/lah mee·ah ee·mayl*
Call/E-mail me.	**Mi chiami/mandi una e-mail.** *mee kyah·mee/mahn·dee oo·nah ee·mayl*
I'll text you.	**Le mando un SMS.** *leh mahn·doh oon ehs·seh ehm·meh ehs·seh*
Hello. This is...	**Pronto. Sono...** *prohn·toh soh·noh...*
Can I speak to...?	**Posso parlare con...?** *pohs·soh pahr·lah·reh kohn...*
Can you repeat that?	**Può ripetere?** *pwoh ree·peh·teh·reh*
I'll call back later.	**Richiamo più tardi.** *ree·kyah·moh pyoo tahr·dee*
Bye.	**Arrivederla.** *ahr·ree·veh·dehr·lah*
Where's the post office?	**Dov'è un ufficio postale?** *doh·veh oon oof·fee·chyoh poh·stah·leh*
I'd like to send this to...	**Vorrei inviare questo a...** *vohr·ray een·vyah·reh kweh·stoh ah...*
What is the WiFi password?	**Qual è la password Wi-Fi?** *koo·ahl·eh lah pahs·swoh·rd wah·ee fah·ee*

Is the WiFi free?	**Il WiFi è gratis?** *eel wah•ee fah•ee eh grah•tees*
Do you have bluetooth?	**Avete il Bluetooth?** *ah•veh•teh eel bloo•too•th*
Can I...?	**Posso...?** *pohs•soh...*
access the internet	**collegarmi (a Internet)** *kohl•leh•gahr•mee (ah een•tehr•neht)*
check e-mail	**controllare le e-mail** *kohn•trohl•lah•reh leh ee-mayl*
print	**stampare** *stahm•pah•reh*
plug in/charge my laptop/iPhone/ iPad/BlackBerry?	**collegare/ricaricare il mio portatile/iPhone/iPad?** *kohl•leh•gah•reh eel mee•oh pohr•tah•tee•leh/ahy•fon/ ahy•pad*
access Skype?	**usare Skype?** *oo•sah•reh skah•eep*
Do you have a scanner?	**Avete uno scanner?** *ah•veh•teh oo•noh skahn•nehr*

Social Media

Are you on Facebook/ Twitter?	**È su Facebook/Twitter?** *(polite form)* *eh soo feh•eez•book/tweet•tehr*
	Sei su Facebook/Twitter? *(informal form)* *seh•ee soo feh•eez•book/tweet•tehr*
What's your user name?	**Qual è il suo nome utente?** *(polite form)* *koo•ahl eh eel soo•oh noh•meh oo•tehn•teh*
	Qual è il tuo nome utente? *(informal form)* *Koo•ahl•eh eel too•oh noh•meh oo•tehn•teh*
I'll add you as a friend.	**La aggiungerò come amico.** *(polite form)* *lah ah•djoon•djeh•roh koh•meh ah•mee•koh*
	Ti aggiungerò come amico. *(informal form)* *tee ah•djoon•djeh•roh koh•meh ah•mee•koh*
I'll follow you Twitter.	**La seguirò su Twitter.** *(polite form)* *lah seh•gwee•roh soo tweet•tehr*
	Ti seguirò su Twitter. *(informal form)* *tee seh•gwee•roh soo tweet•tehr*

Are you following...? **Segue...?** *(polite form)* seh·gweh...

Seguite...? *(informal form)* seh·gwee·teh...

I'll put the pictures on **Metterò le foto su Facebook/Twitter.**
Facebook/Twitter. *meht·teh·roh leh foh·toh soo feh·eez·book/tweet·tehr*

Conversation

Hello!/Hi!	**Salve!/Ciao!** *sahl·veh/chah·oh*
How are you?	**Come sta?** *koh·meh stah*
Fine, thanks.	**Bene, grazie.** *beh·neh grah·tsyeh*
Excuse me!	**Scusi!** *skoo·zee*
Do you speak English?	**Parla inglese?** *pahr·lah een·gleh·zeh*
What's your name?	**Come si chiama?** *koh·meh see kyah·mah*
My name is...	**Mi chiamo...** *mee kyah·moh...*
Nice to meet you.	**Piacere.** *pyah·cheh·reh*
Where are you from?	**Di dov'è?** *dee doh·veh*
I'm American.	**Sono americano m/americana f.** *soh·noh ah·meh·ree·kah·noh/ah·meh·ree·kah·nah*
I'm English.	**Sono inglese.** *soh·noh een·gleh·zeh*
What do you do for a living?	**Cosa fa?** *koh·zah fah*
I work for...	**Lavoro per...** *lah·voh·roh pehr...*
I'm a student.	**Studio.** *stoo·dyoh*
I'm retired.	**Sono in pensione.** *soh·noh een pehn·syoh·neh*

Romance

Would you like to go out for a drink/dinner?	**Le va di andare a bere qualcosa/cena?** *leh vah dee ahn·dah·reh ah beh·reh kwahl·koh·zah/cheh·nah*
What are your plans for tonight/tomorrow?	**Che programmi ha per stasera/domani?** *keh proh·grahm·mee ah pehr stah·seh·rah/doh·mah·nee*
Can I have your number?	**Mi dà il suo numero?** *mee dah eel soo·oh noo·meh·roh*

Can I join you?	**Mi posso sedere con te?** *mee pohs•soh sed•ehr•eh con te*
Can I buy you a drink?	**Posso offrirle qualcosa?** *pohs•soh ohf•freer•leh kwahl•koh•zah*
I love you.	**Ti amo.** *tee ah•moh*

Accepting & Rejecting

I'd love to.	**Mi piacerebbe moltissimo.** *mee pyah•cheh•rehb•beh mohl•tees•see•moh*
Where should we meet?	**Dove ci vediamo?** *doh•veh chee veh•dyah•moh*
I'll meet you at the bar/your hotel.	**Vediamoci al bar/nel suo hotel.** *veh•dyah•moh•chee ahl bahr/nehl soo•oh oh•tehl*
I'll come by at…	**Passo alle…** *pahs•soh ahl•leh…*
What is your address?	**Mi dà il suo indirizzo?** *mee dah eel soo•oh een•dee•ree•tsoh*
I'm busy.	**Ho da fare.** *oh dah fah•reh*
I'm not interested.	**Non m'interessa.** *nohn meen•teh•rehs•sah*
Leave me alone.	**Mi lasci in pace.** *mee lah•shee een pah•cheh*
Stop bothering me!	**Smetta d'infastidirmi!** *smeht•tah deen•fah•stee•deer•mee*

Food & Drink

Eating Out

Can you recommend a good restaurant/bar?	**Può consigliarmi un buon ristorante/bar?** *pwoh kohn•see•llyahr•mee oon bwohn ree•stoh•rahn•teh/bahr*
Is there a traditional/an inexpensive restaurant nearby?	**C'è un ristorante tipico/economico qui vicino?** *cheh oon ree•stoh•rahn•teh tee•pee•koh/ eh•koh•noh•mee•koh kwee vee•chee•noh*
A table for…, please.	**Un tavolo per…, per favore.** *oon tah•voh•loh pehr… pehr fah•voh•reh*

Can we sit...?	**Possiamo sederci...?**
	pohs-syah-moh seh-dehr-chee...
here/there	**qui/là** *kwee/lah*
outside	**fuori** *fwoh-ree*
in a (non-)	**in una sala per (non) fumatori**
smoking area	*een oo-nah sah-lah pehr (nohn) foo-mah-toh-ree*
I'm waiting for	**Sto aspettando qualcuno.** *stoh ah-speht-tahn-doh*
someone.	*kwahl-koo-noh*
Where are the toilets?	**Dov'è la toilette?** *doh-veh lah twah-leht*
The menu, please.	**Il menù, per favore.** *eel meh-noo pehr fah-voh-reh*
What do you	**Cosa mi consiglia?** *koh-zah mee*
recommend?	*kohn-see-llyah*
I'd like...	**Vorrei...** *vohr-ray...*
Some more ...,	**Un po' di più..., per favore**
please.	*oon poh dee pyoo, pehr fah-voh-reh*
Enjoy your meal!	**Buon appetito!** *bwohn ahp-peh-tee-toh*
The check [bill],	**Il conto, per favore.** *eel kohn-toh pehr*
please.	*fah-voh-reh*
Is service included?	**Il servizio è compreso?** *eel sehr-vee-tsyoh*
	eh kohm-preh-zoh
Can I pay by credit	**Posso pagare con carta di credito/avere**
card/have a receipt?	**una ricevuta?** *pohs-soh pah-gah-reh kohn kahr-tah*
	dee kreh-dee-toh/ah-veh-reh oo-nah ree-cheh-voo-tah

YOU MAY SEE...

COPERTO	cover charge
PREZZO FISSO	fixed-price
MENÙ (DEL GIORNO)	menu (of the day)
SERVIZIO (NON) COMPRESO	service (not) included
SPECIALITÀ DEL GIORNO	daily specials

Breakfast

la pancetta *lah pahn·cheht·tah*	bacon
il pane *eel pah·neh*	bread
il pane tostato *eel pah·neh toh·stah·toh*	toast
il formaggio *eel fohr·mah·djoh*	cheese
la frittata *lah freet·tah·tah*	omelet
l'uovo... *lwoh·voh...*	...egg
fritto *freet·toh*	fried
sodo/alla coque *soh·doh/ahl·lah kohk*	hard-/soft-boiled
strapazzato *strah·pah·tsah·toh*	scrambled
lo yogurt *loh yoh·goort*	yogurt
il burro *eel boor·roh*	butter
la marmellata *lah mahr·mehl·lah·tah*	jam
la salsiccia *lah sahl·see·chyah*	sausage
gli affettati *llyee ahf·feht·tah·tee*	cold cuts [charcuterie]

Appetizers

la buridda *lah boo·reed·dah*	fish stew
la zuppa di pollo *lah dzoop·pah dee pohl·loh*	chicken soup
la zuppa di pomodoro *lah dzoop·pah dee poh·moh·doh·roh*	tomato soup
la zuppa di verdure *lah dzoop·pah dee vehr·doo·reh*	vegetable soup
l'insalata *leen·sah·lah·tah*	salad

Meat

il maiale *eel mah·yah·leh*	pork
il manzo *eel mahn·dzoh*	beef
il pollo *eel pohl·loh*	chicken
il vitello *eel vee·tehl·loh*	veal
l'agnello *lah·nyehl·loh*	lamb
la bistecca *lah bee·stehk·kah*	steak

YOU MAY HEAR...

al sangue *ahl sahn•gweh*	rare
mediamente cotta	medium
meh•dyah•mehn•teh koht•tah	
ben cotta *behn koht•tah*	well-done

Fish & Seafood

il merluzzo *eel mehr•loo•tsoh*	cod
il branzino *eel brahn•dzee•noh*	sea bass
l'aringa *lah•reen•gah*	herring
il salmone *eel sahl•moh•neh*	salmon
l'aragosta *lah•rah•goh•stah*	lobster
i gamberi *ee gahm•beh•ree*	shrimp

Vegetables

la carota *lah kah•roh•tah*	carrot
il cavolo *eel kah•voh•loh*	cabbage
la cipolla *lah chee•pohl•lah*	onion
i fagioli *ee fah•jyoh•lee*	beans
la patata *lah pah•tah•tah*	potato
i piselli *ee pee•tsehl•lee*	peas
il pomodoro *eel poh•moh•doh•roh*	tomato

Sauces & Condiments

salt	**sale** *sah•leh*
pepper	**pepe** *peh•peh*
mustard	**senape** *seh•nah•peh*
ketchup	**ketchup** *keh•chyahp*

Fruit & Dessert

l'arancia *lah-rahn-chah*	orange
la banana *lah bah-nah-nah*	banana
la fragola *lah frah-goh-lah*	strawberry
il limone *eel lee-moh-neh*	lemon
la mela *lah meh-lah*	apple
la pera *lah peh-rah*	pear
il gelato *eel jeh-lah-toh*	ice cream
la torta *lah tohr-tah*	cake
il cioccolato *eel chyohk-koh-lah-toh*	chocolate
la vaniglia *lah vah-nee-llyah*	vanilla
la crema *lah kreh-mah*	custard
gli amaretti *llyee ah-mah-reht-tee*	almond cookies

Drinks

Can I have the wine/ drink menu, please?	**La carta dei vini/lista delle bevande, per favore.** *lah kahr-tah day vee-nee/lee-stah dehl-leh beh-vahn-deh pehr fah-voh-reh*
What do you recommend?	**Cosa mi consiglia?** *koh-zah mee kohn-see-llyah*
I'd like a bottle/ glass of red/ white wine.	**Vorrei una bottiglia/un bicchiere di vino rosso/bianco.** *vohr-ray oo-nah boht-tee-llyah/ oon beek-kyeh-reh dee vee-noh rohs-soh/byahn-koh*
The house wine, please.	**Il vino della casa, per favore.** *eel vee-noh dehl-lah kah-zah pehr fah-voh-reh*
Another bottle/ glass, please.	**Un'altra bottiglia/Un altro bicchiere, per favore.** *oo-nahl-trah boht-tee-llyah/oo-nahl-troh beek-kyeh-reh pehr fah-voh-reh*
I'd like a local beer.	**Vorrei una birra locale.** *vohr-ray oo-nah beer-rah loh-kah-leh*
Cheers!	**Salute!** *sah-loo-teh*

Can I buy you a drink?	**Posso offrirle qualcosa?** _pohs_•soh ohf•_freer_•leh kwahl•_koh_•sah
A coffee/tea, please.	**Un caffè/tè, per favore.** oon kahf•_feh_/teh pehr fah•_voh_•reh
Black.	**Nero.** _neh_•roh
With...	**Con...** kohn...
some milk	**un po' di latte** _oon_ poh dee _laht_•teh
sugar	**lo zucchero** loh _dzook_•keh•roh
artificial sweetener	**il dolcificante** eel dohl•chee•fee•_kahn_•teh
..., please.	**..., per favore.** ...pehr fah•_voh_•reh
A juice	**Un succo.** oon _sook_•koh
A soda	**Una bibita.** _oo_•nah _bee_•bee•tah
A (sparkling/still) water.	**Un bicchiere d'acqua (frizzante/naturale).** oon beek•_kyeh_•reh _dah_•kwah (free•_dzahn_•teh/ nah•too•_rah_•leh)

Leisure Time

Sightseeing

| Where's the tourist information office? | **Dov'è l'ufficio informazioni turistiche?** doh•_veh_ loof•_fee_•chyoh een•fohr•mah•_tsyoh_•nee too•_ree_•stee•keh |
| What are the main sights? | **Cosa c'è da vedere?** _koh_•zah ceh dah veh•_deh_•reh |

> **YOU MAY SEE...**
> **APERTO/CHIUSO**   open/closed
> **ENTRATA/USCITA**   entrance/exit

| Do you offer tours in English? | **Ci sono visite guidate in inglese?** *chee soh·noh vee·zee·teh gwee·dah·teh een een·gleh·zeh* |
| Can I have a map/guide? | **Mi può dare una cartina/guida?** *mee pwoh dah·reh oo·nah kahr·tee·nah/gwee·dah* |

Shopping

Where's the market/ mall [shopping centre]?	**Dov'è il mercato/centro commerciale?** *doh·veh eel mehr·kah·toh/chehn·troh kohm·mehr·chyah·leh*
I'm just looking.	**Sto solo guardando.** *stoh soh·loh gwahr·dahn·doh*
Can you help me?	**Può aiutarmi?** *pwoh ah·yoo·tahr·mee*
I'm being helped.	**Mi stanno servendo.** *mee stahn·noh sehr·vehn·doh*
How much?	**Quant'è?** *kwahn·teh*
That one, please.	**Quello, per favore.** *kwehl·loh pehr fah·voh·reh*
That's all.	**Basta così.** *bah·stah koh·zee*
Where can I pay?	**Dove posso pagare?** *doh·veh pohs·soh pah·gah·reh*
I'll pay in cash/ by credit card.	**Pago in contanti/con carta di credito.** *pah·goh een kohn·tahn·tee/kohn kahr·tah dee kreh·dee·toh*
A receipt, please.	**Una ricevuta, per favore.** *oo·nah ree·cheh·voo·tah pehr fah·voh·reh*

Sport & Leisure

When's the game?	**A che ora c'è la partita?** *ah keh oh·rah cheh lah pahr·tee·tah*
Where's...?	**Dov'è...?** *doh·veh...*
the beach	**la spiaggia** *lah spyah·djah*
the park	**il parco** *eel pahr·koh*
the pool	**la piscina** *lah pee·shee·nah*
Is it safe to swim here?	**Si può nuotare?** *see pwoh nwoh·tah·reh*
Can I hire golf clubs?	**Posso noleggiare delle mazze?** *pohs·soh noh·leh·djah·reh dehl·leh mah·tseh*

How much per hour?	**Qual è la tariffa per un'ora?** _kwah·leh lah_ _tah·reef·fah pehr oo·noh·rah_
How far is it to…?	**Quanto dista a…?** _kwahn·toh dee·stah ah…_
Can you show me on the map?	**Può indicarmelo sulla cartina?** _pwoh een·dee·kahr·meh·loh sool·lah kahr·tee·nah_

Going Out

What's there to do at night?	**Cosa si fa di sera?** _koh·zah see fah dee seh·rah_
Do you have a program of events?	**Mi può dare un calendario degli eventi?** _mee pwoh dah·reh oon kah·lehn·dah·ryoh deh·llyee eh·vehn·tee_
What's playing tonight?	**Cosa c'è in programma stasera?** _koh·zah cheh een proh·grahm·mah stah·seh·rah_
Where's…?	**Dov'è…?** _doh·veh…_
the downtown area	**il centro** _eel chehn·troh_
the bar	**il bar** _eel bahr_
the dance club	**la discoteca** _lah dee·skoh·teh·kah_
Is this area safe at night?	**Questa zona è sicura di notte?** _Kweh·stah·dzoh·nah eh see·koo·rah dee noht·teh?_

Baby Essentials

Do you have…?	**Avete…?** _ah·veh·teh…_
a baby bottle	**un biberon** _oon bee·beh·rohn_
baby food	**del cibo per neonati** _dehl chee·boh pehr neh·oh·nah·tee_
baby wipes	**delle salviette per neonati** _dehl·leh sahl·vyeht·teh pehr neh·oh·nah·tee_
a car seat	**un seggiolino per auto** _oon seh·djoh·lee·noh pehr ow·toh_
a children's menu/portion	**il menù/le porzioni per bambini** _eel meh·noo/leh pohr·tsyoh·nee pehr bahm·bee·nee_

a child's seat/ highchair	**un seggiolino/seggiolone per bambini** *oon seh·djoh·lee·noh/seh·djoh·loh·neh pehr bahm·bee·nee*
a crib/cot	**una culla/un lettino** *oo·nah kool·lah/ oon leht·tee·noh*
diapers [nappies]	**dei pannolini** *day pahn·noh·lee·nee*
formula [baby food]	**del latte in polvere** *dehl laht·teh een pohl·veh·reh*
a pacifier [dummy]	**un ciucciotto** *oon chyoo·chyoht·toh*
a playpen	**un box** *oon bohks*
a stroller[pushchair]	**un passeggino** *oon pah·seh·djee·noh*
Can I breastfeed the baby here?	**Posso allattare il bambino?** *poh·soh ahl·laht·tah·reh eel bahm·bee·noh*
Where can I breastfeed/change the baby?	**Dove posso allattare/cambiare il bambino?** *doh·veh poh·soh ahl·laht·tah·reh/ kahm·byah·reh eel bahm·bee·noh*

Disabled Travelers

Is there...?	**C'è...?** *cheh...*
access for the disabled	**l'accesso ai disabili** *lah·cheh·soh ah·ee dee·zah·bee·lee*
a wheelchair ramp	**la rampa per le sedie a rotelle** *lah rahm·pah pehr leh seh·dyeh ah roh·tehl·leh*
a disabled-accessible toilet	**la toilette per i disabili** *lah twah·leht pehr ee dee·zah·bee·lee*
I need...	**Mi serve...** *mee sehr·veh...*
assistance	**assistenza** *ah·see·stehn·tsah*
an elevator [a lift]	**un ascensore** *oon ah·shehn·soh·reh*
a ground-floor room	**una stanza al pianterreno** *oo·nah stahn·tsah ahl pyahn·tehr·reh·noh*
Please speak louder	**Per favore, potrebbe parlare più forte?** *pehr fah·voh·reh, poh·treb·beh par·lahr·eh pyoo for·teh*

Health & Emergencies

Emergencies

Help!	**Aiuto!** *ah-yoo-toh*
Go away!	**Se ne vada!** *seh neh vah-dah*
Stop, thief!	**Fermi, al ladro!** *fehr-mee ahl lah-droh*
Get a doctor!	**Un medico!** *oon meh-dee-koh*
Fire!	**Al fuoco!** *ahl fwoh-koh*
I'm lost.	**Mi sono perso m/persa f.** *mee soh-noh pehr-soh/pehr-sah*
Can you help me?	**Può aiutarmi?** *pwoh ah-yoo-tahr-mee*
Call the police!	**Chiami la polizia!** *kyah-mee lah poh-lee-tsee-ah*
Where's the police station?	**Dov'è il commissariato?** *doh-veh eel kohm-mee-sah-ryah-toh*
My son/daughter is missing.	**Il mio bambino m/La mia bambina f è scomparso m/scomparsa f.** *eel mee-oh bahm-bee-noh/lah mee-ah bahm-bee-nah eh skohm-pahr-soh/skohm-pahr-sah*

YOU MAY HEAR...

Riempia questo modulo. *ree-ehm-pyah kweh-stoh moh-doo-loh*

Fill out this form.

Un documento, per favore. *oon doh-koo-mehn-toh pehr fah-voh-reh*

Your identification, please.

Quando/Dove è successo? *kwahn-doh/doh-veh eh soo-cheh-soh*

When/Where did it happen?

Che aspetto aveva? *keh ah-speht-toh ah-veh-vah*

What does he/she look like?

In an emergency, dial: **112** for the police
115 for the fire brigade
118 for the ambulance.

Health

I'm sick [ill].	**Sto male.** stoh _mah_•leh
I need an English-speaking doctor.	**Ho bisogno di un medico che parli inglese.** oh bee•_soh_•nyoh dee oon _meh_•dee•koh keh _pahr_•lee een•_gleh_•zeh
It hurts here.	**Mi fa male qui.** mee fah _mah_•leh kwee
Where's the pharmacy?	**Dov'è una farmacia?** doh•_veh_ _oo_•nah fahr•mah•_chee_•ah
I'm pregnant.	**Sono incinta.** _soh_•noh een•_cheen_•tah
I'm on…	**Prendo…** _prehn_•doh…
I'm allergic to antibiotics/penicillin.	**Sono allergico m/allergica f agli antibiotici/alla penicillina.** _soh_•noh ahl•_lehr_•jee•koh/ahl•_lehr_•jee•kah _ah_•llyee ahn•tee•_byoh_•tee•chee/ahl•lah peh•nee•cheel•_lee_•nah

Dictionary

acetaminophen/il paracetamolo
paracetamol [BE]
adapter l'adattatore
American americano
and e
antiseptic cream la crema antisettica
aspirin l'aspirina

baby il bebè
backpack lo zaino
bag la borsa
  bandage la benda
battleground il campo di battaglia
beige beige
bikini il bikini; ~ **wax** la ceretta all'inguine

bird l'uccello
black nero
bland insipido
blue blu
bottle la bottiglia; ~ **opener** l'apribottiglie
bowl la coppa
boy il ragazzo; ~**friend** il ragazzo
bra il reggiseno
British britannico(a)
brown marrone
camera la macchina fotografica
can opener l'apriscatole
castle il castello
cigarette la sigaretta
cold (sickness) il raffreddore; ~ **(temperature)** freddo
comb il pettine
computer il computer
condom il preservativo
contact v contattare; ~ **lens** la lente a contatto; ~ **lens solution** la soluzione per lenti a contatto
corkscrew il cavatappi
cup la tazza
dangerous pericoloso
deodorant il deodorante
diabetic diabetico
doll la bambola
earlier prima
early presto
earrings gli orecchini
east est

easy facile
eat v mangiare
economy class la classe economica
elbow il gomito
electric outlet la presa elettrica
elevator l'ascensore
e-mail v inviare e-mail; ~ n l'e-mail; ~ **address** l'indirizzo e-mail
fork la forchetta
girl la ragazza; ~**friend** la ragazza
glass (drinking) il bicchiere; ~ **(material)** il vetro; ~**es** gli occhiali
good n il bene
gray grigio
green verde
hairbrush la spazzola ; ~**spray** la lacca;
hot (temperature) caldo; ~ **(spicy)** piccante
husband il marito
ibuprofen l'ibuprofene
ice il ghiaccio
icy gelato
insect repellent il repellente per gli insetti
Irish irlandese
jeans i jeans
kilo il chilo; ~**gram** il chilogrammo; ~**meter** il chilometro
kiss v baciare

kitchen la cucina; ~ **foil** la carta stagnola
knee il ginocchio
knife il coltello
lactose intolerant intollerante al lattosio
large grande
lighter l'accendino
lotion la lozione
love v (someone) amare; ~ n l'amore
match n (wooden stick) il fiammifero
medium (size) medio
museum il museo
nail file la lima
napkin il tovagliolo
nurse l'infermiere
or o
orange (color) arancione
park il parco
pen la penna
pink rosa
plate il piatto
purple viola
rain la pioggia; ~**coat** l'impermeabile
razor blade la lametta
red rosso
sandals i sandali
sauna la sauna
scissors le forbici
shampoo lo shampoo
shoes le scarpe

small piccolo
sneakers le scarpe da ginnastica
snow neve
soap il sapone
sock il calzino
spicy piccante
spoon il cucchiaio
stamp v (a ticket) convalidare; ~ n (postage) il francobollo
suitcase la valigia
sun il sole; ~**glasses** gli occhiali da sole; ~**screen** il filtro solare;
sweater il maglione
sweatshirt la felpa
swimsuit il costume da bagno
tampon il tampone
terrible terribile
tie (clothing) la cravatta
tissue il fazzoletto di carta
toilet paper la carta igienica
tooth il dente; ~**brush** spazzolino da denti; ~**paste** il dentifricio
tough (food) duro
toy il giocattolo
T-shirt la maglietta
underwear la biancheria intima
vegen vegeno
vegetarian vegetariano
white bianco; ~ **gold** l'oro bianco
wife la moglie
with con
without senza
yellow giallo; ~ **gold** l'oro giallo
zoo lo zoo

Portuguese

Essentials

Hello.	**Olá.**	_aw·lah_
Goodbye.	**Adeus.**	_uh·dehoosh_
Yes/No/O.K.	**Sim/Não/O.K.**	_seeng/nohm/aw·kay_
Excuse me! (attention)	**Desculpe!**	_deh·skoolp_
Excuse me. (to get past)	**Com licença.**	_kohng lee·sehn·suh_
Sorry!	**Perdão!**	_pehr·dohm_
I'd like something...	**Queria algo...**	_keh·ree·uh ahl·goo..._
How much/many?	**Quanto/Quantos?**	_kwuhn·too/kwuhn·toos_
And/or	**e/ou**	_ee/oo_
Where is the...?	**Onde está...?**	_aund ee·stah..._
My name is...	**Chamo-me... [Meu nome é...]**	_shuh·moo meh... [mehoo nau·mee eh...]_
I'm going to...	**Vou para...**	_vauoo puh·ruh..._
Please.	**Se faz favor [Por favor].**	_seh fahz fuh·vaur [poor fuh·vaur]_
Thank you.	**Obrigado m/Obrigada f.**	_aw·bree·gah·doo/ aw·bree·gah·duh_
You're welcome.	**De nada.**	_deh nah·duh_
Could you speak more slowly?	**Pode falar mais devagar?**	_pawd fuh·lahr meyez deh·vuh·gahr_
Could you repeat that?	**Importa-se de repetir?**	_eeng·pawr·tuh·seh deh reh·peh·teer_
I don't understand	**Não compreendo.**	_nohm kaum·pree·ehn·doo_
Do you speak English?	**Fala inglês?**	_fah·luh eng·lehz_
I don't speak (much) Portuguese.	**Não falo (bem) português.**	_nohm fah·loo (beng) poor·too·gehz_
Where are the restrooms [toilets]?	**Onde são as casas de banho [os banheiros]?**	_aund sohm uhz kah·zuhz deh buh·nyoo [ooz bah·nyay·rooz]_
Help!	**Ajuda!**	_uh·zsoo·duh_

143

You'll find the pronunciation of the Portuguese letters and words written in gray after each sentence to guide you. Simply pronounce these as if they were English, noting that any underlines and bolds indicate an additional emphasis or stress or a lengthening of a vowel sound. As you hear the language being spoken, you will quickly become accustomed to the local pronunciation and dialect.

Numbers

0	**zero** _zeh_·roo
1	**um** *m*/**uma** *f* oong/_oo_·muh
2	**dois** *m*/**duas** *f* doyz/_thoo_·uhz
3	**três** trehz
4	**quatro** _kwah_·troo
5	**cinco** _seeng_·koo
6	**seis** sayz
7	**sete** seht
8	**oito** _oy_·too
9	**nove** nawv
10	**dez** dehz
11	**onze** aunz
12	**doze** dauz
13	**treze** trehz
14	**catorze** kuh·_taurz_
15	**quinze** keengz
16	**dezasseis [dezesseis]** dehz·eh·_sayz_
17	**dezassete [dezessete]** dehz·eh·_seht_
18	**dezoito** dehz·_oy_·too
19	**dezanove [dezenove]** deh·zuh·_nawv_
20	**vinte** veent
21	**vinte e um** *m*/**uma** *f* veent ee oong/_oo_·muh

30	**trinta** _treeng_·tuh
40	**quarenta** kwuh·_rehn_·tuh
50	**cinquenta** seeng·_kwehn_·tuh
60	**sessenta** seh·_sehn_·tuh
70	**setenta** seh·_tehn_·tuh
80	**oitenta** oy·_tehn_·tuh
90	**noventa** noo·_vehn_·tuh
100	**cem** sehn
101	**cento e um** m/**uma** f _sehn_·too ee oong/_oo_·muh
200	**duzentos** m/**duzentas** f doo·_zehn_·tooz/doo·_zehn_·tuhz
500	**quinhentos** m/**quinhentas** f kee·_nyehn_·tooz/
	kee·_nyehn_·tuhz
1,000	**mil** meel
10,000	**dez mil** dehz meel
1,000,000	**um milhão** oong mee·_lyohm_

Time

What time is it?	**As horas, por favor?** uhz _aw_·ruhz poor fuh·_vaur_
It's noon [mid-day].	**É meio-dia.** eh _may_·oo _dee_·uh
Twenty past four	**Quatro e vinte.** _kwah_·troo ee veent
A quarter to nine.	**Um quarto para as nove.**
	oong _kwahr_·too _puh_·ruh uhz nawv
5:30 a.m./p.m.	**Cinco e meia de manhã/da tarde.**
	seeng·koo ee _may_·uh deh muh·_nyuh_/duh tahrd

Days

Monday	**segunda-feira** seh·_goon_·duh _fay_·ruh
Tuesday	**terça-feira** _tehr_·suh _fay_·ruh
Wednesday	**quarta-feira** _kwahr_·tuh _fay_·ruh
Thursday	**quinta-feira** _keen_·tuh _fay_·ruh
Friday	**sexta-feira** _say_·stuh _fay_·ruh
Saturday	**sábado** _sah_·buh·thoo
Sunday	**domingo** doo·_meeng_·goo

Dates

yesterday	**ontem**	_awn_-teng
today	**hoje**	_auzseh_
tomorrow	**amanhã**	uh-muh-_nuh_
day	**o dia**	oo _dee_-uh
week	**a semana**	uh seh-_muh_-nuh
month	**o mês**	oo mehz
year	**o ano**	oo _uh_-noo
Happy New Year!	**Feliz Ano Novo!**	_feh_-leez _uh_-noo noh-voh
Happy Birthday!	**Feliz Aniversário!**	_feh_-leez _uh_-nee-vehr-sahr-ee-oo

Months

January	**Janeiro**	zher-_nay_-roo
February	**Fevereiro**	feh-_vray_-roo
March	**Março**	_mahr_-soo
April	**Abril**	uh-_breel_
May	**Maio**	_meye_-oo
June	**Junho**	_zsoo_-nyoo
July	**Julho**	_zsoo_-lyoo
August	**Agosto**	uh-_gaus_-too
September	**Setembro**	seh-_tehm_-broo
October	**Outubro**	aw-_too_-broo
November	**Novembro**	noo-_vehm_-broo
December	**Dezembro**	deh-_zehm_-broo

Arrival & Departure

I'm on vacation [holiday]/business.	**Estou de férias/em negócios.** ee-_stawoo_ deh _feh_-ree-uhz/eng neh-_gaw_-see-yooz
I'm going to…	**Vou para…** vawoo _puh_-ruh…
I'm staying at the… Hotel.	**Permaneço no hotel…** pehr-muh-_neh_-soo noo aw-_tehl_…

Money

Where's...?	**Onde é...?** *aund eh...*
the ATM	**o multibanco [a caixa automática]** *oo mool·tee·buhn·koo [uh keye·shuh aw·too·mah·tee·kuh]*
the bank	**o banco** *oo buhn·koo*
the currency exchange office	**o câmbio** *oo kuhm·bee·oo*
What time does the bank open/close?	**A que horas é que o banco abre/fecha?** *uh keh aw·ruhz eh keh oo buhn·koo ah·breh/feh·shuh*
I'd like to change dollars/pounds into euros/reais.	**Queria trocar dólares/libras em euros/reais.** *keh·ree·uh troo·kahr daw·luhrz/lee·bruhz eng ehoo·rooz/rree·eyez*
I want to cash some traveler's checks [cheques].	**Quero cobrar [trocar] cheques de viagem.** *keh·roo koo·brahr [troo·kahr] sheh·kehz deh vee·ah·zseng*
I'll pay...	**Pago...** *pah·goo...*
in cash	**com dinheiro** *kaum dee·nyay·roo*
by credit card	**com o cartão de crédito** *kaum oo kuhr·tohm deh kreh·dee·too*

For Numbers, see page 144.

YOU MAY SEE...

The currency in Portugal is the **euro (€)**, divided into 100 **cêntimos** (cents).
Coins: 1, 2, 5, 10, 20, 50 **cêntimos**; €1,2
Notes: €5, 10, 20, 50, 100, 200, 500

Getting Around

How do I get to the city center?	**Como é que vou para o centro da cidade?** _kau•moo eh keh vawoo puh•ruh oo sehn•troo duh see•dahd_
Where's...?	**Onde é...?** _aund eh..._
the airport	**o aeroporto** _oo uh•eh•rau•paur•too_
the train station [the railway station]	**a estação de caminho de ferro [a estação ferroviária]** _uh ee•stuh•sohm deh kuh•mee•nyoo deh feh•rroo [uh ee•stuh•sohm feh•rroo•vee•ah•ree•uh]_
the bus station	**a estação de camionetas [ônibus]** _uh ee•stuh•sohm deh kah•meeoo•neh•tuhz [aw•nee•boos]_
the metro [underground] station	**a estação de metro** _uh ee•stuh•sohm deh meh•troo_
How far is it?	**A que distância fica?** _uh keh dee•stuhn•see•uh fee•kuh_
Where can I buy tickets?	**Onde posso comprar bilhetes?** _aund paw•soo kaum•prahr bee•lyehtz_
A one-way/return-trip ticket to...	**Um bilhete de ida/de ida e volta para...** _oong bee•lyeht deh ee•thuh/deh ee•thuh ee vaul•tuh puh•ruh..._
How much?	**Quanto custa?** _kwuhn•too koo•stuh_
Which...?	**Qual...?** _kwahl..._
gate	**porta** _port•uh_
line	**linha** _lee•nyuh_
platform	**plataforma** _plah•tuh•fawr•muh_
Where can I get a taxi?	**Onde posso apanhar [pegar] um táxi?** _aund paw•soo uh•puh•nyar [peh•gahr] oong tahk•see_
Please take me to this address.	**Leve-me a esta morada [neste endereço].** _leh•veh•meh uh eh•stuh maw•rah•duh [nehst ehn•deh•reh•soo]_

To...Airport, please.	**Ao aeroporto de..., por favor.**
	ahoo uh·eh·rau·paur·too deh...poor fuh·vaur
I'm in a hurry.	**Estou com pressa.** *ee·stawoo kaum preh·suh*
Could I have a map?	**Pode dar-me um mapa?** *pawd dahr·meh*
	oong mah·puh

Tickets

When's...to...?	**A que horas é...para...?**
	uh kee aw·ruhz eh...puh·ruh...
the (first) bus	**a (primeira) camioneta [o (primeiro) ônibus]**
	uh (pree·may·ruh) kah·meeoo·neh·tuh
	[oo (pree·may·roo) aw·nee·boos]
the (next) flight	**o (próximo) vôo** *oo (praw·see·moo) vau·oo*
the (last) train	**o (último) comboio [trem]**
	oo (ool·tee·moo) kaum·baw·eeoo [treng]
Where can I buy tickets?	**Onde posso comprar bilhetes?**
	aund paw·soo kaum·prahr bee·lyehtz
One/Two ticket(s), please.	**Um bilhete/Dois bilhetes, se faz favor.**
	oong bee·lyeht/doyz bee·lyehtz seh fahz fuh·vaur
For today/tomorrow.	**Para hoje/amanhã.** *puh·ruh auzseh/uh·muh·nyuh*
A(n)...ticket.	**Um bilhete...** *oong bee·lyeht...*
one-way	**de ida** *deh ee·thuh*
return-trip	**de ida e volta** *deh ee·thuh ee vaul·tuh*
first-class	**em primeira classe** *eng pree·may·ruh klah·she*
I have an e-ticket.	**Eu tenho um bilhete electrónico.**
	ehoo teh·nyoo oong bee·lyeht ee·lek·tro·nee·kuh
How long is the trip?	**Quanto tempo demora a viagem?**
	kwuhn·too tehm·poo deh·maw·ruh uh vee·ah·zseng
Is it a direct train?	**É um comboio directo?** *eh oong kaum·baw·eeoo*
	dee·reh·too
Could you tell me when to get off?	**Pode-me dizer quando eu devo sair?**
	paw·deh meh dee·zehr kwuhn·doo deh·voo suh·eer

Is this the bus to...?	**Este ônibus vai para ...?** *ehst aw·nee·boos vay parah ...*
I'd like to...my reservation.	**Queria...a minha reserva.** *keh·ree·uh...uh mee·nyuh reh·zehr·vuh*
cancel	**cancelar** *kuhn·seh·lahr*
change	**mudar** *moo·dahr*
confirm	**confirmar** *kaum·feer·mahr*

For Time, see page 145.

Car Hire

Where can I rent a car?	**Onde posso alugar um carro?** *aund paw·soo uh·loo·gahr oong kah·rroo*
I'd like to rent...	**Queria alugar...** *keh·ree·uh uh·loo·gahr...*
a cheap/small car	**um carro barato/pequeno** *oong kah·rroo buh·rah·too/peh·keh·noo*

YOU MAY HEAR...

sempre em frente *sehm·preh eng frehn·teh*	straight ahead
à esquerda *ah ee·skehr·duh*	on the left
à direita *ah dee·ray·tuh*	on the right
depois de/ao dobrar da esquina *deh·poyz deh/ahoo doo·brahr duh ees·kee·nuh*	on/around the corner
em frente de *eng frehn·teh deh*	opposite
por trás de *poor trahz deh*	behind
a seguir ao *m***/à** *f* *uh seh·geer ahoo/ah*	next to
depois do *m***/da** *f* *deh·poyz thoo/duh*	after
norte/sul *nawrt/sool*	north/south
leste/oeste *lehs·the/aw·ehs·teh*	east/west
no semáforo *noo seh·mah·fau·roo*	at the traffic light
no cruzamento *noo croo·zuh·mehn·too*	at the intersection

a 2-/4-door car	**um carro de duas/quatro portas** *oong kah·rroo deh thoo·uhz/kwah·troo pawr·tuhz*
a(n) automatic/ manual	**um carro automático/de mudanças** *oong kah·rroo awoo·too·mah·tee·koo/deh moo·thuhn·suhz*
a car with air conditioning	**um carro com ar condicionado** *oong kah·rroo kaum ahr kawn·dee·seeoo·nah·thoo*
a car seat	**um assento de carro de bebé** *oong uh·sehn·too deh kah·rroo deh beh·beh*
How much...	**Quanto é...?** *kwuhn·too eh...*
per day/week	**por dia/semana** *poor dee·uh/seh·muh·nuh*
Are there any discounts?	**Há descontos?** *ah dehs·kaum·tooz*

Places to Stay

Can you recommend a hotel?	**Pode recomendar-me um hotel?** *pawd reh·kaw·mehn·dahr·meh oong aw·tehl*
I have a reservation.	**Tenho uma reserva.** *teh·nyoo oo·muh reh·zehr·vuh*
My name is...	**Chamo-me... [Meu nome é...]** *shuh·moo·meh... [mehoo naum·eh eh...]*
Do you have a room...?	**Tem um quarto...?** *teng oong kwahr·too...*
for one/two	**para um/dois** *puh·ruh oong/doyz*
with a bathroom	**com quarto de banho [banheiro]** *kaum kwahr·too deh buh·nyoo buh·nyay·roo*
with air conditioning	**com ar condicionado** *kaum ar kawn·dee·seeoo·nah·thoo*
For...	**Para...** *puh·ruh...*
tonight	**hoje à noite** *auzseh ah noyt*
two nights	**duas noites** *thoo·uhz noytz*
one week	**uma semana** *oo·muh seh·muh·nuh*
How much is it?	**Quanto custa?** *kwuhn·too koo·stuh*
Do you have anything cheaper?	**Há mais barato?** *ah meyez buh·rah·too*

What time is check-out?	**A que horas temos de deixar o quarto?** *uh kee <u>aw</u>•ruhz teh•mooz deh thay•<u>shahr</u> oo kwahr•too*
Can I leave this in the safe?	**Posso deixar isto no cofre?** *paw•soo thay•<u>shahr</u> ee•stoo noo <u>kaw</u>•freh*
Can I leave my bags?	**Posso deixar a minha bagagem?** *paw•soo day•<u>shahr</u> uh <u>mee</u>•nyuh buh•<u>gah</u>•geng*
Can I have the bill/ a receipt?	**Pode dar-me a conta/uma factura [um recibo]?** *pawd <u>dahr</u>•meh uh <u>kaum</u>•tuh/<u>oo</u>•muh fah•<u>too</u>•ruh [oong reh•<u>see</u>•boo]*
I'll pay in cash/by credit card.	**Pago com dinheiro/com o cartão de crédito.** *<u>pah</u>•goo kaum dee•<u>nyay</u>•roo/kaum oo kuhr•<u>tohm</u> deh <u>kreh</u>•dee•too*

Communications

Where's an internet café?	**Onde fica um internet café?** *aund <u>fee</u>•kuh oong een•tehr•<u>neht</u> kuh•<u>feh</u>*
Can I access the Internet here?	**Tenho acesso à internet aqui?** *<u>teh</u>•nyoo uh•<u>seh</u>•soo ah een•tehr•<u>neht</u> uh•<u>kee</u>*
Can I check e-mail here?	**Posso ler o meu e-mail aqui?** *<u>paw</u>•soo lehr oo mehoo ee•<u>mehl</u> uh•<u>khee</u>*
How much per (half) hour?	**Quanto é por (meia) hora?** *kwuhn•too eh poor (<u>may</u>•uh) <u>aw</u>•ruh*
How do I connect/ log on?	**Como conecto/faço o logon?** *<u>kau</u>•moo koo•<u>nehk</u>•too/<u>fah</u>•soo oo <u>law</u>•gawn*
A phone card, please.	**Um credifone [cartão telefónico], se faz favor.** *oong kreh•dee•<u>faun</u> [kuhr•<u>tohm</u> tehl•eh•<u>fawn</u>•ee•koo] seh fahz fuh•<u>vaur</u>*
Can I have your phone number?	**Pode dar-me o seu número de telefone?** *pawd <u>dahr</u>•meh oo sehoo <u>noo</u>•meh•roo deh tehl•<u>fawn</u>*
Here's my number/ e-mail address.	**Este é o meu número/e-mail.** *ehst eh oo mehoo <u>noo</u>•meh•roo/ee•<u>mehl</u>*

Call me/Text me.	**Telefone-me/Manda-me uma mensagem de texto.** *tehl·fawn·eh·meh/muhn·duh·meh oo·muh mehn·sah·zseng deh tehk·stoo*
E-mail me.	**Envie-me um e-mail.** *ehn·vee·eh meh oong ee·mehl*
Hello. This is...	**Estou [Alô]. Fala...** *ee·stawoo [aw·lah]. fah·luh...*
I'd like to speak to...	**Queria falar com...** *keh·ree·uh fuh·lahr kaum...*
Could you repeat that, please?	**Importa-se de repetir, por favor?** *eem·pawr·tuh·seh deh reh·peh·teer poor fuh·vaur*
I'll call back later.	**Chamo mais tarde.** *shuh·moo meyez tahr·deh*
Bye.	**Adeus.** *uh·deeoosh*
Where's the post office?	**Onde são os correios?** *aund sohm ooz koo·rray·ooz*
I'd like to send this to...	**Gostaria de mandar isto para...** *goo·stuh·ree·uh deh muhn·dahr ee·stoo puh·ruh...*
Can I...?	**Posso...?** *paw·soo...*
access the internet	**aceder a internet** *uh·seh·dehr uh een·tehr·neht*
check e-mail	**ler o meu e-mail** *lehr oo mehoo ee·mehl*
print	**imprimir [impressar]** *eeng·pree·meer [eeng·preh·sahr]*
plug in/charge my laptop/iPhone/iPad/BlackBerry	**ligar/carregar o meu laptop/iPhone/iPad/Blackberry** *lee·gahr/kahr·reh·gahr oo mehoo laptop/iPhone/iPad/Blackberry*
What is the WiFi password?	**Qual é a senha do WiFi?** *kwahl eh uh seh·nyuh doo WiFi*
Is the WiFi free?	**O WiFi é grátis?** *oo WiFi eh grah teez*
Do you have bluetooth?	**Tem bluetooth?** *teng bluetooth*
Do you have a scanner?	**Tem um scanner?** *teng oong scanner*

Social Media

Are you on Facebook/Twitter?	**Está no Facebook/Twitter?** *ee·stah noo facebook/twitter*
What's your user name?	**Qual é o seu nome de utilizador?** *kwahl eh oo sehoo naum·eh deh oo·tee·lee·zuh·daur*
I'll add you as a friend.	**Vou adicioná-lo como amigo.** *vawoo·oo uh·dee·seeoo·nah·loo kau·moo uh·mee·goo*
I'll follow you on Twitter.	**Vou segui-lo no Twitter.** *vawoo·oo seh·gee·loo noo Twitter*
Are you following...?	**Está a seguir...?** *ee·stah uh seh·geer...*
I'll put the pictures on Facebook/Twitter.	**Vou colocar as fotos no Facebook/Twitter.** *vawoo koo·loo·khahr uhz faw·tawz noo Facebook/Twitter*
I'll tag you in the pictures.	**Vou identificá-lo nas fotos.** *vawoo ee·dehnt·tee·fee·kah·loo nuhz faw·tawz.*

Conversation

Hello.	**Olá.** *aw·lah*
How are you?	**Como está?** *kau·moo ee·stah*
Fine, thanks.	**Bem, obrigado m/obrigada f.** *behm aw·bree·gah·doo/aw·bree·gah·duh*
Excuse me! (to get attention)	**Desculpe!** *dehz·kool·peh*
Do you speak English?	**Fala inglês?** *fah·luh eeng·lehz*
What's your name?	**Como se chama?** *kau·moo seh shuh·muh*
My name is...	**Chamo-me... [Meu nome é...]** *shuh·moo meh... [mehoo naum·ee eh...]*
Nice to meet you.	**Muito prazer.** *mooee·too pruh·zehr*
Where are you from?	**De onde é?** *deh aund eh*
I'm from the U.S./U.K.	**Sou dos Estados Unidos/da Inglaterra.** *soh dooz ee·stah·dooz oo·nee·dooz/duh eeng·luh·teh·rruh*
What do you do?	**O que é que faz?** *oo kee eh keh fahz*

I work for...	**Trabalho para...** *truh•bah•lyoo puh•ruh...*
I'm a student.	**Sou estudante.** *sauoo ee•stoo•duhnt*
I'm retired.	**Sou reformado** *m*/**reformada** *f* **[aposentado** *m*/**aposentada** *f*]. *soh reh•foor•mah•thoo/ reh•foor•mah•thuh [uh•poo•zehn•tah•doo/ uh•poo•zehn•tah•duh]*

Romance

Would you like to go out for a drink/dinner?	**Queres ir tomar uma bebida/comer fóra?** *keh•rehz eer too•mahr oo•muh beh•bee•thuh/ koo•mehr faw•ruh*
What are your plans for tonight/tomorrow?	**Quais são os seus planos para hoje à noite/ amanhã?** *kweyez sohm ooz sehooz pluh•nooz puh•ruh auzseh ah noyt/uh•muh•nyuh*
Can I have your number?	**Podes dar-me o teu número de telefone?** *pawd•ehz dahr•meh oo tehoo noo•meh•roo deh tehl•fawn*
Can I join you?	**Posso acompanhar-te?** *paw•soo uh•kaum•puh•nyahr•teh*
Can I buy you a drink?	**O que quer beber?** *oo keh kehr beh•behr*
I love you.	**Amo-te [Te amo].** *uh•moo teh [teh uh•moo]*

Accepting & Rejecting

I'd love to.	**Adorava [adoraria] ir.** *uh•daw•rah•vuh [uh•doo•ruh•ree•uh] eer*
Where should we meet?	**Onde nos vamos encontrar?** *aund nooz vuh•mooz ehng•kaun•trahr*
I'll meet you at the bar/your hotel.	**Vou ter contigo [te encontrar] ao bar/hotel.** *vauoo tehr kaun•tee•goo [tee ehn•kaun•trahr] ahoo bahr/aw•tehl*
I'll come by at...	**Eu passo por lá às...** *ehoo pah•soo poor lah ahz...*

What's your address?	**Qual é a sua morada [endereço]?** *kwahl eh uh*
	soo·uh maw·rah·duh [ehn·deh·reh·soo]
I'm busy.	**Mas tenho imenso [muito] que fazer.** *muhz*
	teh·nyoo ee·mehn·soo [mooee·too] keh fuh·zehr
I'm not interested.	**Não estou interessado m/interessada f.** *nohm*
	ee·stawoo een·treh·sah·thoo/een·treh·sah·thuh
Leave me alone.	**Deixe-me em paz.** *day·sheh· meh eng pahz*
Stop bothering me!	**Está quieto!** *ee·stah kee·eh·too*

Food & Drink

Eating Out

Can you recommend a good restaurant/bar?	**Pode recomendar-me um bom restaurante/bar?** *pawd reh·kaw·mehn·dahr·meh oong bohng reh·stahoo·ruhnt/bar*
Is there a(n) traditional Portuguese/ inexpensive restaurant near here?	**Há um restaurante tradicional português/ barato perto daqui?** *ah oong reh·stuhoo·ruhnt truh·dee·see·oo·nahl por·too·gehz/buh·rah·too pehr·too duh·kee*
A table for…, please.	**Uma mesa para…, se faz favor.** *oo·muh meh·zuh puh·ruh… seh fahz fuh·vaur*
Could we sit…?	**Podemos sentar-nos…?** *poo·deh·mooz sehn·tahr·nooz…*
here/there	**aqui/ali** *uh·kee/uh·lee*
outside	**lá fora** *lah faw·ruh*
in a non-smoking area	**na área para não-fumadores [não-fumantes]** *nuh ah·ree·uh puh·ruh nohmfoo·muh·daur·ehs [nohmfoo·muhnts]*

YOU MAY SEE...

COUVERT	cover charge
PREÇO-FIXO	fixed-price
EMENTA	menu
UMA EMENTA DO DIA	menu of the day
SERVIÇO (NÃO) INCLUÍDO	service (not) included
ESPECIAIS	specials

I'm waiting for someone.	**Estou à espera de alguém.** ee·*stawoo* ah ee·*speh*·ruh deh ahl·*gehm*
Where's the restroom [toilet]?	**Onde são as casas de banho [os banheiros]?** aund sohmuhz *kah*·zuhz deh *buh*·nyoo [ooz buh·*nyay*·rooz]
A menu, please.	**Uma ementa, por favor.** *oo*·muh ee·*mehn*·tuh poor fuh·*vaur*
What do you recommend?	**O que é que me recomenda?** oo keh eh keh meh reh·koo·*mehn*·duh
I'd like...	**Queria...** keh·*ree*·uh...
Some more..., please.	**Mais..., se faz favor.** meyez... seh fahz fuh·*vaur*
Enjoy your meal.	**Bom apetite.** bohng uh·peh·*tee*·teh
The check [bill], please.	**A conta, por favor.** uh *kaum*·tuh poor fuh·*vaur*
Is service included?	**O serviço está incluído?** oo sehr·*vee*·soo ee·*stah* een·kloo·*ee*·thoo
Can I pay by credit card?	**Posso pagar com cartão de crédito?** *paw*·soo puh·*gahr* kaumkuhr·*tohm* deh *kreh*·dee·too
Could I have a receipt, please?	**Pode darme uma factura [um recibo], por favor?** pawd *dahr*·meh *oo*·muh fah·*too*·ruh [oong reh·*see*·boo] poor fuh·*vaur*

Breakfast

as carnes frias *uhz kahr·nehz free·uhz*	cold cuts
o doce de fruta [geleia] *oo dau·seh deh froo·tuh [zseh·lay·uh]*	jam
a manteiga *uh muhn·tay·guh*	butter
a omelete *uh aw·meh·leh·tuh*	omelet
o ovo... *oo au·voo...*	...egg
muito fervido/fervido macio *mooee·too fehr·vee·thoo/fehr·vee·thoo muh·see·oo*	hard-boiled/ soft-boiled
estrelado [frito] *ee·struh·lah·doo [free·too]*	fried
mexido *meh·shee·doo*	scrambled
o pão *oo pohm*	bread
o queijo *oo kay·zsoo*	cheese
as salsichas *uhz sahl·see·shuhz*	sausages
as torradas *uhz too·rrah·duhz*	toast
o toucinho *oo tau·see·nyoo*	bacon
o yogurte *oo yaw·goort*	yogurt

Appetizers

a sopa à pescador *uh sau·puh ah pehs·kuh·daur*	fish soup
a sopa transmontana *a sau·puh truhnz·moo·tuh·nuh*	vegetable soup with bacon and bread
a sopa canja *keng·zsuh*	chicken and rice soup
a sopa de tomate *a sau·puh deh too·maht*	tomato soup
o paio *oo peye·oo*	smoked pork fillet (Port.)

Meat

o bife [filete] *oo beef [fee·leh·chee]*	steak
o borrego [carneiro] *oo boo·rreh·goo [kuhr·nay·roo]*	lamb
a carne de porco *uh kahrn deh paur·koo*	pork
a carne de vaca *uh kahrn deh vah·kuh*	beef

YOU MAY HEAR...

mal passado *m*/**passada** *f*
mahl puh·sah·thoo/puh·sah·thuh
rare

meio passado *m*/**passada** *f*
may·oo puh·sah·thoo/puh·sah·thuh
medium

bem passado *m*/**passada** *f*
beng puh·sah·thoo/puh·sah·thuh
well-done

o frango *oo fruhn·goo* — chicken
a vitela *uh vee·tehl·uh* — veal

Fish & Seafood

o bacalhau *oo buh·kuh·lyahoo* — cod
as almôndegas *uhz ahl·mawn·deh·guhz* — fishballs
o arenque *oo uh·rehn·keh* — herring
a lagosta *uh luh·gau·stuh* — lobster
o salmão (fumado) [defumado] — (smoked) salmon
oo suh·mohm (foo·mah·thoo) [deh·foo·mah·do]
os camarões *ooz kuh·muh·roings* — shrimp [prawns]

Vegetables

as batatas *uhz buh·tah·tuhz* — potatoes
as cebolas *uhz seh·bau·luhz* — onions
a cenoura *uh seh·nau·ruh* — carrot
os cogumelos *ooz koo·goo·meh·looz* — mushrooms
a couve *uh kaw·veh* — cabbage
as ervilhas *uhz eer·vee·lyuhz* — peas
as favas *uhz fah·vuhz* — broad beans
o feijão *oo fay·zsohm* — kidney beans
o tomate *oo too·maht* — tomato

Sauces & Condiments

o sal *o sahl*	salt
a pimenta *uh pee·mehn·tuh*	pepper
mostarda *mooz·tahr·duh*	mustard
ketchup *ketchup*	ketchup

Fruit & Dessert

a banana *uh buh·nuh·nuh*	banana
a laranja *uh luh·ruhn·zsuh*	orange
o limão *oo lee·mohm*	lemon
a maçã *uh muh·suh*	apple
os morangos *ooz moo·ruhn·gooz*	strawberries
a pêra *uh peh·ruh*	pear
o gelado *oo zseh·lah·thoo*	ice cream
o chocolate *oo shoo·koo·laht*	chocolate
a baunilha *uh bahoo·nee·lyuh*	vanilla
a tarte *uh tahrt*	tart
a mousse *uh moo·seh*	mousse
o creme leite *oo krehm layt*	custard

Drinks

The wine list/drink menu, please.	**A carta dos vinhos/ementa de bebidas, se faz favor.** *uh kahr·tuh dooz vee·nyooz/ee·mehn·tuh deh beh·bee·duhz seh fahz fuh·vaur*
What do you recommend?	**O que é que me recomenda?** *oo keh eh keh meh reh·koo·mehn·duh*
I'd like a bottle/glass of red/white wine.	**Queria uma garrafa/um copo de vinho tinto/branco.** *keh·ree·uh oo·muh guh·rrah·fuh/oong kaw·poo deh vee·nyoo teen·too/bruhn·koo*
The house wine, please.	**O vinho da casa, se faz favor.** *oo vee·nyoo duh kah·zuh seh fahz fuh·vaur*

Another bottle/glass, please.	**Outra garrafa/Outro copo, se faz favor.** _auoo•truh guh•rrah•fuh/auoo•troo kaw•poo ser fahz fuh•vaur_
I'd like a local beer.	**Gostaria uma cerveja local.** _goo•stuh•ree•uh oo•muh sehr•vay•zsuh loo•kahl_
Can I buy you a drink?	**Posso oferecer-lhe uma bebida?** _paw•soo aw•freh•sehr•lyeh oo•muh beh•bee•thuh_
Cheers!	**Viva!** _vee•vuh_
A coffee/tea, please.	**Um café/chá, se faz favor.** _oong kuh•feh/shah seh fahz fuh•vaur_
Black.	**Bica [Cafezinho].** _bee•kuh [kuh•feh•zee•nyoo]_
With...	**com...** _kaum..._
milk	**leite** _layt_
sugar	**açúcar** _uh•soo•kuhr_
artificial sweetener	**adoçante** _uh•doo•suhnty_
A..., please.	**..., se faz favor.** _...seh fahz fuh•vaur_
juice	**Um sumo [suco]** _oong soo•moo [soo•koo]_
soda	**Um refresco** _oong reh•freh•skoo_
sparkling/still	**Uma água com/sem gás** _oo•muh ah•gwuh kaum/sehm gahz_
water	
Is the tap water safe to drink?	**A água da torneira é boa para beber?** _uh ah•gwuh duh toor•nay•ruh eh baw•uh puh•ruh beh•behr_

Leisure Time

Sightseeing

Where's the tourist office?	**Onde é o posto de turismo [informações turísticas]?** _aund eh oo pau•stoo deh too•reez•moo [een•foor•muh•soings too•ree•stee•kuhz]_
What are the main points of interest?	**O que há de mais interessante para se ver?** _oo kee ah deh meyez een•tehr•reh•suhnt puh•ruh seh vehr_

YOU MAY SEE...

aberto/fechado	open/closed
entrada/saída	entrance/exit

Do you have tours in English? **Tem excursões em inglês?** teng ee•skoor•*soings* eng eng•*lehz*

Can I have a map/guide? **Pode dar-me um mapa/guia?** pawd *dahr*•meh oong *mah*•puh/gee•uh

Shopping

Where is the market/mall [shopping? **Onde é o mercado/o centro comercial?** aund eh oo mehr•*kah*•thoo/oo *sehn*•troo koo•mehr•see•*ahl*

I'm just looking. **Estou só a ver [vendo].** ee•*stawoo* saw uh vehr [*vehn*•doo]

Can you help me? **Pode ajudar-me?** pawd uh•zsoo•*dahr*•meh

I'm being helped. **Alguém está a [me] ajudar-me.** ahl•*gehng* ee•*stah* uh [meh] uh•zsoo•*dahr*•meh

How much is it? **Quanto é?** *kwuhn*•too eh

I'd like ... **Queria...** keh•*ree*•uh...

That one, please. **Aquele m/Aquela f, por favor.** uh•*kehl*/uh•*keh*•luh poor fuh•*vaur*

That's all, thanks. **É tudo, obrigado m/obrigada f.** eh *too*•doo aw•bree•*gah*•doo/aw•bree•*gah*•thuh

Where can I pay? **Onde pago?** aund *pah*•goo

I'll pay in cash/by credit card. **Pago com dinheiro/com o cartão de crédito.** *pah*•goo kaum dee•*nyay*•roo/kaum oo kuhr•*tohm* deh *kreh*•dee•too

A receipt, please. **Um recibo, se faz favor.** oong reh•*see*•boo seh fahz fuh•*vaur*

Sport & Leisure

When's the game?	**Quando é o jogo?**	_kwuhn•doo eh o zsau•goo_
Where's…?	**Onde é…?**	_aund eh…_
the beach	**a praia**	_uh preye•uh_
the park	**o parque**	_oo pahr•keh_
the pool	**a piscina**	_uh pee•see•nuh_
Is it safe to swim here?	**Pode-se nadar aqui sem perigo?**	_pawd seh nuh•dahr uh•kee sehn peh•ree•goo_
Can I hire golf clubs?	**Posso alugar tacos?**	_paw•soo uh•loo•gahr tah•kooz_
How much per hour?	**Qual é a tarifa por hora?**	_kwahl eh uh tuh•ree•fuh poor aw•ruh_
How far is it to…?	**A que distância fica…?**	_uh keh dee•stuhn•see•uh fee•kuh…_
Can you show me on the map?	**Pode indicar-me no mapa?**	_pawd een•dee•kahr•meh noo mah•puh_

Going Out

What is there to do in the evenings?	**O que há para se fazer à noite?**	_oo keh ah puh•ruh seh fuh•zehr ah noyt_
Do you have a program of events?	**Tem um programa dos espectáculos?**	_teng oong proo•gruh•muh dooz ee•spehk•tah•koo•looz_
What's playing at the movies [cinema] tonight?	**O que há no cinema hoje à noite?**	_oo kee ah noo see•neh•muh auzseh ah noyt_
Where's…?	**Onde é…?**	_aund eh…_
the downtown area	**o centro**	_oo sehn•troo_
the bar	**o bar**	_oo bar_
the dance club	**a discoteca**	_uh deez•koo•teh•kuh_
Is there a cover charge?	**É preciso pagar entrada [ingresso]?**	_eh preh•see•zoo puh•gahr ehn•trah•duh [een•greh•soo]_
Is this area safe at night?	**Esta zona é segura à noite?**	_eh•stuh zau•nuh eh seh•goo•ruh ah noyt?_

Baby Essentials

Do you have…?	**Tem…?** *teng…*
a baby bottle	**um biberom** *oong bee-brohng*
baby wipes	**os toalhetes de limpeza para o bebé [nenê]** *ooz too-ah-lyehtz deh leem-peh-zuh puh-ruh oo beh-beh [neh-neh]*
a car seat	**um assento de carro** *oong uh-sehn-too deh kah-rroo*
a children's menu/ portion	**uma ementa/dose [porção] de criança** *oo-muh ee-mehn-tuh/daw-zeh [poor-sohm] deh kree-uhn-suh*
a child's seat	**uma cadeirinha de criança** *oo-muh kuh-day-ree-nyuh deh kree-uhn-suh*
a crib	**uma cama de bebé [neném]** *oo-muh kuh-muh deh beh-beh [neh-neh]*
diapers [nappies]	**as fraldas** *uhz frahl-duhz*
formula	**fórmula de bebé [neném]** *fawr-moo-luh deh beh-beh [neh-neh]*
a pacifier [dummy]	**uma chupeta** *oo-muh shoo-peh-tuh*
a playpen	**um parque para crianças** *oong pahr-kuh puh-ruh kree-uhn-suhz*
a stroller [pushchair]	**uma cadeira de bebé [neném]** *oo-muh kuh-day-ruh deh beh-beh [neh-neh]*
Can I breastfeed the baby here?	**Posso amamentar o bebé [neném] aqui?** *paw-soo uh-muh-mehn-tahr oo beh-beh [neh-neh] uh-kee*
Where can I change the baby?	**Onde posso mudar o bebé [neném]?** *aund paw-soo moo-thahr oo beh-beh [neh-neh]*

Disabled Travelers

Is there…?	**Há…?** *ah…*
access for the disabled	**acesso para deficientes físicos** *uh-seh-soo puh-ruh deh-fee-see-ehntz fee-see-kooz*
a wheelchair ramp	**uma rampa de cadeira de rodas** *oo-muh ruhm-puh deh kuh-day-ruh deh raw-thuhz*

In Portugal, dial **112** for the police, ambulance or fire brigade.
In Brazil, dial **190** for the police, **192** for the ambulance, and **193**
for the fire brigade.

a handicapped-[disabled-] accessible toilet	**uma casa de banho acessível para deficientes** _oo•muh kah•zuh deh buh•nyoo uh•seh•see•vehl puh•ruh deh•fee•see•ehntz_
I need…	**Preciso de…** _preh•see•zoo deh…_
assistance	**assistência** _uh•see•stehn•see•uh_
an elevator [lift]	**um elevador** _oong eh•leh•vuh•daur_
a ground-floor room	**um quarto no primeiro andar** _oong kwahr•too noo pree•may•roo uhn•dahr_
Please speak louder.	**Por favor, fale mais alto.** _poor fuh•vaur fah•leh mey•ez ahl•too_

Health & Emergencies

Emergencies

Help!	**Socorro!** _soo•kau•rroo_
Go away!	**Vá-se embora!** _vah•seh ehng•baw•ruh_
Call the police!	**Chame a polícia!** _shuh•meh uh poo•lee•see•uh_
Stop thief!	**Pára ladrão!** _pah•ruh luh•drohm_
Get a doctor!	**Chame um médico!** _shuh•meh oong meh•dee•koo_
Fire!	**Fogo!** _fau•goo_
I'm lost.	**Estou perdido** _m_/**perdida** _f._ _ee•stawoo pehr•dee•thoo/pehr•dee•thuh_
Can you help me?	**Pode ajudar-me?** _pawd uh•zsoo•dahr•meh_
Call the police!	**Chame a polícia!** _shuh•meh uh poo•lee•see•uh_

YOU MAY HEAR...

Preencha este formulário.
pree·eng·sheh eh·stuh fawr·muh·lah·reeoo

Fill out this form.

A sua identificação, por favor. *uh soo·uh ee·dehnt·tee·fee·kuh·sohm por fuh·vaur*

Your identification, please.

Quando/Onde é que foi? *kwuhn·doo/ aund eh keh foy*

When/Where did it happen?

Como é ele/ela? *kau·moo eh ehleh/ehluh*

What does he/ she look like?

Where's the police station?	**Onde é a esquadra [delegacia] da polícia?** *aund eh uh ee·skwahr·duh [deh·leh·guh·see·uh] thuh poo·lee·see·uh*
My son/daughter is missing.	**O meu filho/A minha filha desapareceu.** *oo mehoo fee·lyoo/uh mee·nyuh fee·lyuh deh·zuh·puh·ruh·seoo*

Health

I'm sick [ill].	**Estou doente.** *ee·stawoo doo·ehnt*
I need an English-speaking doctor.	**Preciso de um médico que fale inglês.** *preh·see·zoo deh oong meh·dee·koo keh fah·leh eeng·lehz*
It hurts here.	**Dói-me aqui.** *doy·meh uh·kee*
Where's the pharmacy [chemist]?	**Onde fica a farmácia?** *aund fee·kuh uh fuhr·mah·see·uh*
I'm (not) pregnant.	**(Não) Estou grávida.** *(nohm) ee·stawoo grah·vee·thuh*
I'm allergic to antibiotics/penicillin.	**Sou alérgico m/alérgica f a antibióticos/penicilina.** *sawoo uh·lehr·gee·koo/uh·lehr·gee·kuh uh uhn·tee·bee·aw·tee·kuhz/peh·neh·seh·lee·nuh*
I'm on...	**Estou em...** *ee·stawoo eng...*

Dictionary

adaptor o adaptador
American o americano, a americana
and e
antiseptic cream a pomada antiséptica
aspirin a aspirina
at least pelo menos
athletics atletismo
attack o ataque
attendant o empregado, a empregada
attractive atraente
aunt a tia
baby o bebé [neném]
backpack a mochila
bad mau, má
bandage a ligadura [a atadura]
battle site o campo de batalha
beige beige [bege]
bikini o bikini [o biquini]
bird o pássaro
black preto
blue azul
bottle opener o abre-garrafas [o abridor de garrafas]
bowl a malga
boy o rapaz
boyfriend o namorado
bra o sutiã
British britânico
brown o castanho
burger o hambúrguer

camera a máquina fotográfica
can opener o abre-latas [o abridor de latas]
cat o gato [a gata]
castle o castelo
cigarette o cigarro
cold frio; ~ **(illness)** a constipação [o resfriado]
comb o pente
computer o computador
condom o preservativo
contact lens as lentes de contacto
corkscrew o saca-rolhas
cup a chávena
dangerous perigoso
deodorant o desodorizante [o desodorante]
diabetic o diabético
dog o cão
doll a boneca
economy class a classe económica
electricity a electricidade
embassy a embaixada
Europe a Europa
except excepto
excess o excesso
exchange v trocar
exchange rate a taxa de câmbio
excursion a excursão
excuse me (apology) desculpe-me; **(to get attention)** desculpe
fly v voar

fork (utensil) o garfo
girl a menina
girlfriend a namorada
glass (drinking) o copo
glass (material) o vidro
good bom [boa]; ~ **morning** bom dia; ~**night** boa noite
gray o cinzento
green o verde
hairbrush a escova de cabelo; ~**spray** a laca para o cabelo
horse o cavalo
hot (temperature) quente; **(spicy)** picante
husband o marido
ice o gelo
icy adj gelado, gelada
I'd like... Queria...
insect repellent o repelente de insectos
Irish irlandês
jeans as calças de ganga
knife faca
lactose intolerant intolerantes à lactose
large grande
lighter o isqueiro
lotion a loção
love (a person) amar; **(a thing)** gostar de
matches (fire) os fósforos
medium (size) médio; **(cooked)** meio-passado
museum o museu

nail file lima para unhas
napkin o guardanapo
nurse o enfermeiro, a enfermeira
or ou
orange (fruit) a laranja; **(color)** cor-de-laranja
park o parque
partner o companheiro, a companheira
pen a caneta
pink cor-de-rosa
plate o prato
purple roxo
pyjama o pijama
rain v chover
raincoat a gabardine
razor a navalha; ~ **blade** a lâmina de barbear
red vermelho, vermelha
salty salgado
sandals as sandálias
sanitary napkin o penso higiénico [a toalha higiénica]
sauna o sauna
scissors a tesoura
shampoo o shampoo [o xampu]
shoe o sapato
small pequeno, pequena
sneakers as sapatilhas [os ténis]
snow a neve; v nevar
soap o sabonete
sock a peúga, meia [meia curta]
spicy picante
spider a aranha

spoon a colher
stamp o selo
suitcase a mala de viagem
sun o sol
sunglasses os óculos de sol
sweatshirt a sweatshirt
  [blusa de moleton]
swimsuit o fato [maiô] de banho
tampons os tampões higiénicos
ticket o bilhete; ~ **machine** a
  máquina de venda de bilhetes;
  ~ **office** a bilheteira [a bilheteria]
tie (clothing) a gravata
tissue o lenço de papel
toilet paper o papel higiénico
toothbrush a escova de dentes
toothpaste a pasta de dentes
toy o brinquedo
traffic o trânsito; ~ **jam** o
  engarrafamento; ~ **circle** a
  rotunda; ~ **light** o semáforo
trail o caminho; ~ **map** o mapa
train o comboio [o trem];
  ~ **station** a estação de caminho
  de ferro [a estação ferroviária]
transfer (plane, train) o
  transbordo
translate v traduzir
trash o lixo; ~ **can** a lixeira
travel v viajar;
  ~ **agency** a agência de viagens
traveler's check o cheque de
  viagens
T-shirt a T-Shirt [a camiseta]

underwear a roupa interior
vegan vegan
vegetarian vegetariano
walking route o itinerário a pé
wall a parede
wallet a carteira (de documentos)
warm adj morno, morna; v aquecer
wash v lavar
washing machine a máquina de
  lavar
watch n o relógio; v ver
water a água
water skis os skis aquáticos
  [os esquis-aquáticos]
weather o tempo; ~ **forecast**
  a previsão do tempo
wedding o casamento; ~ **ring**
  a aliança **white** branco, branca
wife a mulher [a esposa]
with com
without sem
year o ano
yellow amarelo, amarela
zoo o jardim zoológico, o zoo

Spanish

Essentials

Hello.	**Hola.** _oh_·lah
Goodbye.	**Adiós.** ah·_deeyohs_
Yes/No/OK	**Sí/No/De acuerdo** see/noh/deh ah·_kwehr_·doh
Excuse me! (to get attention)	**¡Disculpe!** dees·_kool_·peh
Excuse me. (to get past)	**Perdón.** pehr·_dohn_
I'm sorry.	**Lo siento.** loh _seeyehn_·toh
I'd like...	**Quiero...** _keeyeh_·roh...
And/or	**y/o** ee/oh
How much?	**¿Cuánto?** _kwahn_·toh
Where is...?	**¿Dónde está...?** _dohn_·deh ehs·_tah_...
My name is...	**Me llamo...** meh _yah_·moh...
I'm going to...	**Voy a...** boy ah...
Please.	**Por favor.** pohr fah·_bohr_
Thank you.	**Gracias.** _grah_·theeyahs
You're welcome.	**De nada.** deh _nah_·dah
Please speak slowly.	**Hable más despacio, por favor.** _ah_·bleh mahs dehs·_pah_·theeyoh pohr fah·_bohr_
Can you repeat that?	**¿Podría repetir eso?** poh·_dree_·ah reh·peh·_teer_ eh·soh
I don't understand.	**No entiendo.** noh ehn·_teeyehn_·doh
Do you speak English?	**¿Habla usted inglés?** _ah_·blah oos·_teth_ een·_glehs_
I don't speak Spanish.	**No hablo español.** noh _ah_·bloh ehs·pah·_nyohl_
Where's the restroom [toilet]?	**¿Dónde están los servicios?** _dohn_·deh ehs·_tahn_ lohs sehr·_bee_·theeyohs
Help!	**¡Socorro!** soh·_koh_·rroh

You'll find the pronunciation of the Spanish letters and words written in gray after each sentence to guide you. Simply pronounce these as if they were English, noting that any underlines and bolds indicate an additional emphasis or stress or a lengthening of a vowel sound. As you hear the language being spoken, you will quickly become accustomed to the local pronunciation and dialect.

Numbers

0	**cero**	_theh_•roh
1	**uno**	_oo_•noh
2	**dos**	dohs
3	**tres**	trehs
4	**cuatro**	_kwah_•troh
5	**cinco**	_theen_•koh
6	**seis**	seyees
7	**siete**	_seeyeh_•teh
8	**ocho**	_oh_•choh
9	**nueve**	_nweh_•beh
10	**diez**	deeyehth
11	**once**	_ohn_•theh
12	**doce**	_doh_•theh
13	**trece**	_treh_•theh
14	**catorce**	kah•_tohr_•theh
15	**quince**	_keen_•theh
16	**dieciséis**	deeyeh•thee•_seyees_
17	**diecisiete**	deeyeh•thee•_seeyeh_•teh
18	**dieciocho**	deeyeh•thee•_oh_•choh
19	**diecinueve**	deeyeh•thee•_nweh_•beh
20	**veinte**	_beyeen_•teh

21	**veintiuno** *beyeen·tee·oo·noh*
30	**treinta** *treyeen·tah*
40	**cuarenta** *kwah·rehn·tah*
50	**cincuenta** *theen·kwehn·tah*
60	**sesenta** *seh·sehn·tah*
70	**setenta** *seh·tehn·tah*
80	**ochenta** *oh·chehn·tah*
90	**noventa** *noh·behn·tah*
100	**cien** *theeyehn*
101	**ciento uno** *theeyehn·toh oo·noh*
200	**doscientos** *dohs·theeyehn·tohs*
500	**quinientos** *kee·neeyehn·tohs*
1,000	**mil** *meel*
10,000	**diez mil** *deeyehth meel*
1,000,000	**un millón** *oon mee·yohn*

Time

What time is it?	**¿Qué hora es?** *keh oh·rah ehs*
It's noon [midday].	**Son las doce del mediodía.** *sohn lahs doh·theh dehl meh·deeyoh·dee·ah*
Five after [past] three.	**Las tres y cinco.** *lahs trehs ee theen·koh*
A quarter to five.	**Las cinco menos cuarto.** *lahs theen·koh meh·nohs kwahr·toh*
5:30 a.m./p.m.	**Las cinco y media de la mañana/tarde.** *lahs theen·koh ee meh·deeyah deh lah mah·nyah·nah/tahr·deh*

Days

Monday	**lunes** *loo·nehs*
Tuesday	**martes** *mahr·tehs*
Wednesday	**miércoles** *meeyehr·koh·lehs*
Thursday	**jueves** *khweh·behs*

Friday	**viernes** _beeyehr_·nehs
Saturday	**sábado** _sah_·bah·doh
Sunday	**domingo** doh·_meen_·goh

Dates

yesterday	**ayer** ah·_yehr_
today	**hoy** oy
tomorrow	**mañana** mah·_nyah_·nah
day	**día** _dee_·ah
week	**semana** seh·_mah_·nah
month	**mes** mehs
year	**año** _ah_·nyoh
Happy New Year!	**Feliz año Nuevo! feh** feh·leez _ah_·nyoh _nweh_·boh
Happy Birthday!	**Feliz cumpleaños!** feh·leez cum·plee· _ah_·nyohz

Months

January	**enero** eh·_neh_·roh
February	**febrero** feh·_breh_·roh
March	**marzo** _mahr_·thoh
April	**abril** ah·_breel_
May	**mayo** _mah_·yoh
June	**junio** _khoo_·neeyoh
July	**julio** _khoo_·leeyoh
August	**agosto** ah·_gohs_·toh
September	**septiembre** sehp·_teeyehm_·breh
October	**octubre** ohk·_too_·breh

YOU MAY SEE...

Spanish currency is the **euro**, €, divided into 100 **céntimos** (cents).
Coins: 1, 2, 5, 10, 20, 50 **cts.**; €1, 2
Notes: €5, 10, 20, 50, 100, 200, 500

| November | **noviembre** *noh·beeyehm·breh* |
| December | **diciembre** *dee·theeyehm·breh* |

Arrival & Departure

I'm on vacation/ business.	**Estoy aquí de vacaciones/en viaje de negocios.** *ehs·toy ah·kee deh bah·kah·theeyohn·ehs/ ehn beeyah·kheh deh neh·goh·theeyohs*
I'm going to...	**Voy a...** *boy ah...*
I'm staying at the... Hotel.	**Me alojo en el Hotel...** *meh ah·loh·khoh ehn ehl oh·tehl...*

Money

Where's...?	**¿Dónde está...?** *dohn·deh ehs·tah...*
the ATM	**el cajero automático** *ehl kah·kheh·roh awtoh·mah·tee·koh*
the bank	**el banco** *ehl bahn·koh*
the currency exchange office	**la casa de cambio** *lah kah·sah deh kahm·beeyoh*
When does the bank open/close?	**¿A qué hora abre/cierra el banco?** *ah keh oh·rah ah·breh/theeyeh·rrah ehl bahn·koh*
I'd like to change dollars/pounds into euros.	**Quiero cambiar dólares/libras a euros.** *keeyeh·roh kahm·beeyahr doh·lah·rehs/lee·brahs ah ew·rohs*
I'd like to cash traveler's checks [cheques].	**Quiero cobrar cheques de viaje.** *keeyeh·roh koh·brahr cheh·kehs deh beeyah·kheh*
I'll pay in cash/by credit card.	**Voy a pagar en efectivo/con tarjeta de crédito.** *boy ah pah·gahr ehn eh·fehk·tee·boh/ kohn tahr·kheh·tah deh kreh·dee·toh*

For Numbers, see page 172

Getting Around

How do I get to town?	**¿Cómo se llega a la ciudad?** _koh·moh seh yeh·gah ah lah theew·dahd_
Where's...?	**¿Dónde está...?** _dohn·deh ehs·tah..._
the airport	**el aeropuerto** _ehl ah·eh·roh·pwehr·toh_
the train [railway] station	**la estación de tren** _lah ehs·tah·theeyohn deh trehn_
the bus station	**la estación de autobuses** _lah ehs·tah·theeyohn deh awtoh·booses_
the metro station	**la estación de metro** _lah ehs·tah·theeyohn deh meh·troh_
Is it far from here?	**¿A qué distancia está?** _ah keh dees·tahn·theeyah ehs·tah_
Where do I buy a ticket?	**¿Dónde se compra el billete?** _dohn·deh seh kohm·prah ehl bee·yeh·teh_
A one-way/return-trip ticket to...	**Un billete de ida/ida y vuelta a...** _oon bee·yeh·teh deh ee·dah/ee·dah ee bwehl·tah ah..._
How much?	**¿Cuánto es?** _kwahn·toh ehs_
Is there a discount?	**¿Hacen descuento?** _ah·then dehs·kwehn·toh_
Which...?	**¿De qué...?** _deh keh..._
gate	**puerta de embarque** _pwehr·tah deh ehm·bahr·keh_
line	**línea** _lee·neh·ah_
platform	**andén** _ahn·dehn_
Where can I get a taxi?	**¿Dónde puedo coger un taxi?** _dohn·deh pweh·doh koh·khehr oon tah·xee_
Take me to this address.	**Lléveme a esta dirección.** _yeh·beh·meh ah ehs·tah dee·rek·theeyohn_
To...Airport, please.	**Al aeropuerto de..., por favor.** _ahl ah·eh·roh·pwehr·toh deh...pohr fah·bohr_
My airline is...	**Mi compañía aérea es...** _mee kohm·pah·nyee·ah ah·eh·reh·ah ehs..._

I'm in a rush.	**Tengo prisa.** *tehn•goh pree•sah*	
Can I have a map?	**¿Podría darme un mapa?** *poh•dree•ah dahr•meh oon mah•pah*	

Tickets

When's…to Madrid?	**¿Cuándo sale…a Madrid?** *kwahn•doh sah•leh…ah mah•dreeth*
the (first) bus	**el (primer) autobús** *ehl (pree•mehr) awtoh•boos*
the (next) flight	**el (próximo) vuelo** *ehl (proh•xee•moh) bweh•loh*
the (last) train	**el (último) tren** *ehl (ool•tee•moh) trehn*
Where do I buy a ticket?	**¿Dónde se compra el billete?** *dohn•deh seh kohm•prah ehl bee•yeh•teh*
One/Two ticket(s), please.	**Un/Dos billete(s), por favor.** *oon/dohs bee•yeh•teh(s) pohr fah•bohr*
For today/tomorrow.	**Para hoy/mañana.** *pah•rah oy/mah•nyah•nah*
A…ticket.	**Un billete…** *oon bee•yeh•teh…*
one-way	**de ida** *deh ee•dah*
return-trip	**de ida y vuelta** *deh ee•dah ee bwehl•tah*
first class	**de primera clase** *deh pree•meh•rah klah•she*
I have an e-ticket.	**Tengo un billete electrónico.** *tehn•goh oon bee•yeh•teh eh•lehk•troh•nee•koh*
How long is the trip?	**¿Cuánto dura el viaje?** *kwahn•toh doo•rah ehl veeyah•kheh*
Is it a direct train?	**¿Es un tren directo?** *ehs oon trehn dee•rehk•toh*
Can you tell me when to get off?	**¿Podría decirme cuándo me tengo que bajar?** *poh•dree•ah deh•theer•meh kwahn•doh meh tehn•goh keh bah•khahr*
Is this the bus to…?	**¿Es éste el autobús a…?** *ehs ehs•teh ehl awtoh•boos ah…*
I'd like to…my reservation.	**Quiero…mi reserva.** *keeyeh•roh…mee reh•sehr•bah*

cancel	**cancelar** kahn·theh·*lahr*
change	**cambiar** kahm·*beeyahr*
confirm	**confirmar** kohn·feer·*mahr*

For Time, see page 173.

Car Hire

Where's the car hire?	**¿Dónde está el alquiler de coches?**
	dohn·deh ehs·*tah* ehl ahl·kee·*lehr* deh *koh*·chehs
I'd like...	**Quiero...** *keeyeh*·roh...
a cheap/small car	**un coche económico/pequeño**
	oon *koh*·cheh eh·koh·*noh*·mee·koh/peh·*keh*·nyoh
an automatic/ a manual	**un coche automático/con transmisión manual**
	oon *koh*·cheh awtoh·*mah*·tee·koh/ kohn trahns·mee·*seeyohn* mah·noo·*ahl*

YOU MAY HEAR...

todo recto *toh*·doh *rehk*·toh	straight ahead
a la izquierda ah lah eeth·*keeyehr*·dah	left
a la derecha ah lah deh·*reh*·chah	right
en/doblando la esquina	on/around the corner
ehn/doh·*blahn*·doh lah ehs·*kee*·nah	
frente a *frehn*·teh ah	opposite
detrás de deh·*trahs* deh	behind
al lado de ahl *lah*·doh deh	next to
después de dehs·*pwehs* deh	after
al norte/sur ahl *nohr*·teh/soor	north/south
al este/oeste ahl *ehs*·teh/oh·*ehs*·teh	east/west
en el semáforo en ehl seh·*mah*·foh·roh	at the traffic light
en el cruce en ehl *kroo*·theh	at the intersection

air conditioning	**un coche con aire acondicionado** *oon koh•cheh kohn ayee•reh ah•kohn•dee•theeyoh•nah•doh*
a car seat	**un asiento de niño** *oon ah•seeyehn•toh deh nee•nyoh*
How much...?	**¿Cuánto cobran...?** *kwahn•toh koh•brahn...*
per day/week	**por día/semana** *pohr dee•ah/seh•mah•nah*
Are there any discounts?	**¿Ofrecen algún descuento?** *oh•freh•thehn ahl•goon dehs•kwehn•toh*

Places to Stay

Can you recommend a hotel?	**¿Puede recomendarme un hotel?** *pweh•deh reh•koh•mehn•dahr•meh oon oh•tehl*
I have a reservation.	**Tengo una reserva.** *tehn•goh oo•nah reh•sehr•bah*
My name is...	**Me llamo...** *meh yah•moh...*
Do you have a room...?	**¿Tienen habitaciones...?** *teeyeh•nehn ah•bee•tah•theeyoh•nehs...*
for one/two	**individuales/dobles** *een•dee•bee•doo•ah•lehs/doh•blehs*
with a bathroom	**con baño** *kohn bah•nyoh*
with air conditioning	**con aire acondicionado** *kohn ayee•reh ah•kohn•dee•theeyoh•nah•doh*
For...	**Para...** *pah•rah...*
tonight	**esta noche** *ehs•tah noh•cheh*
two nights	**dos noches** *dohs noh•chehs*
one week	**una semana** *oo•nah seh•mah•nah*
How much?	**¿Cuánto es?** *kwahn•toh ehs*
Is there anything cheaper?	**¿Hay alguna tarifa más barata?** *aye ahl•goo•nah tah•ree•fah mahs bah•rah•tah*
When's check-out?	**¿A qué hora hay que desocupar la habitación?** *ah keh oh•rah aye keh deh•soh•koo•pahr lah ah•bee•tah•theeyohn*

Can I leave this in the safe?	**¿Puedo dejar esto en la caja fuerte?** _pweh_-doh deh-_khahr_ ehs-toh ehn lah _kah_-khah _fwehr_-teh
Can I leave my bags?	**¿Podría dejar mi equipaje?** poh-_dree_-ah deh-_khahr_ mee eh-kee-_pah_-kheh
Can I have the bill/ a receipt?	**¿Me da la factura/un recibo?** meh dah lah fahk-_too_-rah/oon reh-_thee_-boh
I'll pay in cash/by credit card.	**Voy a pagar en efectivo/con tarjeta de crédito.** boy ah pah-_gahr_ ehn eh-fehk-_tee_-boh/ kohn tahr-_kheh_-tah deh _kreh_-dee-toh

Communications

Where's an internet cafe?	**¿Dónde hay un cibercafé?** _dohn_-deh aye oon thee-behr-kah-_feh_
Can I access the internet/check e-mail?	**¿Puedo acceder a Internet/revisar el correo electrónico?** _pweh_-doh ahk-theh-_dehr_ ah een-tehr-_neht_/reh-bee-_sahr_ ehl koh-_rreh_-oh eh-lehk-_troh_-nee-koh
How much per (half) hour?	**¿Cuánto cuesta por (media) hora?** _kwahn_-toh _kwehs_-tah pohr (_meh_-deeyah) _oh_-rah
How do I connect/ log on?	**¿Cómo entro al sistema/inicio la sesión?** _koh_-moh _ehn_-troh ahl sees-_teh_-mah/ ee-nee-_theeyoh_ lah seh-_seeyohn_
A phone card, please.	**Una tarjeta telefónica, por favor.** _oo_-nah tahr-_kheh_-tah teh-leh-_foh_-nee-kah pohr fah-_bohr_
Can I have your phone number?	**¿Me puede dar su número de teléfono?** meh _pweh_-deh dahr soo _noo_-meh-roh deh teh-_leh_-foh-noh
Here's my number/ e-mail address.	**Aquí tiene mi número/dirección de correo electrónico.** ah-_kee_ teeyeh-neh mee _noo_-meh-roh/ dee-rehk-_theeyohn_ deh koh-_rreh_-oh eh-lehk-_troh_-nee-koh

Call me/Text me	**Llámeme/Envíame un mensaje de texto**
	yah·meh·meh/ehn·beeyah·meh oon mehn·sah·kheh
	deh tehx·toh
I'll text you.	**Te enviaré un mensaje de texto.**
	teh ehn·beeyah·reh oon mehn·sah·kheh deh tehx·toh
E-mail me.	**Envíeme un correo.** *ehn·bee·eh·meh oon koh·rreh·oh*
Hello. This is...	**Hola. Soy...** *oh·lah soy...*
Can I speak to...?	**¿Puedo hablar con...?** *pweh·doh ah·blahr kohn...*
Can you repeat that?	**¿Puede repetir eso?** *pweh·deh reh·peh·teer eh·soh*
I'll call back later.	**Llamaré más tarde.** *yah·mah·reh mahs tahr·deh*
Bye.	**Adiós.** *ah·deeyohs*
Where's the post office?	**¿Dónde está la oficina de correos?**
	dohn·deh ehs·tah lah oh·fee·thee·nah
	deh koh·rreh·ohs
I'd like to send this to...	**Quiero mandar esto a...** *keeyeh·roh*
	mahn·dahr ehs·toh ah...
What is the WiFi password?	**¿Cuál es la contraseña de WiFI?** *kwahl ehs lah*
	kohn·trah·seh·nyah deh weeh·feeh
Is the WiFi free?	**¿Es gratuito el acceso WiFi?**
	esh grah·too·ee·toh ehl ahk·theh·soh weeh·feeh
Do you have bluetooth?	**¿Tiene Bluetooth?** *teeyeh·neh blue·tooth*
Can I...?	**¿Puedo...?** *pweh·doh...*
access the internet	**acceder a Internet** *ahk·theh·dehr ah*
	een·tehr·neht
check e-mail	**revisar el correo electrónico** *reh·bee·sahr ehl*
	koh·rreh·oh eh·lehk·troh·nee·koh
print	**imprimir** *eem·pree·meer*
plug in/charge my laptop/iPhone/ iPad/BlackBerry?	**enchufar/cargar el portátil/iPhone/ iPad/Blackberry?** *ehn·choo·fahr/ kahr·gahr ehl pohr·tah·teel/i·fon/i·pad/Blackberry*
access Skype?	**acceder a Skype?** *ahk·theh·dehr ah skype*

Social Media

Are you on Facebook/ Twitter?	**¿Está en Facebook/Twitter?** *(polite form)*
	ehs•tah ehn Facebook/Twitter
	¿Estás en Facebook/Twitter? *(informal form)*
	ehs•tahs ehn Facebook/Twitter
What's your user name?	**¿Cuál es su nombre de usuario?** *(polite form)*
	kwahl ehs soo nohm•breh deh oo•soo•ah•reeyoh
	¿Cuál es tu nombre de usuario? *(informal form)*
	kwahl ehs too nohm•breh deh oo•soo•ah•reeyoh
I'll add you as a friend.	**Le añadiré como amigo.** *(polite form)*
	leh ah•nyah•dee•reh koh•moh ah•mee•goh
	Te añadiré como amigo. *(informal form)*
	teh ah•nyah•dee•reh koh•moh ah•mee•goh
I'll follow you on Twitter.	**Le seguiré en Twitter.** *(polite form)*
	leh seh•gee•reh ehn Twitter
	Te seguiré en Twitter. *(informal form)*
	teh seh•gee•reh ehn Twitter
Are you following...?	**¿Sigue a...?** *(polite form)* *see•geh ah*
	¿Sigues a...? *(informal form)* *see•gehs ah*
I'll put the pictures on Facebook/Twitter.	**Subiré las fotos a Facebook/Twitter.**
	soo•bee•reh lahs foh•tohs ah Facebook/Twitter
I'll tag you in the pictures.	**Le etiquetaré en las fotos.** *(polite form)*
	leh eh•tee•keh•tah•reh ehn lahs foh•tohs
	Te etiquetaré en las fotos. *(informal form)*
	teh eh•tee•keh•tah•reh ehn lahs foh•tohs

Conversation

Hello!	**¡Hola!** *oh•lah*
How are you?	**¿Cómo está?** *koh•moh ehs•tah*
Fine, thanks.	**Bien, gracias.** *beeyehn grah•theeyahs*

Excuse me! (to get attention)	**¡Perdón!** *pehr-dohn*
Do you speak English?	**¿Habla inglés?** *ah-blah een-glehs*
What's your name?	**¿Cómo se llama?** *koh-moh seh yah-mah*
My name is...	**Me llamo...** *meh yah-moh...*
Nice to meet you.	**Encantado m/Encantada f.** *ehn-kahn-tah-doh/ehn-kahn-tah-dah*
Where are you from?	**¿De dónde es usted?** *deh dohn-deh ehs oos-teth*
I'm from the U.S./U.K.	**Soy de Estados Unidos/del Reino Unido.** *soy deh ehs-tah-dohs oo-nee-dohs/ dehl reyee-noh oo-nee-doh*
What do you do for a living?	**¿A qué se dedica?** *ah keh seh deh-dee-kah*
I work for...	**Trabajo para...** *trah-bah-khoh pah-rah...*
I'm a student.	**Soy estudiante.** *soy ehs-too-deeyahn-teh*
I'm retired.	**Estoy jubilado m/jubilada f.** *ehs-toy khoo-bee-lah-doh/khoo-bee-lah-dah*

Romance

Would you like to go out for a drink/dinner?	**¿Le gustaría salir a tomar una copa/cenar?** *leh goos-tah-ree-ah sah-leer ah toh-mahr oo-nah koh-pah/theh-nahr*
What are your plans for tonight/tomorrow?	**¿Qué planes tiene para esta noche/mañana?** *keh plah-nehs teeyeh-nehs pah-rah ehs-tah noh-cheh/ mah-nyah-nah*
Can I have your number?	**¿Puede darme su número?** *pweh-deh dahr-meh soo noo-meh-roh*
Can I join you?	**¿Puedo acompañarle m/acompañarla f?** *pweh-doh ah-kohm-pah-nyahr-leh/ ah-kohm-pah-nyahr-lah*

| Can I buy you a drink? | **¿Puedo invitarle _m_/invitarla _f_ a una copa?** _pweh·doh een·bee·tahr·leh/een·bee·tahr·lah ah oo·nah koh·pah_ |
| I love you. | **Te quiero.** _teh keeyeh·roh_ |

Accepting & Rejecting

I'd love to.	**Me encantaría.** _meh ehn·kahn·tah·ree·yah_
Where should we meet?	**¿Dónde quedamos?** _dohn·deh keh·dah·mohs_
I'll meet you at the bar/your hotel.	**Quedamos en el bar/su hotel.** _keh·dah·mohs ehn ehl bahr/soo oh·tehl_
I'll come by at…	**Pasaré a recogerle _m_/recogerla _f_ a las…** _pah·sah·reh ah reh·koh·khehr·leh/ reh·koh·khehr·lah ah lahs…_
What is your address?	**¿Cuál es su dirección?** _kwahl ehs soo dee·rehk·theeyohn_
I'm busy.	**Estoy ocupado _m_/ocupada _f_.** _ehs·toy oh·koo·pah·doh/oh·koo·pah·dah_
I'm not interested.	**No me interesa.** _noh meh een·teh·reh·sah_
Leave me alone.	**Déjeme en paz.** _deh·kheh·meh ehn pahth_
Stop bothering me!	**¡Deje de molestarme!** _deh·kheh deh_

Food & Drink

Eating Out

| Can you recommend a good restaurant/bar? | **¿Puede recomendarme un buen restaurante/bar?** _pweh·deh reh·koh·mehn·dahr·meh oon bwehn rehs·taw·rahn·teh/bahr_ |

YOU MAY SEE...

CARTA	menu
MENÚ DEL DÍA	menu of the day
SERVICIO (NO) INCLUIDO	service (not) included

Is there a traditional Spanish/an inexpensive restaurant nearby?
¿Hay un restaurante típico español/barato cerca de aquí? *aye oon rehs‧taw‧rahn‧teh tee‧pee‧koh ehs‧pah‧nyohl/ bah‧rah‧toh thehr‧kah deh ah‧kee*

A table for..., please.
Una mesa para..., por favor. *oo‧nah meh‧sah pah‧rah... pohr fah‧bohr*

Can we sit...?
¿Podemos sentarnos...? *poh‧deh‧mohs sehn‧tahr‧nohs...*

here/there
aquí/allí *ah‧kee/ah‧yee*

outside
fuera *fweh‧rah*

in a non-smoking area
en una zona de no fumadores *ehn oo‧nah thoh‧nah deh noh foo‧mah‧doh‧rehs*

I'm waiting for someone.
Estoy esperando a alguien. *ehs‧toy ehs‧peh‧rahn‧doh ah ahl‧geeyehn*

Where are the toilets?
¿Dónde están los servicios? *dohn‧deh ehs‧tahn lohs sehr‧bee‧theeyohs*

A menu, please.
Una carta, por favor. *oo‧nah kahr‧tah pohr fah‧bohr*

What do you recommend?
¿Qué me recomienda? *keh meh reh‧koh‧meeyehn‧dah*

I'd like...
Quiero... *keeyeh‧roh...*

Some more..., please.
Quiero más..., por favor. *keeyeh‧roh mahs... pohr fah‧bohr*

Enjoy your meal!
¡Que aproveche! *keh ah‧proh‧beh‧cheh*

The check [bill], please.
La cuenta, por favor. *lah kwen‧tah pohr fah‧bohr*

Food & Drink

Is service included?	**¿Está incluido el servicio?** ehs·*tah* een·kloo·*ee*·doh ehl sehr·*bee*·theeyoh
Can I pay by credit card?	**¿Puedo pagar con tarjeta de crédito?** *pweh*·doh pah·*gahr* kohn tahr·*kheh*·tah deh *kreh*·dee·toh
Can I have a receipt?	**¿Podría darme un recibo?** poh·*dree*·ah *dahr*·meh oon reh·*thee*·boh

Breakfast

los fiambres lohs fee·*ahm*·brehs	cold cuts [charcuterie]
el huevo... ehl *weh*·boh...	egg...
duro/pasado por agua *doo*·roh/ pah·*sah*·doh pohr *ah*·gwah	hard-/soft-boiled
frito *free*·toh	fried
revuelto reh·*bwehl*·toh	scrambled
la mantequilla lah mahn·teh·*kee*·yah	butter
la mermelada/la jalea lah mehr·meh·*lah*·dah/khah·*leh*·ah	jam/jelly
el pan ehl pahn	bread
el queso ehl *keh*·soh	cheese
la salchicha lah sahl·*chee*·chah	sausage
el tocino ehl toh·*thee*·noh	bacon
la tortilla lah tohr·*tee*·yah	omelet
la tostada lah tohs·*tah*·dah	toast
el yogur ehl yoh·*goor*	yogurt

Appetizers

la sopa... lah *soh*·pah...	...soup
de mariscos deh mah·*rees*·kohs	seafood
de pollo deh *poh*·yoh	chicken
de tomate deh toh·*mah*·teh	tomato

de verduras *deh behr·doo·rahs* — vegetable
el pan con tomate *ehl pahn kohn toh·mah·teh* — toasted bread with garlic, tomato and olive oil

YOU MAY HEAR...

muy poco hecho *m*/**hecha** *f* — rare
mooy poh·koh eh·choh/eh·chah
medio hecho *m*/**hecha** *f* — medium
meh·deeyoh eh·choh/eh·chah
bien hecho *m*/**hecha** *f* — well-done
beeyehn eh·choh/eh·chah

Meat

la carne de cerdo *lah kahr·neh deh thehr·doh* — pork
la carne de vaca *lah kahr·neh deh bah·kah* — beef
el cordero *ehl kohr·deh·roh* — lamb
el filete *ehl fee·leh·teh* — steak
el pollo *ehl poh·yoh* — chicken
la ternera *lah tehr·neh·rah* — veal

Fish & Seafood

el arenque *ehl ah·rehn·keh* — herring
el bacalao *ehl bah·kah·laoh* — cod
la gamba *lah gahm·bah* — shrimp
la langosta *lah lahn·gohs·tah* — lobster
el salmón *ehl sahl·mohn* — salmon
la lubina *lah loo·bee·nah* — sea bass

Vegetables

la cebolla *lah theh-boh-yah*	onion
el guisante *ehl gee-sahn-teh*	pea
la judía *lah khoo-dee-ah*	bean
la patata *lah pah-tah-tah*	potato
el repollo *ehl reh-poh-yoh*	cabbage
la seta *lah seh-tah*	mushroom
el tomate *ehl toh-mah-teh*	tomato
la zanahoria *lah thah-nah-oh-reeyah*	carrot

Sauces & Condiments

la sal *lah sahl*	salt
la pimienta negra *lah pee-meeyehn-tah neh-grah*	black pepper
mostaza *mohs-tah-thah*	mustard
ketchup *keht-choop*	ketchup

Fruit & Dessert

la fresa *lah freh-sah*	strawberry
el limón *ehl lee-mohn*	lemon
la manzana *lah mahn-thah-nah*	apple
la naranja *lah nah-rahn-khah*	orange
la pera *lah peh-rah*	pear
el plátano *ehl plah-tah-noh*	banana
el helado *ehl eh-lah-doh*	ice cream
el chocolate *ehl choh-koh-lah-teh*	chocolate
el churro *ehl choo-rroh*	deep-fried fritter sprinkled with sugar
la vainilla *lah bayee-nee-yah*	vanilla
la tarta *lah tahr-tah*	tart
las natillas *lahs nah-tee-yahs*	custard

Drinks

Can I see the wine list/ drink menu, please?	**La carta de vinos/bebidas, por favor.** *lah kahr·tah deh bee·nohs/beh·bee·dahs pohr fah·bohr*
What do you recommend?	**¿Qué me recomienda?** *keh meh reh·koh·meeyehn·dah*
I'd like a bottle/glass of red/white wine.	**Quiero una botella/un vaso de vino tinto/blanco.** *keeyeh·roh oo·nah boh·teh·yah/ oon bah·soh deh bee·noh teen·toh/blahn·koh*
The house wine, please.	**El vino de la casa, por favor.** *ehl bee·noh deh lah kah·sah pohr fah·bohr*
Another bottle/glass, please.	**Otra botella/Otro vaso, por favor.** *oh·trah boh·teh·yah/oh·troh bah·soh pohr fah·bohr*
I'd like a local beer.	**Quiero una cerveza española.** *keeyeh·roh oo·nah thehr·beh·thah ehs·pah·nyoh·lah*
Can I buy you a drink?	**¿Puedo invitarle *m*/invitarla *f* a una copa?** *pweh·doh een·bee·tahr·leh/ een·bee·tahr·lah ah oo·nah koh·pah*
Cheers!	**¡Salud!** *sah·looth*
A coffee/tea, please.	**Un café/té, por favor.** *oon kah·feh/teh pohr fah·bohr*
Black.	**Solo.** *soh·loh*
With...	**Con...** *kohn...*
milk	**leche** *leh·cheh*
sugar	**azúcar** *ah·thoo·kahr*
artificial sweetener	**edulcorante artificial** *eh·dool·khoh·rahn·teh ahr·tee·fee·theeyahl*
A..., please.	**Un..., por favor.** *oon...pohr fah·bohr*
juice	**zumo** *thoo·moh*
soda	**refresco** *reh·frehs·koh*
water	**agua** *ah·gwah*
sparkling/still	**con/sin gas** *kohn/seen gahs*

Leisure Time

Sightseeing

Where's the tourist information office?	**¿Dónde está la oficina de turismo?** _dohn·deh ehs·tah lah oh·fee·thee·nah deh too·rees·moh_
What are the main sights?	**¿Dónde están los principales sitios de interés?** _dohn·deh ehs·tahn lohs preen·thee·pah·lehs see·teeyohs deh een·teh·rehs_
Do you have tours in English?	**¿Hay visitas en inglés?** _aye bee·see·tahs ehn een·glehs_
Can I have a map/guide?	**¿Puede darme un mapa/una guía?** _pweh·deh dahr·meh oon mah·pah/oo·nah gee·ah_

YOU MAY SEE...

ABIERTO/CERRADO	open/closed
ENTRADA/SALIDA	entrance/exit

Shopping

Where's the market/ mall?	**¿Dónde está el mercado/centro comercial?** _dohn·deh ehs·tah ehl mehr·kah·doh/ then·troh koh·mehr·theeyahl_
I'm just looking.	**Sólo estoy mirando.** _soh·loh ehs·toy mee·rahn·doh_
Can you help me?	**¿Puede ayudarme?** _pweh·deh ah·yoo·dahr·meh_
I'm being helped.	**Ya me atienden.** _yah meh ah·teeyehn·dehn_
How much?	**¿Cuánto es?** _kwahn·toh ehs_
That one, please.	**Ése _m_/Ésa _f_, por favor.** _eh·she/eh·sah pohr fah·bohr_
That's all.	**Eso es todo.** _eh·soh ehs toh·doh_
Where can I pay?	**¿Dónde se paga?** _dohn·deh seh pah·gah_

| I'll pay in cash/by credit card. | **Voy a pagar en efectivo/con tarjeta de crédito.** *boy ah pah·gahr ehn eh·fehk·tee·boh/ kohn tahr·kheh·tah deh kreh·dee·toh* |
| A receipt, please. | **Un recibo, por favor.** *oon reh·thee·boh pohr fah·bohr* |

Sport & Leisure

When's the game?	**¿Cuándo empieza el partido?**
	kwahn·doh ehm·peeyeh·thah ehl pahr·tee·doh
Where's...?	**¿Dónde está...?** *dohn·deh ehs·tah...*
the beach	**la playa** *lah plah·yah*
the park	**el parque** *ehl pahr·keh*
the pool	**la piscina** *lah pees·thee·nah*
Is it safe to swim here?	**¿Es seguro nadar aquí?** *ehs seh·goo·roh nah·dahr ah·kee*
Can I rent [hire] golf clubs?	**¿Puedo alquilar palos de golf?** *pweh·doh ahl·kee·lahr pah·lohs deh golf*
How much per hour?	**¿Cuánto cuesta por hora?** *kwahn·toh kwehs·tah pohr oh·rah*
How far is it to...?	**¿A qué distancia está...?** *ah keh dees·tahn·theeyah ehs·tah...*
Can you show me on the map, please?	**¿Puede indicármelo en el mapa, por favor?** *pweh·deh een·dee·kahr·meh·loh ehn ehl mah·pah pohr fah·bohr*

Going Out

What's there to do at night?	**¿Qué se puede hacer por las noches?** *keh seh pweh·deh ah·thehr pohr lahs noh·chehs*
Do you have a program of events?	**¿Tiene un programa de espectáculos?** *teeyeh·neh oon proh·grah·mah deh ehs·pehk·tah·koo·lohs*
What's playing tonight?	**¿Qué hay en cartelera esta noche?** *keh aye ehn kahr·teh·leh·rah ehs·tah noh·cheh*
Where's...?	**¿Dónde está...?** *dohn·deh ehs·tah...*

the downtown area	**el centro**	*ehl thehn·troh*
the bar	**el bar**	*ehl bahr*
the dance club	**la discoteca**	*lah dees·koh·teh·kah*
Is this area safe at night?	**¿Esta zona es segura por la noche?**	
	ehs·tah tho·nah ehs seh·goo·rah pohr lah noh·cheh	

Baby Essentials

Do you have…?	**¿Tiene…?** *teeyeh·neh…*	
a baby bottle	**un biberón** *oon bee·beh·rohn*	
baby food	**la papilla** *lah papeeyah*	
baby wipes	**toallitas** *toh·ah·yee·tahs*	
a car seat	**un asiento para niños** *oon ah·seeyehn toh pah·rah nee·nyohs*	
a children's menu/portion	**un menú/una ración para niños** *oon meh·noo/ oo·nah rah·theeyohn pah·rah nee·nyohs*	
a child's seat/ highchair	**una silla para niños/trona** *oo·nah see·yah pah·rah nee·nyohs/troh·nah*	
a crib/cot	**una cuna/un catre** *oo·nah koo·nah/oon kah·treh*	
diapers [nappies]	**pañales** *pah·nyah·lehs*	
formula	**fórmula infantil** *fohr·moo·lah een·fahn·teel*	
a pacifier [dummy]	**un chupete** *oon choo·peh·teh*	
a playpen	**un parque** *oon pahr·keh*	
a stroller [pushchair]	**un cochecito** *oon koh·cheh·thee·toh*	
Can I breastfeed the baby here?	**¿Puedo darle el pecho al bebé aquí?** *pweh·doh dahr·leh ehl peh·choh ahl beh·beh ah·kee*	
Where can I change the baby?	**¿Dónde puedo cambiar al bebé?** *dohn·deh pweh·doh kahm·beeyahr ahl beh·beh*	

Disabled Travelers

Is there…?	**¿Hay…?** *aye…*
access for the disabled	**acceso para los discapacitados** *ahk·theh·soh pah·rah lohs dees·kah·pah·thee·tah·dohs*

a wheelchair ramp	**una rampa para sillas de ruedas**
	oo·nah rahm·pah pah·rah see·yahs deh rweh·dahs
a disabled-accessible toilet	**un baño con acceso para discapacitados**
	oon bah·nyoh kohn ahk·theh·soh pah·rah dees·kah·pah·th/ee·tah·dohs
I need...	**Necesito...** *neh·theh·see·toh...*
assistance	**ayuda** *ah·yoo·dah*
an elevator [a lift]	**un ascensor** *oon ahs·thehn·sohr*
a ground-floor room	**una habitación en la planta baja**
	oo·nah ah·bee·tah·theeyohn ehn lah plahn·tah bah·khah

Health & Emergencies

Emergencies

Help!	**¡Socorro!** *soh·koh·rroh*
Go away!	**¡Lárguese!** *lahr·geh·seh*
Stop, thief!	**¡Deténgase, ladrón!** *deh·tehn·gah·seh lah·drohn*
Get a doctor!	**¡Llame a un médico!** *yah·meh ah oon meh·dee·koh*
Fire!	**¡Fuego!** *fweh·goh*
I'm lost.	**Me he perdido.** *meh eh pehr·dee·doh*
Can you help me?	**¿Puede ayudarme?** *pweh·deh ah·yoo·dahr·meh*
Call the police!	**¡Llame a la policía!** *yah·meh ah lah poh·lee·thee·ah*
Where's the police station?	**¿Dónde está la comisaría?** *dohn·deh ehs·tah lah koh·mee·sah·ree·ah*

In an emergency, dial: **112** for the police
080 for the fire brigade
061 for the ambulance.

| My son/daughter is missing. | **Mi hijo m /hija f ha desaparecido.** mee ee·khoh/ ee·khah ah deh·sah·pah·reh·thee·doh |

Health

I'm sick [ill].	**Me encuentro mal.** meh ehn·kwehn·troh mahl
I need an English-speaking doctor.	**Necesito un médico que hable inglés.** neh·theh·see·toh oon meh·dee·koh keh ah·bleh een·glehs
It hurts here.	**Me duele aquí.** meh dweh·leh ah·kee
Where's the pharmacy?	**¿Dónde está la farmacia?** dohn·deh ehs·tah lah fahr·mah·theeyah
I'm (. . . months) pregnant.	**Estoy embarazada (de... meses).** esh·toy ehm·bah·rah·thah·dah (deh... meh·sehs)
I'm on...	**Estoy tomando...** ehs·toy toh·mahn·doh...
I'm allergic to antibiotics/penicillin.	**Soy alérgico m/alérgica f a los antibióticos/ la penicilina.** soy ah·lehr·khee·koh/ah·lehr·khee·kah ah lohs ahn·tee·beeyoh·tee·kohs/ lah peh·nee·thee·lee·nah

YOU MAY HEAR...

Rellene este impreso. reh·yeh·neh ehs·teh eem·preh·soh	Fill out this form.
Su documento de identidad, por favor. soo doh·koo·mehn·toh deh ee·dehn·tee·dahd pohr fah·bohr	Your identification, please.
¿Cuándo/Dónde ocurrió? kwahn·doh/ dohn·deh oh·koo·rreeyoh	When/Where did it happen?
¿Puede describirle?/describirla? pweh·deh dehs·kree·beer·leh?/dehs·kree·beer·lah?	What does he/she look like?

adapter el adaptador
American estadounidense
and y
antiseptic cream la crema
  antiséptica
aspirin la aspirina
baby el bebé
backpack la mochila
bad malo
bag la maleta
bandage la tirita
battleground el campo de batalla
beige beis
bikini el biquini
bird el pájaro
black negro
bland soso
blue azul
bottle opener el abrebotellas
bowl el cuenco
boy el niño; **~friend** el novio
bra el sujetador
British británico
brown marrón
camera la cámara
can opener el abrelatas
castle el castillo
cigarette el cigarrillo
cold n (sickness) el catarro; ~ adj
  (temperature) frío
comb el peine
computer el ordenador

condom el preservativo
contact lens solution el líquido de
  lentillas de contacto
corkscrew el sacacorchos
cup la taza
dangerous peligroso
deodorant el desodorante
diabetic diabético
doll la muñeca
early temprano
earrings los pendientes
east el este
easy fácil
eat v comer
economy class la clase económica
elbow el codo
electric outlet el enchufe eléctrico
elevator el ascensor
e-mail v enviar un correo
  electrónico; ~ n el correo
  electrónico; ~ **address** la
  dirección de correo electrónico
emergency la emergencia; ~
  exit la salida de urgencia
empty v vaci
fork el tenedor
girl la niña; **~friend** la novia
glass (drinking) el vaso; ~
  (material) el vidrio
good n el producto
gray gris
green verde

hairbrush el cepillo de pelo;
~**spray** la laca
hot (temperature) caliente; ~
(spicy) picante
husband el marido
ibuprofen el ibuprofeno
ice el hielo; ~ **hockey** el hockey
sobre hielo
icy *adj* helado
ijection infectado
I'd like... Quiero...
insect repellent el repelente de
insectos
Irish irlandés
jeans los vaqueros
jacket la chaqueta
jar el bote
jaw la mandíbula
jazz el jazz; ~ **club** el club de jazz
key la llave; ~ **card** la llave
electrónica; ~ **ring** el llavero
kiddie pool la piscina infantil
kidney (body part) el riñón
kilo el kilo; ~**gram** el kilogramo;
~**meter** el kilómetro
kiss *v* besar
knife el cuchillo
lactose intolerant alérgico a la
lactosa
large grande
lighter el mechero
lotion la crema hidratante
love *v* querer; ~ *n* el amor

match la cerilla
medium (size) mediano
museum el museo
nail file la lima de uñas
napkin la servilleta
nurse el enfermero/la enfermera
or o
orange (color) naranja
park *n* el parque
pen el bolígrafo
pink rosa
plate el plato
purple morado
pyjamas el pijama
rain la lluvia; ~**coat** el
chubasquero
razor blade la hoja de afeitar
red rojo
sandals las sandalias
sanitary napkin la compresa
sauna la sauna
scissors las tijeras
shampoo el champú
shoes los zapatos
small pequeño
sneakers las zapatillas de deporte
snow la nieve
soap el jabón
sock el calcetín
spicy picante
spoon la cuchara
stamp *v* (**a ticket**) picar; ~
n (**postage**) el sello

suitcase la maleta
sun el sol; ~glasses las gafas de sol; ~screen el protector solar
sweater el jersey
sweatshirt la sudadera
swimsuit el bañador
tampon el tampón
terrible terrible
tie (clothing) la corbata
tissue el pañuelo de paper
toilet paper el papel higiénico
tooth brush el cepillo de dientes; ~paste la pasta de dientes
total (amount) el total
tough (food) duro
tourist el turista; ~ information office la oficina de turismo
tour el recorrido turístico
tow truck la grúa
towel la toalla
tower la torre
town la ciudad; ~ hall el ayuntamiento; ~ map el mapa de ciudad; ~ square la plaza
toy el juguete; ~ store la tienda de juguetes
track (train) el andén
traditional tradicional
traffic light el semáforo
T-shirt la camiseta
ugly feo
understand v entender
underwear la ropa interior

United Kingdom (U.K.) el Reino Unido
United States (U.S.) los Estados Unidos
university la universidad
unleaded (gas) la gasolina sin plom
vegan vegan
vegetarian vegetariano
waterfall la cascada
weather el tiempo
week la semana; ~end el fin de semana; ~ly semanal
welcome v acoger
well bien; ~-rested descansado
west el oeste
what (question) qué
wheelchair la silla de ruedas; ~ ramp la rampa para silla de ruedas
when (question) cuándo
where (question) dónde
yellow amarillo
zoo el zoológico

Turkish

Essentials

Hello.	**Merhaba.**	_mehr_·hah·bah
Goodbye. (said by departing party)	**Hoşçakalın.**	hohsh·_chah_·kah·lihn
Goodbye. (said by party staying behind)	**Güle güle.**	gyu·_leh_ gyu·_leh_
Yes/No/OK	**Evet/Hayır/Tamam**	_eh_·vet/_hah_·yihr/tah·_mahm_
Excuse me! (to get past, to get attention)	**Afedersiniz!**	_ahf_·eh·_dehr_·see·neez
Sorry!	**Özür dilerim!**	ur·_zyur_ dee·_leh_·reem
I'd like…	**…istiyorum.**	…ees·_tee_·yoh·room
And/or	**ve/veya**	veh/vehyah
How much?	**Ne kadar?**	_neh_ kah·dahr
Where is…?	**…nerede?**	…_neh_·reh·deh
My name is…	**İsmim…**	ees·meem…
I'm going to…	**…gidiyorum.**	…gee·dee·yoh·room
Please.	**Lütfen.**	_lyut_·fehn
Thank you.	**Teşekkür ederim.**	teh·sheh·_kyur_ eh·deh·reem
You're welcome.	**Bir şey değil.**	beer shay deh·_yeel_
Can you speak more slowly please?	**Daha yavaş konuşur musunuz lütfen?**	dah·_hah_ yah·_vash_ koh·noo·_shoor_ moo·soo·nooz _lyut_·fehn
Can you repeat that please?	**Tekrar eder misiniz lütfen?**	tehk·_rahr_ eh·_dehr_ mee·see·neez _lyut_·fehn
I don't understand.	**Anlamadım.**	ahn·_lah_·mah·dihm
Do you speak English?	**İngilizce biliyor musunuz?**	een·gee·_leez_·jeh bee·_lee_·yohr moo·soo·nooz
I don't speak Turkish.	**Türkçe bilmiyorum.**	_tyurk_·cheh _beel_·mee·yoh·room
Where is the restroom [toilet]?	**Tuvalet nerede?**	too·vah·_let_ _neh_·reh·deh
Help!	**İmdat!**	eem·_daht_

You'll find the pronunciation of the Turkish letters and words written in gray after each sentence to guide you. Simply pronounce these as if they were English, noting that any underlines and bolds indicate an additional emphasis or stress or a lengthening of a vowel sound. As you hear the language being spoken, you will quickly become accustomed to the local pronunciation and dialect.

Numbers

0	**sıfır** _sih·fihr_
1	**bir** _beer_
2	**iki** _ee·kee_
3	**üç** _yuch_
4	**dört** _durrt_
5	**beş** _behsh_
6	**altı** _ahl·tih_
7	**yedi** _yeh·dee_
8	**sekiz** _seh·keez_
9	**dokuz** _doh·kooz_
10	**on** _ohn_
11	**on bir** _ohn beer_
12	**on iki** _ohn ee·kee_
13	**on üç** _ohn yuch_
14	**on dört** _ohn durrt_
15	**on beş** _ohn behsh_
16	**on altı** _ohn ahl·tih_
17	**on yedi** _ohn yeh·dee_
18	**on sekiz** _ohn seh·keez_
19	**on dokuz** _ohn doh·kooz_
20	**yirmi** _yeer·mee_
21	**yirmi bir** _yeer·mee beer_

30	**otuz** *otooz*
40	**kirk** *keerk*
50	**elli** *ehl·lee*
60	**altmış** *ahlt·mihsh*
70	**yetmiş** *yeht·meesh*
80	**seksen** *sehk·sehn*
90	**doksan** *dohk·sahn*
100	**yüz** *yyuz*
101	**yüz bir** *yyuz beer*
200	**ikiyüz** *ee·kee yyuz*
500	**beşyüz** *behsh yyuz*
1,000	**bin** *been*
10,000	**on bin** *ohn been*
1,000,000	**bir milyo** *beer meel·yohn*

Time

What time is it?	**Saat kaç?** *sah·aht kahch*
It's noon [midday].	**Saat on iki.** *sah·aht on ee·kee*
Twenty after [past] four.	**Dördü yirmi geçiyor.** *durr·dyu yeer·mee geh·chee·yohr*
A quarter to nine.	**Dokuza çeyrek var.** *doh·koo·zah chay·rehk vahr*
5:30 a.m./p.m.	**Öğleden önce/sonra beş buçuk.** *ur·leh·dehn urn·jeh/sohn·rah behsh boo·chook*

Days

Monday	**Pazartesi** *pah·zahr·teh·see*
Tuesday	**Salı** *sah·lih*
Wednesday	**Çarşamba** *chahr·shahm·bah*
Thursday	**Perşembe** *pehr·shehm·beh*
Friday	**Cuma** *joo·mah*
Saturday	**Cumartesi** *joo·mahr·teh·see*
Sunday	**Pazar** *pa·zar*

Dates

yesterday	**dün** *dyun*
today	**bugün** <u>*boo*</u>*·gyun*
tomorrow	**yarın** <u>*yah*</u>*·rihn*
day	**gün** *gyun*
week	**hafta** *hahf·*<u>*tah*</u>
month	**ay** *ie*
year	**yıl** *yihl*
Happy New Year!	**Mutlu Yıllar!** *moot·loo yihl·lahr*
Happy Birthday!	**Doğum günün kutlu olsun!** <u>*doh*</u>*·oom gyun·yun koot·loo ol·soon*

Months

January	**Ocak** *oh·*<u>*jahk*</u>
February	**Şubat** *shoo·*<u>*baht*</u>
March	**Mart** *mahrt*
April	**Nisan** *nee·*<u>*sahn*</u>
May	**Mayıs** *mah·*<u>*yihs*</u>
June	**Haziran** *hah·zee·*<u>*rahn*</u>
July	**Temmuz** *tehm·*<u>*mooz*</u>
August	**Ağustos** *ah·oos·*<u>*tohs*</u>
September	**Eylül** *ay·*<u>*lyul*</u>
October	**Ekim** *eh·*<u>*keem*</u>
November	**Kasım** *kah·*<u>*sihm*</u>
December	**Aralık** *ah·rah·*<u>*lihk*</u>

Arrival & Departure

I'm here on vacation [holiday]/business.	**Tatil/İş için buradayım.** *tah·*<u>*teel*</u>*/*<u>*eesh*</u> *ee·cheen* <u>*boo*</u>*·rah·dah·yihm*
I'm going to...	**...gidiyorum.** *...gee·dee·yoh·room*
I'm staying at the...Hotel.	**...otelinde kalıyorum.** *...oh·teh·leen·deh kah·lih·yoh·room*

YOU MAY SEE...

The monetary unit is the Turkish Lira (**Türk Lirası,** abbreviated **TL.**) One **TL** is divided into one hundred **yeni kuruş**, abbreviated **Kr.**

Coins: 1, 5, 10, 25, 50 **Kr** and **1 TL**

Notes: 5, 10, 20, 50 and 100 **TL**

Money

Where's...?	**...nerede?** ..._neh_•reh•deh
the ATM	**Paramatik** _pah_•rah•mah•_teek_
the bank	**Banka** _bahn_•kah
the currency exchange office	**Döviz bürosu** dur•_veez_ byu•roh•soo
What time does the bank open/close?	**Banka saat kaçta açılıyor/kapanıyor?** _bahn_•kah sah•aht kach•_tah_ ah•chih•_lih_•yohr/kah•pah•_nih_•yohr
I'd like to change dollars/pounds into lira.	**Dolar/İngiliz Sterlini bozdurmak istiyorum.** doh•_lahr_/een•gee•_leez_ stehr•lee•_nee_ bohz•door•_mahk_ ees•_tee_•yoh•room
I want to cash some traveler's checks [cheques].	**Seyahat çekleri bozdurmak istiyorum.** seh•yah•_haht_ chek•leh•_ree_ bohz•door•_mahk_ ees•_tee_•yoh•room
I'll pay in cash/by credit card.	**Nakit/Kredi kartı ile ödeyeceğim.** nah•_keet_/kreh•_dee_ kahr•_tih_ ee•leh ur•deh•yeh•_jeh_•yeem

For Numbers, see page 200.

Getting Around

How do I get to town?	**Şehire nasıl gidebilirim?** sheh•hee•_reh_ nah•sıhl gee•deh•bee•_lee_•reem
Where's...?	**...nerede?** ..._neh_•reh•deh
the airport	**Havaalanı** hah•_vah_•ah•lah•nıh
the train [railway] station	**Tren garı** _trehn_ gah•rih

203

the bus station	**Otobüs garajı** oh·toh·*byus* gah·rah·*jih*
the subway [underground] station	**Metro istasyonu** *meht*·roh ees·tahs·yoh·*noo*
How far is it?	**Ne kadar uzakta?** neh kah·dahr oo·zahk·*tah*
Where can I buy tickets?	**Nereden bilet alabilirim?** *neh*·reh·dehn bee·*leht* ah·lah·bee·*lee*·reem
A one-way [single]/round-trip [return] ticket.	**Sadece gidiş/gidiş dönüş bileti.** *sah*·deh·jeh gee·*deesh*/gee·*deesh* dur·*nyush* bee·leh·*tee*
How much?	**Ne kadar?** neh kah·dahr
Are there any discounts?	**İndirim var mı?** een·dee·*reem* *vahr* mih
Which...?	**Hangi...?** *hahn*·gee...
gate?	**kapı?** kah·*pih*
lane?	**hat?** haht
platform?	**peron?** peh·*rohn*
Where can I get a taxi?	**Nerede taksi bulabilirim?** *neh*·reh·deh tahk·*see* boo·lah·bee·*lee*·reem
Please take me to this address.	**Lütfen beni bu adrese götürün.** *lyut*·fehn beh·*nee* boo ahd·reh·*seh* gur·*tyu*·ryun
How long is the trip?	**Yolculuk ne kadar sürüyor?** yohl·joo·*look* neh kah·dahr syu·*ryu*·yohr
Is it a direct train?	**Bu tren doğrudan mı gidiyor?** boo trehn *doh*·roo·dahn mee gee·dee·yoh
Could you tell me when to get off?	**İneceğim yeri söyler misiniz?** ee·neh·jeh·*yeem* yeh·*ree* sur·*ylehr* mee·see·neez
Is this the bus to...?	**Bu ...'a giden otobüs mü?** *boo* ...'ah gee·den oh·toh·*byus* *myul*
Can I have a map?	**Bir harita alabilir miyim?** beer hah·reeh·*tah* ah·lah·bee·*leer*·mee·yeem

For Time, see page 201.

Car Hire

Where can I rent [hire] a car?	**Nereden bir araba kiralayabilirim?** _neh·reh·dehn beer ah·rah·bah kee·rah·lah·yah·bee·lee·reem_	
I'd like to rent [hire]…	**Bir…kiralamak istiyorum.** _beer… kee·rah·lah·mahk ees·tee·yoh·room_	
a 2-/4-door car	**iki/dört kapılı araba** _ee·kee/durrt kah·pih·lih ah·rah·bah_	
an automatic car	**otomatik araba** _oh·toh·mah·teek ah·rah·bah_	
a car with air conditioning	**klimalı araba** _klee·mah·lih ah·rah·bah_	
a car seat	**araba koltuğu** _ah·rah·bah kohl·too·oo_	
How much…?	**…ne kadar?** _…neh kah·dahr_	
per day/week	**Günlüğü/Haftalığı** _gyun·lyu·yu/hahf·tah·lih·ih_	

YOU MAY HEAR…

doğru ilerde _doh·roo ee·lehr·deh_	straight ahead
solda _sohl·dah_	on the left
sağda _sah·dah_	on the right
köşede/köşeyi dönünce _kur·sheh·deh/ kur·sheh·yee dur·nyun·jeh_	on/around the corner
karşısında _kahr·shih·sihn·dah_	opposite
arkasında _ahr·kah·sihn·dah_	behind
yanında _yah·nihn·dah_	next to
…sonra _…sohn·rah_	after…
kuzey/güney _koo·zay/gyu·nay_	north/south
doğu/batı _doh·oo/bah·tih_	east/west
trafik ışıklarında _trah·feek ih·shihk·lah·rihn·dah_	at the traffic light
kavşakta _kahv·shahk·tah_	at the intersection

| Are there any special weekend rates? | **Hafta sonu için indirim var mı?** *hahf·tah soh·noo ee·cheen een·dee·reem vahr mih* |

Places to Stay

Can you recommend a hotel?	**Bir otel tavsiye edebilir misiniz?** *beer oh·tehl tahv·see·yeh eh·deh·bee·leer·mee·see·neez*
I have a reservation.	**Yer ayırtmıştım.** *yehr ah·yihrt·mihsh·tihm*
My name is…	**İsmim…** *ees·meem…*
Do you have a room……**odanız var mı?** *…oh·dah·nihz vahr mih*
for one/two	**Bir/İki kişilik** *beer/ee·kee kee·shee·leek*
with a bathroom	**Banyolu** *bahn·yoh·loo*
with air conditioning	**Klimalı** *klee·mah·lih*
For tonight.	**Bu gecelik.** *boo geh·jeh·leek*
For two nights.	**İki geceliğine.** *ee·kee geh·jeh·lee·yee·neh*
For one week.	**Bir haftalığına.** *beer hahf·tah·lih·ih·nah*
How much?	**Ne kadar?** *neh kah·dahr*
Do you have anything cheaper?	**Daha ucuz yer var mı?** *dah·hah oo·jooz yehr vahr mih*
When's check-out?	**Saat kaçta otelden ayrılmamız gerekiyor?** *sah·aht kahch·tah oh·tehl·dehn ie·rihl·mah·mihz geh·reh·kee·yohr*
Can I leave this in the safe?	**Bunu kasaya koyabilir miyim?** *boo·noo kah·sah·yah koh·yah·bee·leer mee·yeem*
Can I leave my bags?	**Eşyalarımı bırakabilir miyim?** *ehsh·yah·lah·rih·mih bih·rah·kah·bee·leer mee·yeem*
Can I have the bill/ a receipt?	**Fiş/Hesap alabilir miyim?** *feesh/heh·sahp ah·lah·bee·leer mee·yeem*
I'll pay in cash/by credit card.	**Nakit/Kredi kartı ile ödeyeceğim.** *nah·keet/ kreh·dee kahr·tih ee·leh ur·deh·yeh·jeh·yeem*

Communications

Where's an internet cafe?	**İnternet kafe nerede?** een·tehr·<u>neht</u> kah·<u>feh</u> <u>neh</u>·reh·deh
Can I access the internet/check e-mail here?	**Burada internete girebilir/postalarımı kontrol edebilir miyim?** <u>boo</u>·rah·dah een·tehr·neh·<u>teh</u> gee·reh·bee·<u>leer</u>/pohs·tah·lah·rih·<u>mih</u> kohn·<u>trohl</u> eh·deh·bee·<u>leer</u> mee·yeem
How much per hour/ half hour?	**Saati/Yarım saati ne kadar?** sah·ah·<u>tee</u>/ yah·<u>rihm</u> sah·ah·<u>tee</u> neh kah·dahr
How do I connect/ log on?	**Nasıl bağlanabilirim/girebilirim?** <u>nah</u>·sihl bah·lah·nah·bee·lee·reem/gee·reh·bee·<u>lee</u>·reem
I'd like a phone card, please.	**Bir telefon kartı lütfen.** beer teh·leh·<u>fohn</u> kahr·<u>tih</u> <u>lyut</u>·fehn
Can I have your phone number?	**Telefon numaranızı öğrenebilir miyim?** teh·leh·<u>fohn</u> noo·<u>mah</u>·rah·nih·zih ur·reh·neh·bee·<u>leer</u> mee·yeem
Here's my number/ e-mail address.	**İşte numaram/e-posta adresim.** <u>eesh</u>·teh noo·<u>mah</u>·rahm/eh·pohs·<u>tah</u> ahd·reh·seem
Call me/Text me	**Beni arayın/Bana yazın** beh·<u>nee</u> ah·<u>rah</u>·yihn/ bah·<u>nah</u> yah·zihn
I'll text you.	**Size yazarım.** see·<u>zeh</u> yah·<u>zah</u>·rihm
E-mail me.	**Bana yazın.** bah·<u>nah</u> yah·zihn
Hello, this is…	**Merhaba, ben…** <u>mehr</u>·hah·bah behn…
I'd like to speak to…	**…ile konuşmak istiyorum.** …ee·leh koh·noosh·<u>mahk</u> ees·<u>tee</u>·yoh·room
Can you repeat that, please?	**Tekrar eder misiniz lütfen?** tehk·<u>rahr</u> eh·<u>dehr</u> mee·see·neez <u>lyut</u>·fehn
I'll call back later.	**Daha sonra arayacağım.** dah·<u>hah</u> sohn·rah ah·rah·yah·<u>jah</u>·ihm
Goodbye. (said by first person)	**Hoşçakalın.** hosh·<u>chah</u> kah·lihn

Goodbye. (said by the other person)	**Güle güle.** *gyu·leh gyu·leh*
Where is the post office?	**Postane nerede?** *pohs·tah·neh neh·reh·deh*
I'd like to send this to…	**Bunu…göndermek istiyorum.** *boo·noo… gurn·dehr·mehk ees·tee·yoh·room*
What is the WiFi password?	**Kablosuz ağın şifresi nedir?** *kahb·loh·sooz ah·ihn sheef·reh·see neh·deer*
Is the WiFi free?	**Kablosuz ağ ücretsiz mi?** *kahb·loh·sooz ah yuch·reht·seez·mee*
Do you have bluetooth?	**Bluetooth var mı?** *Bluetooth vahr mih*
Can I…?	**…bilir miyim?** *…bee·leer mee·yeem*
access the internet here	**Buradan internete bağlana** *boo·rah·dahn een·tehr·neh·teh bah·lah·nah*
check e-mail	**E-postaya baka** *eh·poh·stah·yah bah·kah*
print	**Basa** *bah·sah*
plug in/charge my laptop/iPhone/iPad/BlackBerry?	**diz üstü bilgisayarımı/iPhone'umu/iPad'imi fişe takabilir miyim/şarj edebilir miyim?** *Deez yus·tyu beel·gee·sah·yah·rih·mi/iPhone'um·hu/ iPad'im·hi feesh·eh tah·kah·bee·leer mee·yeem/sharj eh·deh·bee·leer mee·yeem*
access Skype?	**Skype'ı kullanabilir miyim?** *Skype'ih kool·lah·nah·bee·leer mee·yeem*
Do you have a scanner?	**Tarayıcınız var mı?** *tahr·ah·yee·jee·neez vahr mih*

Social Media

Are you on Facebook/Twitter?	**Facebook/Twitter'da mısın?** *Facebook/Twitter'dah mih·sihn*
What's your user name?	**Kullanıcı adın ne?** *kool·lah·nih·jih ah·dihn neh*
I'll add you as a friend.	**Seni arkadaş olarak ekleyeceğim.** *seh·nee ahr·kah·dash oh·lah·rahk ehk·leh·yeh·jeh·yeem*

I'll follow you on Twitter.	**Seni Twitter'da takip edeceğim.** seh·nee Twitter'dah tah·keep eh·deh·jeh·yeem
Are you following…?	**… takip ediyor musun?** … tah·keep eh·dee·yohr moo soon
I'll put the pictures on Facebook/Twitter.	**Resimleri Facebook/Twitter'a koyacağım.** reh·seem·leh·ree Facebook/Tweeter'ah koh·yah·jah·yihm
I'll tag you in the pictures.	**Seni resimlerde etiketleyeceğim.** seh·nee reh·seem·lehr·deh eh·tee·keht·lih·yeh·jeh·yeem

Conversation

Hello.	**Merhaba.** _mehr_·hah·bah
Hi!	**Selam!** seh·_lahm_
How are you?	**Nasılsınız?** _nah_·sihl·sih·nihz
Fine, thanks.	**İyiyim, teşekkürler.** ee·_yee_·yeem teh·shehk·kyur·_lehr_
Excuse me!	**Afedersiniz!** _ahf_·eh·dehr·see·neez
Do you speak English?	**İngilizce biliyor musunuz?** een·gee·_leez_·jeh bee·_lee_·yohr moo·soo·nooz
What's your name?	**İsminiz nedir?** ees·mee·_neez_ neh·deer
My name is…	**İsmim…** ees·_meem_…
Pleased to meet you.	**Tanıştığımıza memnun oldum.** tah·nihsh·tih·ih·mih·_zah_ mehm·_noon_ ohl·doom
Where are you from?	**Nerelisiniz?** _neh_·reh·lee·see·neez
I'm from the U.S./U.K.	**Amerikadanım/Birleşik Krallıktanım.** ah·meh·_ree_·kah·dah·nihm/beer·leh·_sheek_ krahl·lihk·_tah_·nihm
What do you do?	**Ne iş yapıyorsunuz?** _neh_ eesh yah·_pih_·yohr·soo·nooz
I work for…	**…için çalışıyorum.** …ee·_cheen_ chah·lih·_shih_·yoh·room
I'm a student.	**öğrenciyim.** ur·rehn·_jee_·eem
I'm retired	**Emekliyim.** eh·mehk·_lee_·yeem

Romance

Would you like to go out for a drink/meal?	**Dışarı çıkıp birşeyler içmek/yemek ister misiniz?** *dih-shah-rih chih-kihp beer shay-lehr eech-mehk/yeh-mehk ees-tehr mee-see-neez*
What are your plans for tonight/tomorrow?	**Bu gece/yarın için planınız ne?** *boo geh-jeh/yah-rinn ee-cheen plah-nih-nihz neh*
Can I have your number?	**Telefon numaranızı öğrenebilir miyim?** *teh-leh-fohn noo-mah-rah-nih-zih ur-reh-neh-bee-leer mee-yeem*
Can I join you?	**Size katılabilir miyim?** *see-zeh kah-tih-lah-bee-leer mee-yeem*
Let me buy you a drink.	**Size bir içki ısmarlayayım.** *see-zeh beer eech-kee ihs-mahr-lah-yah-yihm*
I love you.	**Sizi seviyorum.** *see-zee seh-vee-yoh-room*

Accepting & Rejecting

Thank you. I'd love to.	**Teşekkür ederim. Sevinirim.** *teh-shehk-kyur eh-deh-reem seh-vee-nee-reem*
Where shall we meet?	**Nerede buluşalım?** *neh-reh-deh boo-loo-shah-lihm*
I'll meet you at the bar/your hotel.	**Sizi barda/otelinizde bulurum.** *see-zee bahr-dah/oh-teh-lee-neez-deh boo-loo-room*
I'll come by at…	**…uğrarım.** *…oo-rah-rihm*
What's your address?	**Adresin nedir?** *ahd-reh-seen neh-deer*
Thank you, but I'm busy.	**Teşekkür ederim ama meşgulüm.** *teh-shehk-kyur eh-deh-reem ah-mah mehsh-goo-lyum*
I'm not interested.	**İlgilenmiyorum.** *eel-gee-lehn-mee-yoh-room*
Leave me alone!	**Beni yalnız bırakın lütfen!** *beh-nee yahl-nihz bih-rah-kihn lyut-fehn*
Stop bothering me!	**Canımı sıkmayı kesin!** *jah-nih-mih sihk-mah-yih keh-seen*

Essentials

Food & Drink

Eating Out

Can you recommend a good restaurant/bar?	**İyi bir lokanta/bar önerebilir misiniz?** *ee-yee beer loh-kahn-tah/bahr ur-neh-reh-bee-leer mee-see-neez*
Is there a traditional Turkish/an inexpensive restaurant near here?	**Yakınlarda geleneksel Türk yemekleri/ucuz yemek sunan bir lokanta var mı?** *yah-kihn-lahr-dah geh-leh-nehk-sehl tyurk yeh-mehk-leh-ree/oo-jooz yeh-mehk soo-nahn beer loh-kahn-tah vahr mih*
A table for…, please.	**…kişi için bir masa lütfen.** *…kee-shee ee-cheen beer mah-sah lyut-fehn*
Could we sit…?	**…oturabilir miyiz?** *…oh-too-rah-bee-leer mee-yeez*
here/there	**Burada/Orada** *boo-rah-dah/oh-rah-dah*
outside	**Dışarda** *dih-shah-rih-dah*
in a non-smoking area	**Sigara içilmeyen bir yerde** *see-gah-rah ee-cheel-meh-yehn beer yehr-deh*
I'm waiting for someone.	**Birini bekliyorum.** *bee-ree-nee behk-lee-yoh-room*
Where are the restrooms [toilets]?	**Tuvalet nerede?** *too-vah-leht neh-reh-deh*
A menu, please.	**Menü lütfen.** *meh-nyu lyut-fehn*
What do you recommend?	**Ne önerirsiniz?** *neh ur-neh-reer-see-neez*
I'd like…	**…istiyorum.** *…ees-tee-yoh-room*
Some more…, please.	**Biraz daha…istiyorum lütfen.** *bee-rahz dah-hah…ees-tee-yoh-room lyut-fehn*
Enjoy your meal.	**Afiyet olsun.** *ah-fee-yeht ohl-soon*
The check [bill], please.	**Hesap lütfen.** *heh-sahp lyut-fehn*

YOU MAY HEAR...

az pişmiş *ahz peesh•meesh*	rare
orta ateşte *ohr•tah ah•tehsh•teh*	medium
iyi pişmiş *ee•yee peesh•meesh*	well-done

Is service included?	**Servis dahil mi?** *sehr•vees dah•heel mee*
Can I pay by credit card?	**Kredi kartı ile ödeme yapabilir miyim?** *kreh•dee kahr•tih ee•leh ur•deh•meh yah•pah•bee•leer mee•yeem*
Can I have a receipt please?	**Lütfen fiş alabilir miyim?** *lyut•fehn feesh ah•lah•bee•leer mee•yeem*

Breakfast

ekmek *ehk•mehk*	bread
reçel *reh•chehl*	jam
tereyağı *teh•reh•yah•ih*	butter
...yumurta *...yoo•moor•tah*	...eggs
çırpma *chihrp•mah*	scrambled
katı *kah•tih*	boiled
sahanda *sah•hahn•dah*	fried
peynir *pay•neer*	cheese
sosis *soh•sees*	sausages
kızarmış ekmek *kih•zahr•mihsh ehk•mehk*	roasted bread
marmelat *mahr•meh•laht*	marmalade
meyve suyu *may•veh soo•yoo*	fruit juice

Appetizers

tarama *tah•rah•mah*	fish roe pâté
balık çorbası *bah•lihk chohr•bah•sih*	fish soup
sebze çorbası *sehb•zeh chohr•bah•sih*	vegetable soup

tavuk çorbası tah-<u>vook</u> chohr-bah-<u>sih</u>	chicken soup
domates çorbası doh-mah-<u>sih</u> chohr-bah-<u>sih</u>	tomato soup
salatası sah-<u>lah</u>-tah-sih	salad

Meat

bonfile bohn-<u>fee</u>-leh	steak
dana dah-<u>nah</u>	veal
domuz doh-<u>mooz</u>	pork
kuzu koo-<u>zoo</u>	lamb
sığır eti sih-<u>ihr</u> eh-<u>tee</u>	beef
tavuk tah-<u>vook</u>	chicken

YOU MAY SEE...

MASA ÜCRETİ	cover charge
FİKS MENÜ	fixed-price
MENÜ	menu
GÜNÜN MENÜSÜ	menu of the day
HİZMET DAHİL (DEĞİL)	service (not) included
SPESİYALLER	specials

Fish & Seafood

ıstakoz ihs-tah-<u>kohz</u>	lobster
karides kah-ree-<u>dehs</u>	shrimp [prawns]
morina balığı moh-<u>ree</u>-nah bah-lih-<u>ih</u>	cod
ringa balığı reen-<u>gah</u> bah-lih-<u>ih</u>	herring [whitebait]
kalamar kah-lah-<u>mahr</u>	squid

Vegetables

bezelye *beh·zehl·yeh*		peas
domates *doh·mah·tehs*		tomatoes
havuç *hah·vooch*		carrots
lahana *lah·hah·nah*		cabbage
mantar *mahn·tahr*		mushrooms
patates *pah·tah·tehs*		potatoes
soğan *soh·ahn*		onions
fasulye *fah·sool·yeh*		beans

Sauces & Condiments

salt	**tuz** *tooz*	
pepper	**karabiber** *kah·rah·bee·behr*	
mustard	**hardal** *hahr·dahl*	
ketchup	**ketçap** *keht·chahp*	

Fruit & Dessert

çilek *chee·lehk*		strawberries
elma *ehl·mah*		apples
muz *mooz*		bananas
portakal *pohr·tah·kahl*		oranges
muhallebi *moo·hahl·leh·bee*		milk pudding
sütlaç *syut·lahch*		rice pudding
ahududu *ah·hoo·doo·doo*		raspberries
çilek *chee·lehk*		strawberries
elma *ehl·mah*		apples
kiraz *kee·rahz*		cherries
ayva tatlısı *ie·vah taht·lih·sih*		baked quince slices in a syrup

Drinks

May I see the wine list/drink menu, please?	**Şarap listesini/İçecek menüsünü görebilir miyim lütfen?** *shah-rahp lees-teh-see-nee/ ee-cheh-jehk meh-nyu-syu-nyu gur-reh-bee-leer mee-yeem lyut-fehn*
What do you recommend?	**Ne önerirsiniz?** *neh ur-neh-reer-see-neez*
I'd like a bottle/glass of red/white wine.	**Bir şişe/bardak kırmızı/beyaz şarap istiyorum.** *beer shee-sheh/bahr-dahk kihr-mih-zih/ beh-yahz shah-rahp ees-tee-yoh-room*
The house wine, please.	**Ev şarabı lütfen.** *ehv shah-rah-bih lyut-fehn*
Another bottle/glass, please.	**Bir şişe/bardak daha lütfen.** *beer shee-sheh/ bahr-dahk dah-hah lyut-fehn*
May I have a local beer?	**Yerel bir bira alabilir miyim?** *yeh-rehl beer bee-rah ah-lah-bee-leer mee-yeem*
Let me buy you a drink.	**Size bir içki ısmarlayayım.** *see-zeh beer eech-kee ihs-mahr-lah-yah-yihm*
Cheers!	**Şerefe!** *sheh-reh-feh*
A coffee/tea, please.	**Kahve/Çay lütfen.** *kah-hveh/chie lyut-fehn*
Black.	**Sütsüz.** *syut-syuz*
With milk.	**Sütlü.** *syut-lyu*
With sugar.	**Şekerli.** *sheh-kehr-lee*
With artificial sweetener.	**Yapay tatlandırıcılı.** *yah-pie taht-lahn-dih-rih-jih-lih*
...please.	**...lütfen.** *...lyut-fehn*
Fruit juice	**Meyve suyu** *may-veh soo-yoo*
Soda	**Soda** *soh-dah*
Sparkling/still water	**Maden/Sade su** *mah-dehn/sah-deh soo*

Leisure Time

Sightseeing

Where's the tourist office?	**Turist danışma bürosu nerede?** *too·reest dah·nihsh·mah byu·roh·soo neh·reh·deh*
What are the main points of interest?	**Başlıca ilginç yerler nelerdir?** *bahsh·lih·jah eel·geench yehr·lehr neh·lehr·deer*
Do you have tours in English?	**İngilizce turlarınız var mı?** *een·geh·leez·jeh toor·lah·rih·nihz vahr mih*
Can I have a map/guide?	**Harita/Rehber alabilir miyim?** *hah·ree·tah/ reh·ber ah·lah·bee·leer mee·yeem*

> **YOU MAY SEE...**
> **ERKEK GİYİMİ**   men's clothing
> **BAYAN GİYİMİ**   women's clothing
> **ÇOCUK GİYİMİ**   children's clothing

Shopping

Where is the market/mall [shopping centre]?	**Market/Alış veriş merkezi nerede?** *mahr·keht/ah·lihsh veh·reesh mehr·keh·zee neh·reh·deh*
I'm just looking.	**Sadece bakıyorum.** *sah·deh·jeh bah·kih·yoh·room*
Can you help me?	**Bana yardım edebilir misiniz?** *bah·nah yahr·dihm eh·deh·bee·leer mee·see·neez*
I'm being helped.	**Yardım alıyorum.** *yahr·dihm ah·lih·yoh·room*
How much?	**Ne kadar?** *neh kah·dahr*
That one.	**Şunu.** *shoo·noo*
I'd like...	**...istiyorum.** *...ees·tee·yoh·room*
That's all, thanks.	**Hepsi bu, teşekkürler.** *hehp·see boo teh·shehk·kyur·lehr*

Where do I pay?	**Nereye ödeyeceğim?** *neh•reh•yeh ur•deh•yeh•jeh•yeem*
I'll pay in cash/by credit card.	**Nakit/Kredi kartı ile ödeyeceğim.** *nah•keet/ kreh•dee kahr•tih ee•leh ur•deh•yeh•jeh•yeem*
A receipt, please.	**Fatura lütfen.** *fah•too•rah lyut•fehn*

Sport & Leisure

When's the game?	**Maç kaçta?** *mahch kahch•tah*
Where's...?	**...nerede?** *...neh•reh•deh*
the beach	**Plaj** *plahj*
the park	**Park** *pahrk*
the pool	**Yüzme havuzu** *yyuz•meh hah•voo•zoo*
Is it safe to swim/ dive here?	**Burada yüzmek/dalmak güvenli mi?** *boo•rah•dah yyuz•mehk/dahl•mahk gyu•vehn•lee mee*
Can I rent [hire] golf clubs?	**Golf sopalarını kiralayabilir miyim?** *gohlf soh•pah•lah•rih•nih kee•rah•lah•yah•bee•leer mee•yeem*
How much per hour?	**Saatlik ücreti nedir?** *sah•aht•leek yuj•reh•tee neh•deer*
How far is it to...?	**...buradan ne kadar uzakta?** *...boo•rah•dahn neh kah•dahr oo•zahk•tah*
Can you show me on the map?	**Bana haritada gösterebilir misiniz?** *bah•nah hah•ree•tah•dah gurs•teh•reh•bee•leer mee•see•neez*

Going Out

What is there to do in the evenings?	**Geceleri ne yapılır?** *geh•jeh•leh•ree neh yah•pih•lihr*
Do you have a program of events?	**Bir rehberiniz var mı?** *beer reh•beh•ree•neez vahr mih*
What's playing at the movies [cinema] tonight?	**Bu gece hangi filmler oynuyor?** *boo geh•jeh hahn•gee feelm•lehr oy•noo•yohr*

Where's...?	**Nerede...?** _neh_·reh·deh...
the downtown area	**kent merkezi** _kehnt_ mehr·keh·zee
the bar	**bar** bahr
the dance club	**diskotek** dees·koh·_tehk_
Is there a cover charge?	**Giriş ücretli mi?** gee·_reesh_ yuj·reht·_lee_ mee
Is this area safe at night?	**Bu bölge gece güvenli midir?** boo burl·geh geh·jeh gyu·vehn·lih mih·deer

Baby Essentials

Do you have...?	**...var mı?** ..._vahr_ mih
a baby bottle	**Biberon** bee·beh·_rohn_
baby wipes	**Bebek mendili** beh·_behk_ mehn·dee·_lee_
a car seat	**Araba koltuğu** ah·rah·_bah_ kohl·too·_oo_
a children's menu/ portion	**Çocuk menüsü/porsiyonu** choh·_jook_ meh·nyu·_syu_/pohr·see·yoh·_noo_
a child's seat	**Çocuk sandalyesi** choh·_jook_ sahn·dahl·yeh·_see_
a cot	**Çocuk Beşik** choh·_jook_ beh·sheek
a crib	**Çocuk yatağı** choh·_jook_ yah·_tah_·ih
diapers [nappies]	**Bebek bezi** beh·_bek_ beh·zee
formula	**Formül** fohr·_myul_
a highchair	**Çocuk Yüksek sandalye** choh·_jook_ yyuk·_sehk_ sahn·dahl·_yeh_
a pacifier [dummy]	**Yatıştırıcı** yah·tihsh·tih·rih·_jih_
a playpen	**Portatif çocuk** parkı pohr·tah·_teef_ choh·_jook_ pahr·kih
a stroller [push chair]	**Puset** poo·_seht_
Can I breastfeed the baby here?	**Bebeği burda emzirebilir miyim?** beh·beh·_yee_ boor·dah ehm·zee·reh·bee·_leer_ mee·yeem
Where can I change the baby?	**Bebeğin altını nerede değiştirebilirim?** beh·beh·_yeen_ ahl·tih·_nih_ _neh_·reh·deh deh·yeesh·tee·reh·bee·_lee_·reem

Disabled Travelers

Is there…?	**…var mı?**	…vahr mih
access for the disabled	**Engelli girişi**	ehn·gehl·lee gee·ree·shee
a wheelchair ramp	**Tekerlekli sandalye rampası**	teh·kehr·lehk·lee sahn·dahl·yeh rahm·pah·sih
a handicapped [disabled-] accessible restroom [toilet]	**Özürlü tuvaleti**	ur·zyur·lyu too·vah·leh·tee
I need…	**…ihtiyacım var.**	…eeh·tee·yah·jihm vahr
assistance	**Yardımcıya**	yahr·dihm·jih·yah
an elevator [lift]	**Asansöre**	ah·sahn·sur·reh
a ground-floor room	**Zemin-kat odasına**	zeh·meen·kaht oh·dah·sih·nah
Please speak louder.	**Lütfen daha yüksek sesle konuşun.**	lyut·fehn dah·hah yyuk·sehk ses·leh koh·noo·shahn.

Health & Emergencies

Emergencies

Help!	**İmdat!**	eem·daht
Go away!	**Çekil git!**	cheh·keel geet
Stop thief!	**Durdurun, hırsız!**	door·doo·roon hihr·sihz
Get a doctor!	**Bir doktor bulun!**	beer dohk·tohr boo·loon

In an emergency, dial: **155** for the police
110 for the fire brigade
112 for the ambulance.

YOU MAY HEAR...

Bu formu doldurun lütfen. *boo fohr·moo dohl·doo·roon lyut·fehn*

Please fill out this form.

Kimliğiniz lütfen. *keem·lee·yee·neez lyut·fehn*

Your identification, please.

Ne zaman/Nerede oldu? *neh zah·mahn/neh·reh·deh ohl·doo*

When/Where did it happen?

Nasıl biriydi? *nah·sihl bee·reey·dee*

What did he/she look like?

Fire!	**Yangın!** *yahn·gihn*
I'm lost.	**Kayboldum.** *kie·bohl·doom*
Can you help me?	**Bana yardım edebilir misiniz?** *bah·nah yahr·dihm eh·deh·bee·leer mee·see·neez*
Call the police!	**Polis çağırın!** *poh·lees chah·ih·rihn*
Where's the police station?	**Karakol nerede?** *kah·rah·kohl neh·reh·deh*
My child is missing.	**Çocuğum kayıp.** *choh·joo·oom kah·yihp*

Health

I'm sick [ill].	**Hastayım.** *hahs·tah·yihm*
I need an English-speaking doctor.	**İngilizce konuşan bir doktora ihtiyacım var.** *een·gee·leez·jeh koh·noo·shahn beer dohk·toh·rah eeh·tee·yah·jihm vahr*
It hurts here.	**Burası acıyor.** *boo·rah·sih ah·jih·yohr*
Where's the nearest pharmacy [chemist]?	**En yakın eczane nerede?** *ehn yah·kihn ehj·zah·neh neh·reh·deh*

I'm ... months pregnant.	**...aylık hamileyim** ...*ahy·lihk hah·mee·leh·yeem*
I'm on ...	**...dayım.** ....*dah·yihm*
I'm allergic to antibiotics/penicillin.	**Antibiyotiğe/Penisiline alerjim var.** *ahn·tee·bee·yoh·tee·yeh/peh·nee·see·lee·neh ah·lehr·jeem vahr*

Dictionary

acetaminophen parasetamol
adapter adaptör
American *adj* Amerikan; *n* Amerikalı
and ve
antiseptic cream antiseptik krem
aspirin aspirin
baby bebek
backpack sırt çanta
bad kötü
bag çanta
Band-Aid plaster
bandage bandaj
battle site savaş meydanı
bikini bikini
bird kuş
black *adj* siyah
bland mülayim
blue mavi
bottle opener şişe açacağı
bowl kâse
boy erkek çocuk
boyfriend erkek arkadaş
bra sütyen
British Britanyalı

brown kahverengi
camera fotoğraf makinesi
can opener konserve açacağı
castle kale
cat kedi
cigarette sigara
cold *n* **(flu)** soğuk algınlığı; *adj* **(temperature)** soğuk
comb tarak
computer bilgisayar
condom prezervatif
contact lens kontak lens
corkscrew şarap açacağı
cup fincan
dangerous tehlikeli
deodorant deodoran
diabetic (person) şeker hastası
dog köpek
doll bebek
earache kulak ağrısı
earrings küpe
east doğu
easy *adj* kolay
eat *v* yemek
economy class ekonomi sınıfı

eight sekiz
eighteen on sekiz
eighty seksen
electrical outlet elektrik prizi
electronic elektronik
elevator asansör
eleven on bir
England İngiltere
English İngilizce
English-speaking İngilizce konuşan
e-mail n e-posta; v yazmak
e-mail address e-posta adresi
fabric kumaş
facial yüz bakımı
fall sonbahar
family aile
fan (ventilator) vantilatör
far uzak
farm çiftlik
far-sighted yakını görme
  bozukluğu
fast (ahead) adv ileri; **(speed)** hızlı
fast-food restaurant hazır yemek
  lokantası
fax faks
February Şubat
fee komisyon
feed v yemek vermek
female kadın
fly v uçmak
girl kız çocuk
girlfriend kız arkadaş
glass bardak
good adj iyi

gray gri
great mükemmel
green yeşil
hairbrush saç fırçası
hairspray saç spreyi
hot sıcak
husband koca
ibuprofen ibuprofen
ice buz
icy buzlu
I'd like... ...istiyorum.
insect repellent böcek kovucu
Ireland İrlanda
jeans kot pantolon
key ring anahtarlık
kiddie pool çocuk havuzu
kilometer kilometre
kiss v öpmek
kitchen mutfak
kitchen foil [BE] alimünyum kağıtı
knife bıçak
lactose intolerant laktoz
  intoleransı
large büyük
lighter (cigarette) çakmak
lotion losyon
love v **(like)** beğenmek;
  (somebody) sevmek
match kibrit
medium (size) orta
museum müze
nail file tırnak törpüsü
napkin peçete
nurse hemşire

orange (color) portakal rengi
park park
pink pembe
plate tabak
purple mor
pyjamas pijama
rain yağmur
raincoat yağmurluk
razor jilet
razor blades jilet
red kırmızı
salty tuzlu
sandals sandalet
sanitary napkin kadın bağı
sanitary pad [BE] kadın bağı
sauna sauna
scissors makas
Scotland İskoçya
shampoo şampuan
shoe ayakkabı
small küçük
sneakers lastik ayakkabı
snow n kar; v kar yağmak
soap sabun
sock çorap
spicy baharatlı
spoon kaşık
stamp n (postage) pul;
  v mühürletmek
suitcase bavul
sun güneş
sunglasses güneş gözlüğü
sunscreen güneş geçirmez krem
sweater süveter

sweatshirt sweatshirt
swelling şişlik
swimsuit mayo
table masa
tablet tablet
take off çıkartmak
talk v konuşmak
tampon tampon
taxi taksi
taxi stand taksi durağı
team takım
tell v söylemek
ten on
tennis court tenis kortu
tennis match tenis maçı
tent çadır
terminal terminal
terrible berbat; kötü
that o
theft hırsızlık
thermal spring termal kaynağı
thick kalın
thief hırsız
underwear iç çamaşırı
vegan vegan
vegetarian vejetaryen
white beyaz
wife karı
with ile
without olmadan
yellow sarı
zoo hayvanat bahçesi

Berlitz®

speaking your language

phrase book & dictionary
phrase book & CD

Available in: Arabic, Brazilian Portuguese*, Burmese*, Cantonese
Chinese, Croatian, Czech*, Danish*, Dutch, English, Filipino, Finnish*, French,
German, Greek, Hebrew*, Hindi*, Hungarian*, Indonesian, Italian, Japanese,
Korean, Latin American Spanish, Malay, Mandarin Chinese, Mexican Spanish,
Norwegian, Polish, Portuguese, Romanian*, Russian, Spanish, Swedish, Thai,
Turkish, Vietnamese
*Book only